THE
FIRST FIGHTER PILOT
ROLAND GARROS

The Life and Times of the Playboy Who
Invented Air Combat

Lt. Col. Ed Cobleigh

United States Air Force (Retired)
Call Sign "Fast Eddie"

The First Fighter Pilot: Roland Garros
The Life and Times of the Playboy Who Invented Air Combat

First Edition (v1025)

Copyright 2019 by Ed Cobleigh

www.edcobleigh.com

This book is published by Check Six Books, Paso Robles, CA

Cover design by Bespoke Book Covers LTD, UK
Interior layout by Brian Schwartz, USA

All inquires are directed to: Check Six Books, 3750 Sky Ridge Drive, Paso Robles, CA 93446, USA

ISBN: 978-1629671567 (Paperback)
ISBN: 978-1629671574 (Hardcover)
Library of Congress Control Number: 2019905483

Also by Ed Cobleigh
The Pilot: Fighter Planes and Paris
War for the Hell of It: A Fighter Pilot's View of Vietnam

ALSO BY ED COBLEIGH

The Pilot: Fighter Planes and Paris
An aviation/adventure novel.

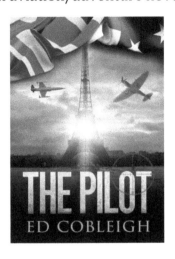

He couldn't shoot down the future,
but his storied past is the key to his present.

War for the Hell of It
A Fighter Pilot's View of Vietnam
A Vietnam War Memoir

A deeply personal account of a fighter pilot's life and his journey into airborne hell and back.

Dedicated To

The Last Fighter Pilot,
He or She is Probably Alive Now

CONTENTS

CHAPTER ONE

A RAPTOR TAKES FLIGHT

The First Fighter Plane

Birthing a new predator can be as hazardous to the midwife as it is to future prey. It is 1915, and starting the first fighter plane is dangerous duty. The wooden propeller needs to be spun by hand until the engine catches. Careless mechanics often lose legs or even their lives to whirling blades. Jules Hue, enlisted chief of the plane's ground crew, has performed this task hundreds, perhaps thousands, of times, but he still takes care to prevent accidental amputation. Standing in front of the silent aircraft, Hue takes a deep breath and calls out to the pilot waiting in the open cockpit.

"*Commutateur est l'arrêt?*" Ignition off? He asks.

The pilot, a dark, slender man, not tall, nods "yes" once. His head, in a leather flying helmet, barely moves. Hue, the pilot's personal mechanic, has worked with the quiet aviator for years. He still does not reach out for the murderous propeller. Standing immobile in front of the cold engine, he stares intently at the cockpit's lone occupant. The silent pilot, a junior officer usually cooperative with enlisted troops, particularly those responsible for the maintenance of his airplane, slowly scans the northeastern sky. What, or who, he searches for is not apparent to the ground crew. Normally as talkative as the car salesman he once was, the pilot's reticence is unusual. The two men holding fast to the aircraft's tail follow his gaze toward the breaking dawn, then look back at each other for a long few seconds before returning their attention to the chief mechanic.

The pilot and his mechanic have launched countless flights together, but this morning is different. No conversation, no banter, no words of encouragement, no shouted challenges.

9

Hue asks again, louder, and more insistently, but still mindful of the difference in rank and status.

"*Est l'arrêt?*" Is it off?

The pilot slowly turns his attention from the horizon toward the man in greasy coveralls barely visible over the plane's nose, and replies softly.

"*Oui, est l'arrêt*" Yes, It's off.

Before starting the engine, the mechanic must rotate the propeller through two full turns, drawing fresh fuel/air mixture into the cylinders. If the cockpit ignition switch is on, the engine might unexpectedly light off. The mechanic could lose his hands grasping the propeller and perhaps the top of his head to the spinning blade. Satisfied at last, he sighs and steps forward to the dangerous task literally at hand.

Hue wraps his callused fingers around the walnut scimitar and pulls down, repeating the process three times. The Le Rhône rotary engine is a bastard to hand crank, usually requiring the services of two men, but Jules Hue prefers to work alone. Heavy, cast-steel cylinders rotate with the propeller around a stationary crankshaft. Straining against the engine's resistance, the crew chief completes two revolutions then stops, his breathing labored.

Hue leans forward, inspecting two metal triangles strapped to the back of the propeller, and facing the pilot. Will they stay attached? The armor plates have not slung off during ground testing, but what effect will they have on the prop's delicate balance when the aircraft takes flight, the engine spinning in anger. How much will they degrade the aerodynamic performance of the propeller? Could vibration be a problem? Will they work when needed? If a plate fails catastrophically, the pilot will probably die as the unbalanced engine shakes itself to pieces, destroying the aircraft. Rough bits of ironmongery, the plates seem unimpressive. However, if they work, today two small triangles will transform an ordinary scout plane into a new breed of killing machine. Jules Hue and his pilot could, although they do not know it, spawn a long lineage of gun-fighter aircraft.

Hue takes another deep breath, retreating a step back out of the propeller's rotational arc.

"Contact," he says.

"Oui, contact," the curt answer comes back from the cockpit.

The pilot stares at Hue as the prospect of flight nears. It is time to waken the plane, to give it life, to use an aircraft to bring death to other men in the air.

The pilot peers over his Gallic nose, a nose sporting a bushy but carefully-trimmed black mustache. Looking at his mechanic, he reaches in the cockpit for a brass switch. He finds it easily, rotating it to the "on" position, energizing the magneto ignition circuit.

One last safety check. The mechanic glances back to the aircraft's tail where two assistants hold tight to delay any forward movement. The Le Rhône, like all rotary engines, is un-throttled. It only operates in one of two modes: turning at full power or off. The airplane mounts no wheel brakes. Once the engine fires, the power of 70 horses will attempt to pull the machine forward, trying to run the mechanic over or suck him into the spinning propeller. Booted heels dug in, the two helpers grip tighter and glance again at each other. Their only task is to hold the aircraft back as long as possible, until Hue moves out of harm's way. Again falling silent, the pilot nods, looking straight ahead but focusing on the lightening sky, not on the ground crew. The mechanic leans forward and presses his palms against the widest portion of the smoothly carved blade, fingers extended straight out. It is bad technique to wrap a hand around the now-live propeller. The secret to surviving the starting process intact is to ensure his body's momentum travels away from the prop while finishing the hand-driven spin. At the same time, as his torso snaps backwards, he needs to keep his head from dipping forward into the deadly disk.

This essential contortion is particularly difficult this morning with poor traction under foot. A nighttime spring shower soaked the aerodrome's grass. This past winter, the war's first, a squadron mechanic slipped on ice while spinning a prop, his fall flung his right leg into the propeller which took it off neatly at the knee. A dishonorable way to be sent home crippled from, and by, the Great War.

The decisive moment. Hue pulls the prop blade sharply down with all his strength, rotating the cylinders. As angular momentum builds, he yanks his hands free and the engine continues turning over. A hurried step back prevents the retreating mechanic from being shredded. A loud pop, two chugs, a blue puff of smoke, a sharp report – internal combustion keeps the rotation going – three more barks, then a feral roar echoes across the airfield. A cloud of acrid smoke envelopes the aircraft as the two assistants cough. Blue haze, blasted by the prop wash, quickly blows away. The polished propeller dissolves into a dancing disc of light, catching and reflecting the rising sun's rays. Nine rotating cylinders spin faster and faster. The iron plates hold tight.

Hue lets out a deep breath, the vapor torn away by the howling engine. He pivots on one foot and jogs along the wing, clearing the aircraft's path to the open airfield, to the primitive runway, to the sky. As soon as Hue passes the wing tip, the pilot thrusts his left arm vertically out of the cockpit, then points forward and down. Spoken commands would be unheard over the engine's din. The straining helpers release their shaking grips and the aircraft immediately starts trundling forward over uneven grass, eager for flight.

The military aerodrome lies outside Arras, in far northern France, almost on the border of German-occupied Belgium. A "flying field," it is just that, a farmer's field deemed fit for flight operations. Once a sheep meadow, the pasture now hosts a key French air base. Oriented east-west to take advantage of the prevailing winds, there is no marked runway on the ground, only a path of worn grass bordered by lines of wood-framed canvas huts. Before engine start, the aircraft had been rolled into place and pointed into the light westerly breeze for take-off.

Lacking brakes on the bicycle-style wheels and dragging a tail with only a fixed metal skid, the diminutive pilot has little control of the aircraft until it generates airflow over the rudder. Only then can he provide some directional input. But now, the little Frenchman from the colonies is along for the ride. Accelerating briskly, the light plane bounces over the rutted field, anxious to be free from the muddy ground. The spindly monoplane is a clumsy thing, bounding across the uneven ground. linen-covered wings flexing, wooden ribs rattling. Its tail skid skips and shakes the fuselage. Despite being state-of-the-art, the combat machine resembles a large, powered kite. Wire-spoked wheels with thin tires and shock cord springs do little to absorb the impacts of terrestrial travel. The pilot feels every bump up through his wooden bench seat. Instead of a box kite, the Morane-Saulnier Model L perhaps more accurately resembles a giant bird; off-white with broad raptor wings ending in squared-off tips. A bird of prey, whose flight appears effortless and graceful when airborne, adept when turning and soaring, but a clumsy and comical creature when running across a sheep field.

Every plane tells its pilot when it is ready to fly. The flight controls evolve from being flaccid and ineffective to being tight and responsive. The little pilot feels the controls, the wooden stick, and the pivoting rudder bar, come alive in his leather-gloved hands and under his fur-booted feet. A quick foot-stab at the rudder keeps the craft pointed into the chilly April wind and a few inches' forward push on the control stick lifts the tail skid off the ground. The pilot has accomplished this basic move countless times. He is one of the most experienced and famous aviators of his era. With less drag now that the tail skid is off the ground, the machine accelerates rapidly and begins to bounce. Each bounce extends longer and higher, each touchdown shorter and softer, until there are no more impacts, no more shocks, no more rattles. Pilot and airplane are airborne, free. Together they climb slowly into the new day, into a new era in warfare, and into the future.

The three mechanics, arms folded, watched intently as the object of their attention for most of their waking hours departs the aerodrome westward into the frigid wind. It turns, banking shallowly to the right, still struggling to climb, lifting a heavy load. A pilot must be careful executing a turn near the ground. A stall, spin, and crash would be fatal. In addition to the unfamiliar and weighty armament the plane is dragging aloft, the primitive craft carries with it the inauguration of true air combat, although no one, particularly the ground crew, suspects as much this April morning. The engine's noise fades into a distant drone as the tiny craft disappears, headed for the opposing spider webs of trenches marking the front lines not so very far to the northeast.

Jules Hue probably wondered if his charge was going to leave the ground, carrying the recently-installed machine gun along with its heavy ammunition clips. Now, the mechanics can grab a quick breakfast meal at the enlisted mem's mess tent and wait until their precious machine returns. If it does. All too often, squadron aircraft fly away into the war zone and never come back.

The Morane-Saulnier Model L is a "parasol" monoplane, its single wing mounted on a spruce frame two feet over the top of the fuselage. A fan of wires in front of the pilot stretches from the tip of a braced pyramid of spindly sticks out to the wings, like a circus tent without the canvas. More wires underneath the plane tie the wings to the undercarriage, giving the correct impression that without the taut strands, the wing's flimsy internal structure would collapse in flight. It is a flying machine held more or less rigid by thin wires in tension. The latest models of the Morane-Saulnier suspend the wing over the body, imitating a parasol, to correct a design flaw, which fixed the wing directly to the fuselage. The space left open between the wing's bottom surface and the engine cowling is intended to improve the pilot's forward view. But today, that gap is partially filled by a machine gun mounted firmly on the cowling, pointed at the whirling propeller. The wooden blades are shielded from bullet impact by the jury-rigged steel plates. Or so the pilot hopes.

The pilot flies northeast alone, engine and propeller clawing for altitude, the brisk west wind pushing him toward the front lines and toward his destiny. His dark, intense eyes are protected by Isinglass goggles, the remainder of his exposed face feels the biting cold of the 60 knot (70 mph) airflow. His curly black hair crammed under his flying helmet offers some welcome cranial insulation. He peers with difficulty around the bulky gun, trying the left side, then the right, as the hazy horizon sinks under the plane's nose in the shallow, labored climb. This fine spring morning, he will seek out German aviators. It will be the first time in history a human being hunts down and kills other men in the air while flying a true fighter plane.

On the first of April 1915, the pilot, Lieutenant Roland Garros of the French Army's Service Aéronautique, a member of Escadrille (Squadron) MS26, became the world's first fighter pilot. That day, the petit Frenchman revolutionized war in the air. In the process, he ended the lives of two German aviators, or as he called them, "Les Boches." They were the first men Garros killed. They would not be the last. The hapless victims probably did not fully appreciate their place in history as participants in the first air-to-air victory, racked up by a real fighter pilot. Garros went on to notch two more shoot-downs in the next fourteen days, sowing alarm among German pilots. At that time, the entire French Air Force had recorded only six downed enemy planes (usually with rifle fire). Garros accounted for half the total.

Roland Garros and Jules Hue, with the help of engineers back at the factory in Paris, invented the fighter plane, a beautiful and terrible machine. A single engine, a lone pilot, a forward-firing, fixed machine gun; all the elements were there on that day over a hundred years ago. From the nimble Nieuports of World War I to the graceful Spitfires of War II; from the sleek, cold-war F-104 Starfighters to today's F-16 Vipers; the basic elements needed to kill other people in the air have not changed, only their effectiveness. How did a car salesman, a *boulevardier,* an indulgent member of Parisian café society, a world-class athlete, along with his mechanic, birth such a century-long progression of focused lethality?

Roland Garros's improbable journey into fighter aviation history and his descent into the man-made hell of World War I began two and half decades earlier in a French colonial paradise.

His story begins on a tropical island in the Indian Ocean east of Madagascar, on the other side of the planet, far from the Great War. It is a tale worth telling.

CHAPTER TWO

FROM PARADISE TO PARIS

As If There's a Difference

Roland Garros took his given name from a famous Frankish knight from Brittany, a Paladin of King Charlemagne. The argument can be made that the weight of this moniker shaped, and perhaps ended, his life. Eugène Adrien Roland Georges Garros arrived in this world on the 6th of October 1888, in the sleepy tropical town of Saint-Denis, the capital of Rèunion, an idyllic island in the western Indian Ocean. About three times the surface area of Singapore, Réunion is often compared to the big island of Hawaii. It has the same tropical climate, same volcanic origin, same wild variation in rainfall between the east and west coasts and the same laid-back native attitude.

Like Hawaii, Réunion is roughly circular, tending toward oval, with two volcanoes, the island's fiery founders, slight right and left of center as seen from an overhead view. Réunion is slightly cooler and less windy, but with even more rain than Hawaii. Saint-Denis, its largest city, sits at the northern tip, beside the warm Indian Ocean. An overseas French Department (French Departments are like American states, but with less political power), it awards French citizenship to all natives born there. The island holds the same legal and political status as Departments in mainland France. French is the only official language. It sends delegates to the French National Assembly, islanders vote in French national elections, and the Napoleonic Code reigns supreme in the island's courts. However, natives of Réunion cannot be drafted into the French military, a fact which will play itself out much later in the life of baby Garros.

Réunion Island is a tiny bit of France, far from Europe, tropical, but France all the same. Visitors and tourists from

17

Europe today land at the Roland Garros International Airport outside Saint-Denis. The airport commemorates Réunion's most famous son, although he earned his fame on the other side of the globe displaying talents few of the inhabitants could conceive of when he was born and which few possess now – proficiency in the air.

Native people of Réunion have always been a mixture, *une mélange*, of African, Indian (mainly Tamils), Europeans, Malays, and Chinese. Most of their ancestors arrived not as free men and women, but as slaves or indentured servants. Racial mixing is now and was back then common and accepted, with everyone born on the island, regardless of ethnic origin, referred to as a "Creole," a local badge of honor, not of shame as it can be elsewhere, such as in the Caribbean and in New Orleans, Louisiana, USA. "Creole" is also the name of the dialect spoken on the island, an offshoot a *patois,* of French.

Roland Garros's father, known as Georges, was not a Creole, but instead came from mainland France and proudly boasted of his ancestral French family's background. His family hailed from the city of Nantes, in Brittany, where the broad and shallow Loire River flows into the cold North Sea. Georges made his way to Réunion by way of Toulouse in southern France.

Georges Garros was also very mindful of his family's history, verbally handed down over the generations. Oral legends said the Garros family called themselves corsairs, or privateers.

Corsairs from Brittany were adventurous sailors on armed civilian vessels, ships empowered by French kings to prey on unarmed merchantmen flying the flags of countries at war with France. When a corsair crew captured a prize ship, they could sell the ship and its cargo, keeping three quarters of the proceeds, the rest going to the royal treasury. If a captured ship was a Spanish galleon returning from plundering the native Americans' gold troves, the monetary rewards could be immense. Not surprisingly, the adversely-affected countries, mainly Great Britain and Spain, viewed these free-lance predatory seaman with distain and alarm, considered them to be nothing more than thinly-disguised pirates. Corsair captains captured by the Royal Navy were sent back to London for a fair trial, followed by a prompt hanging.

Also, in keeping with this romantic martial tradition, Roland bore the name of the famous knight and protagonist in the epic poem, "The Song of Roland." Young Roland Garros enjoyed tales of derring-do; stories spun by his father telling of fearless corsairs and of Sir Roland, the brave French warrior. You can surmise the weight of this family's rich history affected the young lad's attitude toward warfare, honor, and how and when to fight like a man. Early learning influenced how Roland Garros came to view his role in life; how could it not? From early on, he admired the semi-outlaw, the non-conformist, the outsider, the corsair. Garros's inherited value system would later manifest itself during the Great War. Eventually, a lone aviator in his cockpit became Sir Roland the knight on his charger, doing battle with the enemies of France. Growing up, for young Roland, mainland France represented a mythical far-away place, the land of legends, the land of his ancestors.

His place in French life and society is indicated by his surplus of first names. On certain upper societal levels, it was customary to name a child after an extended cast of relatives. Sporting such a list of names indicates where in the social strata his parents felt they belonged, or where they wished to be.

Georges Garros married within his class. Clara Garros, neé Faure, also hailed from the same area in northwest France with the same well-to-do background. However, Clara was born on Réunion, making her a Créole. If anything, the Faures were higher in the pecking order of families whose original fortunes were accumulated by licensed pirates, the corsairs. Georges Garros, a lawyer, was 28 years old when his son was born. The new father was very slowly building a private legal practice in Saint-Denis. It must have been difficult to prosper in litigation, given the local Creoles' *laissez-faire* inclinations and the lack of burning issues on the sleepy island; issues an ambitious lawyer could profitably exploit.

To improve his family's financial prospects, Georges decided to up sticks and move off the island, a decision taken when the young lad reached four years of age. Destination of choice: French Indochina, a vast, prosperous French colony comprising the modern-day states of Vietnam, Laos, and Cambodia, but not Thailand. Saigon was then the capital of Indochina, located in the south of the colony's Vietnamese region, a place now labeled, for the time being, Ho Chi Minh City. Bustling Saigon was to be the promised land for the ambitious young lawyer from Nantes by way of Réunion. Saigon was much bigger and richer than Saint-Denis, with money from rubber, rice, timber, jewels, opium, and colonial activities sloshing around in the French colonizer's comfortable tropical domain.

To be French in Saigon during the colonial era meant a life of relative ease. Colonists attempted, with considerable success, to replicate the life style of the upper middle classes, the *"Bourgeoisie,"* that those people enjoyed in France itself on the globe's far side. They clustered in specified neighborhoods, inhabited comfortable tropical villas, dined in French restaurants, frequented French-only social clubs, and spoke French exclusively. Their children attended local French schools. The curriculum was dictated by educational authorities in Paris, as it is in all French schools wherever they are in the world. Women and young people in their closed-off enclaves would have had little contact with the local Vietnamese people except for their house cleaners, cooks, cleaners, and "house boys," who were numerous, being cheap to employ. The young French scholars would have been taught to pronounce proper Metropolitan French as spoken in Paris. In France, then as now, your status in society was marked by fluency in the French language, to be articulate was the necessary first step on the social ladder. Being well-spoken was, and is, a requirement of acceptance by the upper crust of French society.

Georges Garros, probably for financial reasons, chose to not buy into the circumscribed lifestyle of splendid colonial isolation. Instead, he rented a small house near the languid, muddy Saigon River on the edge of a large ethnic Chinese neighborhood. Vietnamese neighbors lived next door. Young Roland did not enroll in a French school, an "*Ecole Français*," but rather was home-schooled by his mother, thereby avoiding the rigid educational requirements sent out from France. He learned early on some required curriculum elements could be ignored, regardless of the dictates coming from the mandarins in Paris. Roland soon developed a circle of friends from the native Vietnamese and Chinese communities, other young boys who took advantage of outdoor activities available for the adventurous in the tropics. He developed an appreciation of Vietnamese culture from his friends. Years later, this probably affected his choice of a chief mechanic for his aircraft, Jules Hue. Hue, despite being born in a suburb of Paris, was probably of Vietnamese extraction, being named after the old Vietnamese native capital, Hue City. A good crew chief was vital for proper aircraft maintenance; a loose bolt, a slack wire, a leaky pipe could mean the difference between returning from a combat mission or not. Roland later trusted his Vietnamese mechanic as he trusted his Vietnamese friends in Saigon.

Starting with his tricycle on Réunion and then with a bicycle in Saigon, Roland was fascinated with things mechanical, preferably machines that took him places rapidly. Today, we have forgotten the bicycle's dramatic impact on individual freedom in the late 1800s and the 20th century's early years. Trains, trams, and streetcars provided mass transit and the automobile was a rich man's toy. Until the bike's introduction, personal ground mobility was limited to walking or some form of transport involving horses. Bicycles offered an energetic boy the means to range everywhere at will on a moment's notice. Bicycles were always ready, did not need to be saddled or harnessed, and did not eat. Roland took advantage of this new-found ability to roam, exploring not only the city of Saigon, but the rice paddies and bamboo forests outside town. The bicycles of the day, though heavy and with only one gear, captured world-wide interest, affecting a whole generation of young men. Over in America, future aviators got their inspiration for rapid mechanical mobility from the bike. Aviation pioneer Glenn Curtiss and the most famous of the early birdmen, the Wright brothers, started their professional careers with bicycles about the same time Roland Garros pedaled himself all over Saigon.

When Roland turned 11, his father, against the wishes of mother Clara, and without consulting Roland beforehand, dispatched him alone on a steamship to France to attend boarding school. Perhaps his father wished to curtail his son's process of "going native" and associating only with Chinese and Vietnamese playmates. Maybe the idea was to give him a proper French education, in France. Georges might have been living vicariously through young Roland, a common tendency among fathers. It is equally likely the elder Garros merely wanted the best for his son. Whatever the reason, young Roland was not onboard with the plan.

The lad clung to the ship's railing with both hands, leaning over, with the green complexion of seasickness, a malady he would never outgrow. He stared with swollen, red eyes at the heaving ocean. Pacing the boat, a wandering albatross floated on long, thin wings, rising with the lifting air thrust upward by the wavetops, then gliding down into the troughs. A display of aerial proficiency, of effortless flight.

The ship's captain, a family friend charged with looking after the boy during the weeks' long voyage, stood nearby, facing the boy, his arms folded across his chest.

The captain spoke first.

"*As-tu pleuré*? Have you been crying?"

The boy nodded yes without speaking or looking at the captain, continuing to follow the bird's flight paralleling the ship's wake.

"*Ta famille te manqué*? Do you miss your family?"

"My mother and sister, yes. My father, no. He sent me away."

"I know Georges well. He wants the best for you."

The lad's blurry gaze remained locked on the graceful, snow-white bird as tears streamed down his smooth cheeks. The Captain followed the boy's sightline and watched the albatross wheel and soar for a minute, for an eternity, before he went on.

"That is an albatross. Sailors view them as bringing good luck on a long sea voyage. It is forbidden to kill an albatross or to cause one harm."

"The bird is lucky. He can go home whenever he wants," the boy replied.

The old man sighed. "An albatross has no fixed home, wandering the seas endlessly. The sky is his home."

The youth leaned over the rail and vomited, the contents of his stomach joining with his tears, both whipped away by the salty wind before the sad mixture could drop into the churning water below.

Roland admitted years later he cried tears of sadness, missing his mother, and tears of rage at his father. He cried for days on end during the voyage. His relationship with his father never recovered.

Things worsened between them as Roland grew from a lonely, frightened boy in strange country, into a fiercely independent young man in that same country. The Garros's personal finances improved enough and their two families were sufficiently well-connected to get young Roland into the prestigious *Collége Stanislas de Paris*. Movers and shakers of France attended Stanislas; later graduates included Charles De Gaulle and Jacques Cousteau.

Arriving in Paris from Saigon with a cough diagnosed as tropical pneumonia, Roland was sent to a branch campus in the south of France, in Cannes on the *Côte d 'Azur* beside another warm ocean. It is easy to speculate about the sense of isolation, of aloneness, Roland Garros experienced during his reverse exile at age 11 from his tropical home to far-away France, a place he had never seen. He later wrote of acute sadness on leaving his mother, but not his father, behind. Only a sense of self-reliance, of independence tending toward rebellion, would see him through his teen-aged years, the time when he became a man and put away childish things.

The milder climate in the south agreed with Roland and he recovered quickly. At school in Cannes, he prospered, mainly on the athletic fields. He ran track, played soccer/football, and above all, entered bicycle races. One physical education requirement he shunned was fencing. He refused to participate. Skill at fencing was deemed to be essential for a young gentleman. Even now, the French Officer's Club in central Paris hosts a fencing club in its basement, for military officers who wish to hone their swordsmanship and relax from the thrust, cut, and parry of Parisian life. Not for the last time Roland Garros defied convention and marched, or rather

pedaled, to the beat of his own drummer, a boy from the colonies, an outsider, alone in a country he had only heard about.

It was in Cannes that Garros started a mystery still extant today. He learned to play the piano. His father disapproved, indicating he knew about the lessons. Garros Senior felt accomplishment with a musical instrument was a waste of time, while swordsmanship would prove useful. Roland persevered but we do not know how. He is silent about where, when, and for how long he took lessons. Again, according to Roland's autobiography, he became adept at the music of Chopin. If true, this would be remarkable; Chopin's compositions for the piano are notoriously difficult, requiring years of training and constant practice. Yet Garros does not speak of long hours at the keyboard, evidently never owned a piano, and during his later years, had no opportunity to practice. Either Garros possessed immense talent for the piano, or his claims are inflated. History offers few clues, but other observers commented on his playing.

Later, Garros wrote that while in school in Nice, he repeated a dream, one that he couldn't shake. He dreamed of flying. Flying without equipment, just his body. In the dream he circled the city of Nice looking into windows at night. Hovering effortlessly, he noted the love-making techniques of couples. What this reoccurring dream says about young Roland Garros would be important later in his life.

During the summers of 1904 and 1905, Roland, instead of returning to Saigon, spent his vacation months in England at the country home of his extended family's friends. His link with far-off Indochina and his immediate family grew weaker. He perfected his English language skills, grew enamored of the landed English gentry's lifestyle, and learned to play tennis poorly. For the 1906 school year, Georges Garros enrolled Roland in *Lycée Janson-de-Sailly* in Paris. A French *lycée* is the equivalent of an American high school and *Janson-de-Sailly* was famous for training future lawyers, a vocation selected by Georges for Roland without input or assent from the young man in question.

As usual, Roland focused more on athletics than on academics, a sad fact reported monthly to his father in Saigon by scolding letters sent by his disappointed professors. After winning the interscholastic bicycle championship of France, he competed in the very popular professional cycling races under a pseudonym to not jeopardize his amateur standing. He refused to study subjects he considered old-fashioned and useless, notably Greek and Latin, to the facility's consternation, not to mention that of his distant father. However, he managed to graduate with a degree in Philosophy and was promptly enrolled, again by his father *sans* discussion, in a prestigious Parisian law school. How the younger Garros intended to practice law minus the required knowledge of Latin is not known. Perhaps he revealed his plan when he, without his father's knowledge, also enrolled in the business school run by the British Chamber of Commerce in Paris.

While in law and business schools in 1907, he still found time to add rugby to his athletic portfolio, even competing for

France in the Five Nations Cup tourney, a competition still run today. He even dabbled again at tennis, returning to a sport he enjoyed during those long, lazy summers in England. Life must have been good, attending college in Paris, living just off the Champs Elysées in an apartment chosen from Saigon by his father, and walking, or rather strolling, to class.

School for Roland, an indifferent student at best, was a means to several ends. He continued to compete athletically and compete well. Perhaps more importantly, he was making contacts –or as it is called today, networking. At law school, he soon found a circle of friends from the upper reaches of French society who accepted him as a social equal. The Creole from Réunion and Saigon, with his lilting, not-quite classic metropolitan accent, was going places. Realizing the limitations of a Creole accent, Garros worked to prefect a Parisian speech pattern. At this time in France, success in life, whether it be financial, romantic, or social, depended more on your family or "breeding," on your contacts, and the ability to fit in with the upper crust, than on your academic prowess.

Roland spent the summers of 1907 and 1908 at the country home of a famous engineer, Dr. Lulling, located in the Champagne region. *Chateau de Courcelles-Sapicourt* provided a comfortable place to work, unsuccessfully, on his tennis game, and to romance the family's comely female offspring. Saigon was very far away indeed.

At the end of the 1909 school year, Roland Garros graduated from law school without being awarded his license to practice law, but with an additional degree in business. Accepted in the best circles, he lacked the financial means to operate at the expected levels of spending. Financial reverses, including a divorce, prevented his parents from supporting him in the manner to which he had become accustomed. Fortunately, Roland Garros had an idea, one with the possibility of making money, of being accepted, and of living an exciting life at the same time. He needed a way in, a contact to introduce him to the new world of mechanical freedom. The key would be found in *Le Grand Palais* exhibition hall in Paris.

CHAPTER THREE

LA BELLE ÉPOQUE

THE FIRST CAR SALESMAN

The 20th century's first decade and a half witnessed the culmination of what is now called *La Belle Époque*, The Beautiful Era, in France. These 15 years were known later as The Golden Age in Great Britain and called The Gilded Age in America. The precious metal titles came into use only in retrospect. At the time, people did not perceive they were living in a golden age, they thought they inhabited normal times, enjoying the results of inevitable progress. Looking back over the carnage of the Great War and from the depths of the later worldwide depression, the prior extended period of peace and prosperity seemed like a dream, a golden dream. And what an age it was! Cultural highlights we now regard as classically European reached a zenith in the 1900-1915 period, building on groundwork begun in the late 1800s. Nowhere was this more apparent than in Paris, the widely acknowledged epicenter of *La Belle Époque.* While the Gilded Age is usually considered to stretch from the end of the Franco-German War in 1870 to the beginning of World War I in August of 1914, the era's cultural flowering sprouted in earnest during the years following the World Fair of 1889, grew apace through the World Fair of 1900, and reached a bouquet of blooms in the very early 1900s. Both World Fairs were held in Paris, of course. The second fair saw the construction of the *Grand Palais* exhibition hall where Roland Garros's commercial career was about to begin.

During the febrile epoch's final years, rapid advances in technology, medicine, science, the arts, transportation, literature, architecture, entertainment, and cuisine became commonplace, even expected. The art deco school dominated

27

popular architecture. Master chef Georges Escoffier codified French cuisine. The Impressionists finished revolutionizing painting. Popular novels became accessible to more readers. City transportation was mechanized, horses were sent to pasture. Madame Curie won a matched pair of Nobel Prizes and the moneyed classes prospered. Much to the gratification of Roland Garros and his high-spirited young compatriots, French vintners perfected the mass production of champagne. The resurgent champagne industry and the town at its center would prove later to be an important factor in the growth and acceptance of early attempts at manned flight. As a result of all this social and vinous ferment, universal European peace and prosperity reigned, at least for the elite, and at least for the time being.

Construction of the Eiffel Tower in 1887-89 produced a highly visible symbol for the times. Initially hated by some Parisians for being out of scale, in poor taste, looking too industrial, and shamelessly flaunting its naked steel body, the tower was intended to be demolished after the first fair. Spared to highlight the 1900 fair, it became the beloved emblem of the "City of Lights." Even sensitive, artistic Parisians can get used to anything. The Eiffel Tower is still a fitting symbol of that long-ago era when anything seemed possible. A technological marvel, it towers, literally, over today's city, an unmistakable edifice representing French superiority in the culture and technology in that distant time. Along with the Suez Canal and the Paris *Métro* subway system, the tower signified Gallic engineering superiority.

When built, the Eiffel Tower was the world's tallest man-made structure. From the observation deck at the tower's pinnacle in 1908, it might have been possible to discern the ominous storm clouds of war gathering in the east, toward Germany, and over the Austro-Hungarian empire. A small black cloud, initially no bigger than a man's fist but malignant and rapidly growing, the coming darkness approached unseen by the unaware strollers far below the tower on the French capital's serene boulevards.

Those leafy, wide boulevards, broad squares, and sunny open parks we picture in our mind's eye as being typically Parisian were laid down after the clearing of numerous teeming medieval-era slum neighborhoods by Baron Georges-Eugène Haussmann, beginning in the 1850s. Haussmann was born in Paris, but his family came from Alsace, hence the Germanic name. He did not have an engineering education nor was he a recognized civic planner, but he had the ear and the bankroll of Napoleon III, Emperor of France. Paris's main streets, one of which is Boulevard Haussmann, are today straight and broad, not only to accommodate *Belle Époque*-style promenades, but also in part to allow cavalry charges to more easily put down revolts and protests. Lessons taught by the barricades featured in the book and play "*Les Misérables*" were well-learned by the rulers of the City of Lights. Thanks to Haussmann, an army on horseback could easily clear the streets of unruly rabble or dispatch unsavory rioters with a whiff of grapeshot.

In 1908, the *Boulevardiers'* concern was not for cavalry charges or cannon fire but for cars – motorcars – the new subject of Roland Garros's intense interest. Autos were becoming common on those wide avenues, trailing smoke, clattering, chugging, frightening horses and gentle womenfolk alike. Their drivers, sporting oversized goggles, flat cloth hats, and cotton duster coats to ward off the stirred-up dust, were approaching speeds of 20 miles, 30 kilometers, an hour. Here was a mechanical device promising rapid movement, thrills, romance, and money to be made. Garros was infatuated, even abandoning bicycle racing to concentrate on the motorcar.

Early horseless carriages were just that, a marriage of then-new lightweight carriages, minus the horse, with a primitive engine, usually employing internal combustion, although a few were powered by steam engines or electric motors. These crude but elegantly appointed devices were intended to transport wealthy burghers and their families in style. But, by 1908, a new sort of automobile terrified folks on the thoroughfares of Paris – the sports car. Designed to be faster, lower, and with better handling than carriage-based vehicles, sports cars mounted only two leather-lined seats, one for the intrepid driver, and one for his lady of the moment. Sports cars were marketed to well-to-do young men, initially not very successfully. Motorcars tended to be sold from either greasy machine shops by nerdy engineers, or from elegant carriage houses by the carriage trade's elderly Dons. What few garages existed were often converted stables, the resultant irony notwithstanding. Roland Garros intended to address this under-served market, and in the process cash in on a perceived sales void. He had the personal contacts from school. He looked the part of a *Boulevardier.* He spoke the *nouveau riche* language, albeit with a recently-acquired Parisian accent. He loved fast machines and needed a steady income. So, a car salesman he became.

Roland's entry into the domain of commerce, fast automobiles, fast bucks, or rather fast francs, and fast women began with the Paris auto show of 1908. This exhibition of the state of the automotive art was conducted for three weeks in the Grand Palais, just off the Champs Elysées.

The Grand Palais, built for the 1900 World Fair and still in constant use today, is a magnificent monument, large enough for equestrian jumping competitions, and featuring a spectacular barrel-vault glass roof. In French, *"Champs Elysées"* translates to "Elysian Fields" the heaven of Roman mythology, an apt metaphor for Roland Garros's goals for his participation in the *Salon de l'Automobile.* All the big manufacturers of motorcars were there; Renault, De Dion-Bouton, Peugeot, and Levallois. Henry Ford brought over from America his revolutionary Model T. Buyers could order a Model T in any color they wanted, as long as they wanted black. Through his high society contacts, Roland obtained a temporary position with Grégoire Automobiles, a small design and manufacturing company. He worked the exhibit floor, pitching the charms of Grégoire autos. Attracting much attention, the vehicles were low-slung and racy, with red wooden-spoked wheels, gleaming white bodywork, burnished brass fittings throughout, and only two bucket seats. Gréroires were the predecessors of an American classic of 1913, the famous Stutz Bearcat, but without the monocle windshield, and with a French accent.

Garros, exhibiting the boundless self-assurance of his twenty years, quickly proved to have the gift of sales gab, impressing potential customers and management alike with his energy and verbal communication skills. Focused on selling cars, he became frustrated when the President of France, Armand Falliéres, and his entourage took up space in front of the Grégoire stand preventing access by potential customers. Garros had invited many of his classmates from law and business schools to visit the show and perhaps buy a car from him. But he was put off by the dignitaries, horse holders, bureaucrats, and senior personnel milling around, hampering him from selling cars to his compatriots. Resplendent in a bespoke three-piece beige suit; a starched, pinstriped, elegantly tailored shirt with French cuffs, naturally, and a fashionable silk cravat, he smoothly extolled the many virtues of Grégoire sport automobiles. Roland Garros, five years before he became the world's first fighter pilot, was perhaps the world's first professional car salesperson.

Garros's experience at the 1908 auto show confirmed his opinion about the presence of an untapped market for sports cars in his adopted home town; one not being exploited by the larger, establishment car companies. After the show, building on the reputation established in those quick three weeks, Garros canvassed his rich friends and their fathers, pitching not sports cars, but an auto dealership focused on sporting machines. He possessed the sales skills, he could get the franchise for Grégoire products in Paris, he had the customer base, i.e. his friends, now all he needed was financial backing and a place of business.

The *Champs Elysées* runs northeast from the Place de la Concorde, up a slight incline for a little over a mile and a quarter, two kilometers, to the massive *l'Arc de Triomphe*, set in the center of the *Étoile*. The *Étoile*, or "star," is a giant roundabout-cum-demolition derby arena from which many principal streets emanate, and where many traffic accidents occur in the circular *mêlée*. If you carry on eastward in the same direction past the *Étoile* and *Arc*, the street changes its name from the *Champs Elysées* to *l'Avenue de la Grand-Armée*, and runs down another shallow hill to the *Port Maillot* plaza and interchange. Near the top of the slope, at #6, close to the *l'Arc de Triomphe*, and with the backing of various friends and his family, Roland Garros, in late 1909, opened his dealership. An elegantly lettered sign announced, *"Roland Garros Automobiles-Voiturettes de Sport"* or Roland Garros Sports Cars. He was 20 years old.

Commercial success came quickly to the new auto store. Garros's marketing smarts and contacts with the moneyed young paid off. His crowd, the group he socialized with, included his customers, his future customers, his social equals, and his sporting comrades. It was an excellent time to be alive, young, well-to-do, handsome, and in Paris. Parisians, then as now, spent little time in their rather cramped apartments preferring instead to while away the evening hours in cafés, bistros, and restaurants. A domicile was for sleeping, dressing, and returning home to late at night, often alone, sometimes not. During these nighttime *soirees*, the spirited conversations turned to beautiful women, trendy restaurants, sporting events, drink, and music, probably in that order. Cars were also discussed along with mounting interest in the halting first attempts at aviation, the news of which appeared in the many local papers. Roland and his friends occasionally spoke about the loss of the Alsace and Lorraine regions to the hated Germans and what a pity it was, but politics and geopolitical trends did not hover prominently over lifted glasses of Italian vermouth at their favorite bar, Cinzano's.

Across Europe in the wood-paneled *weinstubes* of Berlin, in London's paneled pubs, in the restaurants scattered around the *Grand Place* in Brussels, and in Parisian nightspots, the same scene played out. People, particularly young people, but also including their elders as well, enjoyed the good life of *La Belle Époque*. Europe had treated itself to roughly half a century of peace and ever-increasing prosperity with new delights for the senses continually invented.

The Franco-German War of 1870-71 was but a distant and fading memory, at least in France. This conflict, which should be more accurately called the Franco-Prussian War, was provoked by Prussia to secure the consolidation of imperial Germany, bringing the independent south German states, such as Bavaria, into a united Germany ruled over by the Prussians. The German victory and national unification upset the delicate balance of powers envisioned by the Peace of 1815, the treaty ending the Napoleonic wars. Winning set in motion tensions and rivalries, which would soon result in the most horrific carnage ever endured in warfare. These tectonic tendencies were not apparent to anyone in Cinzano's, or in any other trendy Parisian social setting. What if the Germans now owned Alsace and Lorraine? Most people living there had German names anyway and spoke a German dialect as well as a French *patois*. Intensely more interesting to Garros's crowd were the exploits of early birdmen; the American Wright brothers, the Brazilian Santos-Dumont, and who was sleeping with whom. The party played on across Europe as the political weather worsened and clouds of coming war roiled. People living in what is now known as the Golden Age thought the good times would go on forever. They were wrong.

It is 1908 and Maxim's of Paris holds the title "The World's Most Famous Restaurant," or so the proprietor would have prospective diners believe. It is certainly one of the most expensive, with a fabulous art nouveau interior (still fabulous today), with innovative cuisine, superb service, and with clientele drawn from the upper reaches of British, French, and Continental society. It is the monthly meeting place for the Aero Club of France, the first and most prestigious organization of its kind. Aero club meetings are famous for generating piles of empty champagne bottles. Maxim's is the place to see and be seen for people who crave being seen.

Being seen is particularly easy for good-looking, fashionable women who are invariably seated as if on display, in one of the sidewalk-facing windows, posed there by the unctuous *Maître d'hôtel.*

On this night in late fall, the crowd of passers-by strolling on *Rue Royal* in front of the restaurant are forced to choose between two visual attractions; beautiful women tastefully shown off in the restaurant's windows, and the rakish Grégoire sports car strategically parked just outside the front door. It is brilliant in white, with red wooden wheels lightly dusted by Parisian streets; feline, low and crouching, with two bucket seats upholstered in diamond-stitched glove leather. The driver's seat is on the right, passenger's on the left, the car with its extensive brass trim gleaming in the street lights; it is a sight to see.

Maxim's massive carved wooden door swings open, held there by a uniformed doorman and a couple saunters out. The man leans close to the doorman speaking in a soft voice, their palms touch, and francs are passed. The customer looks at the waiting car and nods. As the door swings shut, the doorman crosses the sidewalk and waits in front of the vehicle. The man, thin, dark, and sporting a bushy moustache, helps his elegant young lady don a long cotton duster, then puts on his own coat while she ties a flowered silk scarf over her elaborate hat, knotting two corners under her chin.

"Ce diner était fabuleux. Les Escargots étaient particulièrement bons, charnusmet juteux." The dinner was fabulous, the snails were particularly good, fat and juicy. She said with a smile.

"I'm glad you enjoyed it. Now, where do we go?"

"Anywhere there is champagne."

"Anywhere?" The man asks.

Her smile returns, sly and discreet, her eyes, looking into his are half-closed. The message could not be clearer.

"Anywhere."

Much to the staring pedestrians' disappointment, the lady manages to mount the white running board and occupy the left-hand bucket seat, helped by her escort, without flashing a forbidden glimpse of a well-turned ankle or even better, a shapely calf below her long skirt.

A struck wooden match and a quick fiddle with tiny valves ignite the acetylene-powered headlights which struggle to illuminate the city's gloom with their pasty yellow beams. *Rue Royal* boasts the new-fangled electric street lights which cast circular pools of light at intervals on the sidewalk. The ornate lamps try to brighten the street with limited success. The winter night's gathering dark and mist is winning the lighting battle.

The driver takes his place behind the wood-rimmed steering wheel. Using two brass levers protruding from the steering column, he retards the ignition timing and sets the throttle to the start position. He nods to the doorman waiting between the shinning headlights. Bending over, the doorman grasps the red crank protruding forward from under the polished brass radiator shell. Carefully, he gives the crank a half-turn. He must be cautious. Hand-cranking an auto, engines often kick back, spinning the crank backward, impacting the starter's forearm, and inflicting a "Ford Fracture." The injury is named after the Model T's propensity to dish out such punishment.

The four-cylinder engine catches, spits, and settles into a grumpy idle. Quick adjustment to the spark lever and throttle produces a contented purr. A grinding of gears, no synchromesh transmissions yet, a jarring clutch release, and the car lurches forward, the lady's comely head and hat bobbing in reaction. The sports car leaves the curb, rolling slowly at first, then gathering speed down the dimly lit *Rue Royal*, the headlights trying to highlight the Belgian-block-paved road. At the expansive *Place de la Concorde,* 100m away, the machine turns right, up the *Champs Elysées* and towards a waiting apartment.

Navigating the nighttime Parisian streets will not be the driver's only challenge this evening. Prior to the invention of zippers, Velcro, and elastic, undressing a fashionable woman was an exercise in patience. Numerous buttons, hooks, laces, ribbons, bows, and layers lay between an excited lover and a well-dressed woman's body, the object of his desire. He might have to open a second bottle of champagne and take a break from such an arduous but amorous task. Fortunately, the sports car's slender pilot is as experienced and proficient at disrobing womenfolk as he is at driving.

CHAPTER FOUR

HUMANKIND TAKES TO THE AIR

GARROS IS DETERMINED TO JOIN IN

In mid-summer 1909, Roland Garros's auto sales business was booming. He obtained sole representation for Grégoire automobiles in the Paris region and quickly succeeded at his newly-chosen profession. Sales poured in, cars rolled out, and commissions piled up in his bank account. Likewise, his social life proved to be relentless, one he shared with numerous like-minded friends at fine restaurants, parties, and cafés with ever-present ladies. However, a new love vied to displace most of the sweet life, a love no one saw coming, least of all Garros himself.

July came and Paris emptied as it still does, most well-off people departed for vacations either in the French countryside or abroad. Garros was no exception; why hang around a deserted car showroom? Once again, he whiled away a few weeks at his friend's castle among several other young bloods, playing tennis and chasing women, with considerably more success at the second endeavor. It was summer camp for adults in the Champagne region.

Late in August, the "clan" as they called themselves, drove their motorcars on a lark to the ancient city of Reims, the region's capitol, to attend *Le Grand Semaine International d'Aviation de la Champagne* the international week of aviation in the Champagne country. The highly profitable sparkling wine industry, based in Reims, collectively intended to brand their bubbly as the tipple of choice for the *avant garde*, the trendsetters, the elite, the young, the rich and powerful. Embryonic aviation drew such people's interest. Hopefully, they would attend a flying exhibition and while doing so, acquire a taste for champagne.

A large field outside Reims was temporarily converted to an airfield, and nearly anything and anyone who could fly was there. Tents, hangers, pavilions, bars, and cafés large and small ringed the expansive grass field. On display were spherical balloons filled with hot air or hydrogen, torpedo-shaped dirigibles also lifted by hydrogen, and heavier-than-air flying machines galore, some more successful at flying than others. Most aviation pioneers attended, except for the Wright brothers, who felt they had nothing to prove, and who were probably worried about other inventors filching their technology. A series of pylons erected on the field served to conduct speed trials and air races. Would any fearless pilot break the 100 kilometers per hour, 60 miles per hour, barrier and survive the attempt?

Day by day, corks popped, champagne flowed, and tales of airborne adventure were shared, enhanced, and shared again in the canvas-covered cafés. It is easy to suspect Garros learned a fundamental aviation truth in Reims, when you cannot fly, talk about flying. If your story is not interesting enough to compete with the other pilots, add some dubious details. Later, published accounts of his aerial exploits would reflect this essential enhancement technique.

Roland Garros always dreamed of flying, who has not, but his dreams continued long after childhood, particularly during his schooling in the south of France. As a boy, he watched the seabirds of Réunion Island wheel and soar effortlessly, masters of the air, and wondered how they did it. Flying looked so easy when he watched birds.

But flying was not easy for humans, and part of the problem lay with birds. For millennia, boys and girls, men and women, dreamed of flying like a bird, riding the wind with rarely a ruffled feather. Greek mythology tells us Daedalus and his son, Icarus, were imprisoned in the dreaded Labyrinth on the Island of Crete. They collected loose feathers, coated their arms with molten candle wax, stuck the feathers on, and flew away furiously flapping. In route back to Greece, Icarus, despite his father's warning, flew too close to the sun and his wax melted, plunging the arrogant lad to his death into the Aegean Sea. Or so the myth goes. Not really a story about flying, but rather a cautionary tale about the classical Greek aversion to excess and hubris. In this case an excess of pride in aerial performance expressed by Icarus as an excess of altitude.

Humankind eventually discovered human-powered flight was very difficult. Leonardo da Vinci sketched detailed drawings of two notional flying machines, both man-powered; a helicopter and an ornithopter, a machine that flies, supposedly, by flapping its wings. The designs were well-thought out. Leonardo studied the flight of birds extensively. There is no record of either machine being constructed. Perhaps Leonardo suspected man-powered flight was doomed to failure, as he also invented the parachute.

An extremely fit, lightweight human, such as the cyclists riding in the *Le Tour de France* bike race, can put out 2.5 horsepower for a few seconds and maybe 0.5 horsepower for an extended period. The Wright brothers, careful engineers, calculated they needed an engine putting out at least ten horsepower to enable their Flyer I to sustain level flight. Master engine builder Charlie Taylor gave them 12 hp. It was not until the 1970's that an airplane, the Gossamer Condor, using space-age materials demonstrated controlled, sustained human-powered flight. Its hard-working pilot was a professional cyclist and hang glider pilot who drove a slow-turning propeller by pedaling. But, until then, human-powered flight was a futile hope. True, powered, heavier-than-air flight of any kind had to wait for internal combustion engine technology to catch up with the dreams of would-be aviators. All the while, birds soared, climbed, dove, and looked down on earth-bound humans with arrogant avian distain.

To fly, heavier-than-air craft must solve four major issues: aerodynamic lift, power production, stability, and control. Unlike surface vehicles, which can be paused for tinkering, machines supported by air must address all four problems simultaneously. By1900, the generation of lift started to be understood from studies of bird's wings and wind tunnel testing. Humankind knew how to build a wing and it could glide producing lift. The gasoline engine's development slowly solved the needed power problem. Concepts of aerodynamic stability and flight control were much harder to grasp. It is in this domain people had always been deceived by birds. Birds make flying look easy, but if you build an accurate replica of a bird and try to fly it, the model bird will tumble end-over-end. Although they do not appear to be so, birds are aerodynamically unstable. They can fly because they employ an avian version of an active control system. Their brains send constant correctional commands to their wing and tail feathers. Introduction of the F-16 Viper fighter plane and the B-2 Spirit bomber proved at last that aerodynamically unstable machines could fly employing active control systems. Even so, the F-16 has a vertical tail, unlike any bird.

Early inventors tended to solve one of the two problems, either stability or control, but not the other. Samuel Langley, a scientist at the American Smithsonian Museum, flew a miniature airplane powered by a tiny steam engine, of all things, in 1896. The model plane flew 1600 meters, almost a mile, a paragon of stability, but with no control. Langley's full-sized "aerodromes" were flops, literally, flopping his luckless pilot into the Potomac river immediately after launch from atop a moored houseboat. Langley gave up.

Germany's Otto Lilienthal convinced himself the stability and control problems could be handled by simply shifting the pilot's weight during flight. He constructed a series of gliders and launched them down steep hills while he balanced underneath on a type of trapeze bar like on a modern hang-glider. Lilienthal tragically demonstrated the limitations of weight-shifting for control when coupled with a lack of inherent stability by killing himself in 1896. He was unable to pull his latest glider out of a dive by shifting his weight. He did invent the biplane though, mounting two wings one atop the other producing a rigid box structure. Today's hang gliders are much more aerodynamically advanced than the German's primitive straight-winged crates. They are both stable and controllable in flight. Their pilots owe a lot to Otto.

The Wrights understood the control issue well and their Flyer I mounted movable surfaces allowing the pilot to command all three axis; roll (banking the wings), pitch (moving the nose up and down), and yaw (nose skewing left and right). Stability was something else, and the Wrights did not see this problem coming. The Flyer I was extremely unstable, even wildly divergent, in the pitch direction. Its nose either wanted to climb or dive violently. Roll stability was neutral, the wings had to be leveled constantly. Yaw stability was acceptable; the airplane would fly straight ahead with little effort required by a neóphyte pilot.

The United States Air Force programmed a flight simulator to mimic the Flyer I and invited test pilots from the famed USAF Aerospace Research Pilot School at Edwards Air Force Base to try and fly it. No one could. Experienced, highly-trained test pilots scored an unbroken series of simulated crashes. Orville and Wilbur Wright could fly their invention only because they were not pilots, yet. Despite all this, the brothers managed the first controlled, sustained flights of a heavier-than-air machine in December of 1903. Sea birds, those effortless wind riders over Kill Devil Hills on North Carolina's Atlantic coast, must have watched the Wrights' first powered flight of 120 feet, about 40 meters, at an altitude of 10 feet, 3 meters, and laughed their little feathered asses off. The Wright brother's first flight was shorter than the wingspan of today's Boeing 747 jumbo jet airliner.

Unmindful of all this history, Roland Garros and his clan visiting at Reims were impressed by the idea of powered flight, although due to bad weather, not as much flying took place at the week-long air display as the promoter had promised. Roland seemed more intrigued than the rest, perhaps due to his re-occurring dreams of flight, or maybe due to a thirst for fame and adventure not fulfilled by the automobile. Many long nights of heated discussion followed later in the fall of 1909 at Cinzano's back in Paris between Garros and his Parisian crowd.

The issue was money. Conventional wisdom held that while flying machines were exciting and perhaps the next big thing, prospects of making a profit building, flying, or selling aircraft were perceived as slim to none.

In October of 1909, Garros attended another, different exposition at the *Grand Palais* in Paris, this time as a wannabe customer, not an exhibitor. *Le Exposition Internationale de Locomotion Aérienne* was the world's premier showplace of aircraft despite being confined to the vast hall's interior where no flying was possible. This trade show grew into the world-famous Paris Air Show and soon moved outside the city to Le Bourget airfield where actual flight is possible, even encouraged. It is held in all odd-numbered years to this day.

The assortment of flying machines, most for sale, at the exposition hardened Garros's resolve to fly. Before electric lights became widespread and efficient, major exhibition halls needed glass roofs to illuminate the exhibits. The Grand Palais featured the monoplane Louis Blériot flew across the English Channel. It hovered over the crowd of attendees, suspended under the glazed half-dome canopy and back-lit by sunlight. Blériot won a prize of 1000 Pounds Sterling, put up by a London newspaper, for the first heavier-than-air flight from France to England. Seen from below, it was as if the sky, visible through the great hall's roof, was inviting the tiny aircraft to return to the air.

Many exhibitors hawked their wares at the air show representing state-of-the-art in aviation, such that it was. In 1910, that state was expressed by artisanal inventors and producers. Airplanes were built one at a time as orders trickled in. Workshops tended to construct each plane separately; no two were exactly alike, even from the same builder. The stick-and-muslin cloth contraptions for sale followed no standard configuration for flight controls; each manufacturer had his own ideas. Today, from the lowliest Cessna 150 trainer to the F-22 Raptor fighter plane, cockpit controls are similar and pilots move easily from one aircraft to another, although probably not from the C-150 directly to the Raptor.

Roland Garros wanted an aircraft and he wanted one badly. Not surprisingly, the issue again was money, or rather the lack thereof. Even with his successful automobile business, his savings, and some small loans from skeptical friends, his bankroll was nowhere near most builders' asking prices for their aerial creations. Then, he saw the Demoiselle and it was boy-meets-girl love at first sight. *"Demoiselle"* in French means, "Damsel" or "Fair Maiden." The word also means "Dragonfly" which is what the designer surely intended. But for Garros "Damsel" fit. He was smitten.

The Demoiselle was the product of a brainstorm by an early aviation pioneer, Alberto Santos-Dumont. Santos-Dumont, his given name is rarely used, was the scion of an aristocratic Brazilian family. Profits from a vast coffee empire in Brazil made them, and him, very wealthy. Santos-Dumont spent most of his life in Paris, not Brazil, and with nothing productive to do there, he became interested in aviation. Few aviation pioneers made contributions to both lighter-than-air flight and to heavier-than-air machines. Santos-Dumont excelled at both. In the 1890s he developed, constructed, and flew dirigibles, rigid-framed airships held aloft by bags of hydrogen gas. In 1901, he won a substantial monetary prize, not that he needed the money, for the first flight of any kind to circle the Eiffel Tower and return. He donated his winnings to the poor people of Paris.

After the turn of the century, Santos-Dumont turned his attention increasingly to airplanes, finding them more exciting, more challenging, than rigid airships. Perhaps he liked to smoke while flying, not a good idea with a gas bag overhead filled with highly flammable hydrogen and with an on-board generator keeping the bag filled. In any case, piloting his 14-bis craft, which looked like a giant box kite, he made the first powered, controlled flight of an airplane in Europe. Taking off from the *Bois de Boulogne*, the large park just outside the built-up area of the city, he brought heavier-than-air flight to Europe. Like the Wrights, Santo-Dumont's plane mounted its pitch control surfaces out in front of the pilot. He encountered the same instability as the boys from Dayton, Ohio had wrestled with on their Flyer I. By this time, the brothers were operating their Flyer III for over half an hour, having moved pitch control surfaces to the tail. However, they conducted their aerial experiments in the United States far from the European limelight. Santos-Dumont's achievement was certified by the *Federation Internationale Aeronautique*, the FIA, of France, as the first powered flight anyone important, meaning anyone French, had seen. As a result, most Brazilians today firmly believe Santos-Dumont was the first heavier-than-air aviator and the Wrights were crass imposters, usurpers of Santos-Dumont's glory. How could two bike mechanics from Ohio outdo a Parisian/Brazilian blue-blood?

Regardless of who was first to fly, Santos-Dumont had a vision for aviation, one which promised the airplane would bring widespread peace and prosperity. People of the world would fly around, visit, get to know and understand each other. To accomplish that goal, he declined to patent his many aviation inventions, allowing anyone to use his technology and his designs free of charge. Having no need of more riches, he devoted his efforts to spreading aviation knowhow. This contrasted with the Wrights, who frequently sued competitors for patent infringement. Hoping to move aviation out of the domain of rich dilettantes and hustling entrepreneurs, Santos-Dumont planned the inexpensive Demoiselle for mass production, aiming for 100 units built and sold. It was the last aircraft he designed and the last one he flew. At the 1909 aviation exhibition in Paris, Demoiselles sold for one-third the price of other contemporary craft, just what Roland Garros was looking for. He put down a deposit and waited for delivery.

Alas, Santos-Dumont's concept of world harmony facilitated by far-ranging airplanes was not to be. Instead, future air power would be instrumental in the Great War's merciless carnage. Dirigibles bombed London, blowing up helpless civilians. Biplanes strafed exposed troops and rained death from the sky. Aerial dogfights killed pilots and observers daily. This shattered dream of global harmony broke Santos-

Dumont and he fell into deep depression. He also suffered a chronic debilitating disease. Mourning the killing wrought by his precious aircraft and the loss of his physical well-being, Alberto Santos-Dumont took his own life after the first world war but before the next one.

War clouds were only just darkening the horizon in late 1909 when Santos-Dumont, ever the philanthropist, encouraged the Clément-Bayard workshop outside Paris to build and sell Demoiselles. Winter floods in northern France halted production. In Paris, the Seine River burst its banks and inundated large areas of the city. His auto business comatose as a result of widespread street flooding, Roland Garros left for *La Côte d'Azur*, the French Rivera, in January. He marked time in the south of France, gambling at the Monte Carlo casino, eating at the famous *Café de Paris* in Monaco, and waiting for delivery of his aircraft. Life on the Rivera was sweet with nothing much to do than to indulge in idle pleasure.

But, Garros was restless, his life-long dreams of flying without care or machine, were replaced by visions of cruising over the Bay of Nice in his own aircraft. In April of 1910, Roland Garros returned to Paris and at last took delivery of his first airplane at the factory. Now, he had to learn how to fly it.

CHAPTER FIVE

THE FLEDGLING

PILOTING, SELF-TAUGHT

Roland Garros was about to realize his new dream of owning and flying an aircraft, but just barely. Not that he did not own the Demoiselle, he bought and paid for it. No, his problem stemmed from the fact that the Demoiselle was barely an airplane. Today, the tiny bird would be classed as an "ultra-light." It weighed less than 135 kilos, 300 pounds, all up without the pilot. Powered by a 30-35 hp Dutheil et Chalmers two-cylinder, air-cooled engine swinging a huge propeller with paddle-shaped blades, the Demoiselle's performance was decidedly marginal at best. It was one of those airplanes which can barely kill you. But, kill people it did; so many that the tricky-to-fly craft earned the nickname, *"Tueuse d'Homme,"* or killer of men.

The tiny plane consisted primarily of bamboo stalks, undoubtedly shipped from the Indochina colony of Garros's childhood. Bamboo is light, rigid, and strong for its weight, more so than the woods normally used for aircraft, ash and spruce. However, it does not tolerate metal fasteners, such as screws and bolts, and its shiny surface repels glue. So, the Demoiselle was held together by lashing cotton cords and thin brass wire around the spindly bamboo poles, and joining the disparate parts together with a few metal bracket clamps. Its wings were outlined in bamboo. Arched ash ribs spanned the width of each wing, held there by knotted string. Muslin cloth stretched over the wing's top structure and was fixed in place using stitches which would not look out of place on a baseball.

Three longer, thicker bamboo poles comprised the fuselage, clamped in a triangular structure by steel posts and left uncovered by fabric and open to the airflow. At the rear, the plane's tail swiveled on a universal joint for pitch and yaw control and was built, like the wings, of bamboo, light wood, and cloth. Warping the wings effected roll control, this mechanism being the Wright brothers' patented invention. There is no record of the designer, Alberto Santos-Dumont, licensing the Wright's technology, but it is hard to imagine he did not. The brothers were famous for suing aviators who "borrowed" their inventions without compensation. Mounted on the wing's leading edge, the engine drank gasoline from a shiny, torpedo-shaped copper tank on metal stalks above the wing's top surface. Gravity kept the engine fed with fuel.

The tricycle landing gear employed flimsy bicycle wheels, aided by a steel tail skid. Successful use of aluminum for aircraft structures would be years in the future. The wheels were fixed rigidly to a spider web of small steel tubing slung beneath the fuselage. Without springs or dampers to absorb the shock, any hard touchdown resulted in bent wheels, buckled tubes, and a damaged airplane.

Seemingly a design afterthought, the pilot sat low, squarely behind the two main wheels, their axle under his feet, his butt scant inches above the ground. His seat was a canvas strap suspended between two tubes. No seat belt. Spinning in front of the pilot, the prop waited on a careless landing, one that would pitch the pilot forward into the walnut blade. One hand operated a lever for yaw control, as with a rudder on a boat. The other hand held a similar lever for pitch control, up and down. A foot pedal, as on a car, controlled the throttle. To warp the wings for roll control, the pilot leaned left or right. Input reached the wings by a lever attached to the pilot's back with a leather harness. In contemporary photos of Roland Garros, he is pictured wearing the wing-warping harness over his impeccably tailored vest, shirt, and tie.

Garros, normally the face of fearlessness, must have grasped the danger inherent in the skill he was about to learn. He wrote an old friend a letter, really a hand-written last will and testament, instructing his friend what to do if Roland was killed. His assets were to be liquidated, his debts paid, and the balance sent to his mother in Saigon. There was no mention of his father, now divorced from his mother.

In the early days of aviation, learning to fly was very much a teach-it-to-yourself process. All early birdmen, the Wrights, Glen Curtiss, Santos-Dumont, Louis Blériot, taught themselves how to pilot a plane. No one knew how to do something which had never been done before. Otto Lilienthal might have provided some helpful tips, but he was dead. Samuel Langley's hapless pilot had nothing to offer other than swimming lessons. There were no instructors, no syllabus, no manuals, no simulators, no check rides, and no dual-control aircraft. Indeed, few aircraft could carry more than one (light) human. At least the Wright brothers could compare piloting techniques with each other. Orville and Wilbur alternated flights, but even when they built a two-place Flyer, no in-flight instruction between them ensued. They promised their father they would never fly together in case the worst happened. Younger than most fledgling pilots, Roland Garros eagerly stepped into this new, dangerous world of aviation, the teach-your-self-how-to-fly domain, determined to be both an apt student and good teacher, to himself.

Garros took delivery of his Demoiselle at the factory-cum-workshop at Issy-les-Moulineaux, outside Paris. He was impatient to get into the air, but had to wait. The airfield was controlled by the French army, who conducted drills, marching to and fro most of the day, leaving only a few hours for flying; just after dawn and late in the afternoon.

During World War II, boastful pilots when encountering a new aircraft would often claim, "Just show me how to start it," announcing their prowess at flying anything. This technique was not as far-fetched as you might think. After the war, legendary American fighter pilot Robin Olds survived his first flight in a Royal Air Force Meteor jet just this way. A squadron mate standing on the wing showed him where the switches were in the cockpit, helped him start the airplane, and sent Olds off alone into lousy weather. While this attitude prevailed in some quarters of aviation until mid-century, mainly in the world of single-seat fighters, at the dawn of the air age it was the norm.

Thus, prior to World War I, Pilots were expected to figure things out for themselves. At Issy-les-Moulineaux, the chief mechanic, a dowdy chap named "Romain," briefed Garros on the control levers of his aircraft and helped Roland adjust to the rudimentary cockpit; the canvas seat, the single foot pedal, and the leather wing warping straps. Eager to fly, Garros was told by Romain his initial flight would have to wait, first-time pilots were not to venture forth unless the wind was dead calm, until the smoke from a cigarette floated straight up. Sadly, the late-afternoon breeze was too brisk.

Next day, the Demoiselle's engine would not start; another opportunity lost. The third day; more engine trouble. Garros was not unfamiliar with temperamental engines; the expertise came with the territory for a sports car driver and dealer. After fiddling with the magneto and carburetor, Garros and Romain got the two-cylinder motor turning over. However, its reliability was highly suspect. The beginning flight plan included taxiing, slowly at first, then faster and faster, getting the feel of the controls and the aircraft, and then attempting a short hop before reaching the flying field's far end. Garros's first flight would also be his first solo and hopefully not his last. Unfortunately, the future first fighter pilot would experience his first crash before his first flight.

Learning to fly an airplane is a lot like learning to ride a bicycle, but the penalties for a major mistake are much more severe, tending towards fatal. A child on his or her training bike needs to process error information quickly, think about what corrective action is needed, and then decide how to act. Bike is falling to the left, must turn handlebars to the left now. With a parent jogging alongside, and some scraped knees and elbows, most kids learn bike riding. From then on, balancing a bike becomes second nature. No conscious thought is ever needed to keep the bike upright and moving. A more mature cyclist can think of other things while riding; race strategy, tonight's hot date, or catching the peloton.

Once learned, techniques on how to keep an aircraft under control also become second nature with no thoughts expended. Left wing down, move the controls slightly to raise left wing. Commands flow from your eyes seeing the drooping wing, directly to the hand holding the control stick. An accomplished pilot can devote his or her attention to tonight's love interest or shooting down enemy aircraft, or both.

The Frenchman's initial attempt at aviation was always going to be dicey, no parent running alongside, no instructor pilot giving guidance. Just how risky his inaugural airborne adventure turned out to shock him. It was almost a fatal surprise.

From one day of their careers, student pilots are taught a major precaution to exercise before taking the runway. No matter whether they are turning on to a 10,000-foot concrete expanse at Los Angeles International Airport, or the local crop-duster's grass strip, it is imperative to clear the final approach path. You must look back up the glide slope leading to the active runway to ensure there is no aircraft about to touch down on the space you desire for take-off. A cardinal rule of aviation safety is to never have two aircraft occupy the same point in space and time.

Eager to get into the air, Roland Garros had not yet learned this key lesson. How could he? Romain was not a pilot and Garros received no formal instruction. After all, he did not take driving lessons, why would he need flying lessons?

Late afternoon at Issy-les-Moulineaux; the smoke from a cigarette ascended vertically, time to fly. With Romain pulling the propeller through and two helpers holding on to the tail plane keeping the spindly craft pointed down the grass field, the engine sputtered into life. As soon as Romain was clear, Garros nodded to the holders, they released their grips, and the aircraft began to move forward. Attention directed straight ahead, his brain struggling to remember how to move the controls, Garros sensed rather than saw the presence of another plane, but where was it? He looked right, barely in time to spot a large biplane, a Farman, about to touch down on the patch of grass a few meters ahead. Without brakes and no ground steering, all he could do was press the engine kill switch and prepare for impact. Roland later remarked he assumed a fetal position, as he used in the bottom of a rugby scrum, an instinctive maneuver that probably saved him from going through the still-turning propeller.

The crash was spectacular, a whirlwind of flapping white cloth, shards of bamboo, splinters of wood, broken pieces of the propeller, and dust flying everywhere. Silence came as quickly as the impact but lasted far longer. Romain and his helpers came running, found Garros curled up during the wreckage, and extracted him intact. The Farman, a much bigger aircraft constructed of wood, not bamboo, was only slightly damaged, but Garros's precious Demoiselle was demolished, a total write-off.

Maurice Clément, the aircraft manufacturing company's CEO, soon surveyed the crumpled pile of wreckage and allowed as the engine was reusable, another Demoiselle airframe could be had for the modest sum of one-half of the original purchase price.

Garros was devastated; all his savings were tied up in the heap of debris lying crumpled on the field. His family was less than enthusiastic about funding his aeronautical adventures, and his friends still had no idea how an investment in an aircraft would pay off. Both groups would be no help. Fortunately, the Farman's pilot came to the rescue, taking complete blame for the accident. He opined it was his craft that landed on Garros's delicate bird. Perhaps he should have cleared the touchdown zone before committing to alighting. This was a generous act of charity for the gentleman. While it is true that in 1910 there were few formal rules of aviation, common sense should have dictated an aircraft committed to land would have precedence over a taxing plane. In fact, Roland Garros should have cleared the final approach path before proceeding. The Farman pilot instructed Clément to assemble Garros a new plane and put the bill on his account.

As darkness fell, the two men, one an established aviator and the other not, retired to a nearby hanger for some verbal instruction and advice flowing one way, to Roland Garros. Later that night at Cinzano's, Roland regaled the clan with the tale of how his first attempt at flight was almost his last.

Several days later, another Demoiselle awaited another attempt at aviation. Without hesitation, Garros tried again – after checking to see if any other aircraft were intent on landing. The tiny aircraft gathered speed over the grass parade ground, bumped and bounced, and responded to more power by lifting off. Roland Garros was finally flying! The flight, which covered about 100 meters, 330 feet, at a maximum altitude of one meter, three feet, was not a thing of beauty. "Wobbly" would be an accurate adjective, the wings banked slightly left, then right as the beginning pilot over-corrected, then straightened up. The aircraft's nose pulsed up and down, the random flight path resembled that of an actual demoiselle, a dragonfly. Looking through the spinning propeller, Garros saw the end of the parade ground/airfield approaching. A line of parked aircraft was arranged on the perimeter. He chopped the throttle with his right foot and the diminutive craft dropped from the sky, hitting hard on the un-sprung wire wheels. More wobbles as the stick-and-cloth contraption lurched to a stop, bobbing up and down and rocking side to side. The impact bent both bicycle-style wheels. Looking down on the pair from his seat, he saw the rims in a figure-eight distortion. But he had flown!

That night at Cinzano's, the champagne flowed like aviation fuel.

CHAPTER SIX

THERE IS NO BUSINESS LIKE SHOW BUSINESS

GARROS TAKES HIS ACT ON THE ROAD

As the spring of 1910 warmed into early summer and the days grew longer, much longer in northern Europe, Roland Garros took every opportunity to fly, honing his fast-developing piloting skills. His wind-up alarm clock went off at 0400 every morning, just before the slow-breaking dawn. Wakened by the clanging bell, he checked the leaves on the tree growing just outside his apartment. If the leaves were dead still, he leapt out of bed, dressed rapidly, and cranked up his roadster. He sped the five kilometers, four miles, out to the aerodrome in the southwest suburbs of Paris, driving as fast as the primitive roads of the day would permit.

If the early morning winds remained calm, he flew. His self-training flights became longer and more skilled, aided on the ground by the ever-trusty Romain. His aircraft pitch control improved and along with it, his altitude control. Leveling the wings became easier for him with less overcorrecting, less rocking side to side. By trial and error, he learned how to use the rudder along with the wings to effect gentle, coordinated turns while remaining over the flying field. This skill set is vital for a smooth flight, but it was a technique still in question among the worldwide flying community. Some pilots persisted in performing the flat turn, applying full rudder, left or right, while keeping the wings level, skidding around an aerial corner. The aerodynamics of powered flight were not well understood by all and existing knowledge was typically not shared with other birdmen. Both small and insular, the nascent aviation community was scattered across Europe and the United States, with little conversation between members due to distance and the lack of a rapid communication means other than the telephone or telegraph. Also, for competitive reasons, there was little exchange of information on best practices, particularly from the secretive, litigious Wright brothers. So, the wrong-headed idea of the inefficient skid turn survived. At the week-long exhibition of flying Roland and his clan attended in Reims the previous summer, American aviation pioneer Glenn Curtiss beat the famous French aviator Louis Blériot, conqueror of the English Channel. Louis lost the first Gordon Bennett Trophy race to Curtiss, despite Blériot flying the fastest aircraft and setting a world speed record during the meet. Curtiss won by flying tighter, coordinated turns around the pylons marking the circuit, not wasting energy and speed in skids and by flying a shorter route.

Beginning pilots displayed extreme caution when banking their aircraft at low altitude. To them, there seemed to be some mysterious aerodynamic effect present in flight near the ground which penalized a clumsy banked turn and resulted in a snap roll into mother earth. Hence the preference of some pilots for skidding around turns when flying low. It felt more comfortable to keep the wings level. But, once the aircraft is above half a wingspan's length in altitude, the ground has no more supporting effect on the airflow around the craft.

Not every pioneer pilot grasped the aerodynamic stall phenomenon. A stall occurs when the smooth airflow over the wing separates into chaotic turbulence, killing all lift and sometimes the inept pilot as well. Crashes near the ground were not caused by proximity to Terra Firma, but were caused by too steep a bank angle at too slow an airspeed, as can happen immediately after takeoff, resulting in the classic stall, spin, crash, and burn scenario.

Roland Garros was unafraid to perform banking turns near the ground, despite a dearth of flying experience. His native talent was soon recognized among the small, local aviation community. Perhaps this absence of fear stemmed from his background as a bicycle racer. During fast, steep mountain descents on narrow, curvy roads, the intrepid racer must lay his bike over to heart-stopping angles to navigate around the sharp turns without losing precious speed. Glenn Curtiss, an ex-bike racer, had demonstrated this type of courage at Reims. Still, despite his bravery and rapid progress, Garros had not completed the five-kilometer cross-country flight required for his French pilot's license. That is if a five-kilometer, four-mile, flight can be considered "cross-country." More importantly, he learned to let the Demoiselle down gently, returning to lightly to earth without bending any delicate tubing or warping a spindly spoked wheel.

After a few short flights in the morning calm, Garros would return to Paris and his automotive dealership, abandoning the grass aerodrome to the French army and its daily marching drills. The troops practiced for the war many people saw coming, but no one seemed to know when or why the fighting would break out. A sense of unease about the raging political rivalries prevailed in Europe among the chattering classes. A collision was coming, sometime, somewhere, and it would involve Germany and France. The newspapers were full of speculation, but few predictions. Likewise, the role of aircraft in the approaching conflict remained undefined and un-thought-of, because no military planner was yet familiar with what heavier-than-air craft could do.

Few people in Europe or America had ever seen a human being take to the air. Many skeptics refused to believe such a thing was even possible, thinking heavier-than-air aviation an elaborate hoax. Their descendants today are certain the American landings on the moon were staged in New Mexico. Yes, hot air balloons were well known then. Benjamin Franklin witnessed the ascent of such a craft in Paris over a century earlier and marveled at the sight. Hydrogen-filled balloons and dirigibles were also common. It was easy for the layperson, or the senior army officer, to comprehend flight in balloons and dirigibles. They floated effortlessly in the ocean of air, steadier than a boat bobs on the ocean of water. Heavier-than-air craft were something else, something so far removed from the everyday experiences of humankind despite birds having mastered the technique eons earlier. It was hard to imagine a man flying in a contraption consisting of an engine, cloth, and wood. Or, in Garros's aircraft, an engine, cloth, and bamboo.

Enter the promoter. Manned flight was such a novelty and so widely doubted, people would pay to see it done. These promoters were proficient in organizing shows, traveling around putting on circuses, rodeos, and auto races. The enterprising entertainment entrepreneur would rent a venue, hire or promise prize money to the performers, grease the local authorities' palms, advertise, and sell tickets to the event. After all expenses were paid, or dodged, the promoter would pocket the profits and leave town, sometimes rapidly. Today, such folks put on rock concerts, beauty pageants, and professional wrestling matches. Horse racing tracks were the promoters' favored venues for air shows. Most large towns had one, a grandstand was available, and the logistics for staging an event; ticket sales, parking, crowd control, and transportation, were already in place. All that was needed was a spectacle and what better one than the novelty of manned flight with its promise of thrills, chills, and spills. Successful, read profitable, exhibitions of aerial derring-do had been staged in half a dozen French towns during the years before 1910. The market was there, waiting.

In July of 1910, a promoter proposed to mount an air show in the small town of Cholet in the Loire valley of western France. The hustler enlisted the support of the city council, money surely changing hands under the nearest café's table. He promised to present a flying display of two monoplanes and two biplanes at the local horse track, or hippodrome. The word "hippodrome" is derived from the Latin word for "horse," and is not a place where hippos are raced. The track outside Cholet was booked, adverts were posted, and advanced tickets sales made. Already counting his monetary chickens prior to hatching, the promoter felt well-placed. Then, due to either some contractual dispute or the smell of something financially fishy, two aviators pulled out. The promoter held a leaking bag.

He came to the Issy-des-Moulineaux flying field looking for aviators, any aviators. Like all civilian airfields, then and now, there lingered numerous hangers-about willing to offer free advice, worth what it cost. They pointed to young Roland Garros as an obviously talented, up-and-coming pilot who would also not be able to command a high appearance fee due to his lack of a pilot's license. Garros was probably thrilled to be considered for the role of air show pilot, despite having only a few hours, minutes actually, in the air. Desperate, the promoter was not bothered by the licensing legalities of the Aero Club of France. He was certain the brash young man would show up and if he crashed, well, the public would get their money's worth one way or the other.

Roland enlisted the help of several friends and the chief mechanic, Romain. In school, he thrived on the spectacle of bike racing, but had not been interested in the growing auto racing scene. Auto racers then were blue-collar types, ex-mechanics with grease under their fingernails and working-class accents. America's future flying ace, racecar driver Eddie Rickenbacker, fit this plebian mold. Such an image did not match Garros's view of himself and his place in polite French society. But, being an air show pilot was a good fit for him, leap-frogging from bike racing over the auto-racing fad directly to competing in the skies. Garros signed the offered contract and started to prepare for his debut as a demonstration pilot.

Easily disassembled, the Demoiselle's bamboo poles fit together with brass ferules, rather like a split-bamboo fly-fishing rod. Only a few bolts attached the two-cylinder engine to the aircraft. Disassembled and looking like the stacked wreckage of a complicated tent, the aircraft components were piled into a boxcar and sent to Cholet by rail. Flying there was beyond the capability of both the fledgling pilot and his primitive aircraft.

Arriving at Cholet, the four air show pilots found themselves domiciled at the best hotel in town and invited to an elaborate dinner the night before the big show. Local Loire valley wine flowed like the river itself and the party broke up late, establishing an air show tradition persisting into the 21st century.

The next day, a Wednesday, the aircraft parts were deposited in makeshift hangers erected beside the racetrack. It took the Demoiselle team about two hours to re-assemble the little aircraft. However, nature refused to cooperate. A cold, wet wind gusted in from the Atlantic Ocean to the west. Driving rain showers scudded across the temporary aerodrome. 7000 to 8000 spectators, dry under the grandstand roof, waited impatiently for the show. It was not a good day for flying unless you happened to be a seagull.

Waiting and hoping for the weather to improve, the promoter told the pilots and mechanics to start their engines, to tune them up, and to take their time doing it. One by one, the four aircraft engines sputtered to life, the mechanics made a show of fiddling with the carburetors and ignition systems, then the barking motors fell silent. This charade ate up the best part of two hours and the crowd became more restless. They had come to see men fly, not to watch them tinker with engines.

Facing a revolt from the dissatisfied patrons in the grandstand who were angry at the delays, the promoter possessed few effective ways to quiet the crowd. In the days before high-fidelity electronic loud speakers, the word about the show situation had to be shouted through a primitive public-address system to the buzzing spectators. This crude means of communication did not lend itself to explaining the subtleties of aviation. Also, few customers could understand why a gusty breeze should hamper flight operations. Trains ran despite the weather, ships sailed, streetcars trundled, horses raced, birds flew, why couldn't aircraft fly? Unless of course, this whole heavier-than-air flying thing was a chimera after all. Grasping at straws now blowing away in the wind, the promoter begged the waiting aviators to do something, anything that looked like flying. A Blériot monoplane cranked up and taxied out of its canvas hanger into the teeth of the stiff breeze, the pilot obviously nervous.

Like most European tracks, the makeshift aerodrome was a turf venue with un-cut grass instead of the smooth, bare dirt common on racecourses in the United States. Bouncing along the main straightaway, the Blériot never exceeded 20 kilometers per hour, about 12 miles per hour, and never got close to lifting off. It must have been a handful for the pilot, keeping the flimsy monoplane straight down the home stretch with wind gusts trying to overturn his bird. He had to cope with the craft's lousy ground handling; no steering and no brakes, amid the skeptical crowd's attention.

Scared white, the Blériot pilot retired to his hanger. Now it was Garros's turn to try and taxi in front of the jeering, mostly male, crowd, whose anger was no doubt enhanced by local brandy consumed while waiting. A sudden, drenching rain shower put an end to all aeronautical activities. The Demoiselle's cloth-covered wings and tail would adsorb heavy rainwater like a sponge, the ignition would short out, and the unvarnished wood ribs could warp. Fair weather birds indeed were the aircraft of 1910.

With great trepidation, the panicked promoter shouted through his microphone that the promised air show was delayed until tomorrow. Angrier and drunker by the minute, the crowd poured from the grandstand demanding full refunds for all. The promoter and the complicit city council members fled on foot, making their escape through a nearby woods, running through the forest in the rain, a howling crowd in hot pursuit.

That night in the Cholet hotel, the quartet of would-be aviators kept a sober, low profile and hoped for better weather on the morrow.

Thursday, 14 July 1910, was the French national holiday, the equivalent of Independence Day, the Fourth of July, in the USA. Strangely, the day is known as Bastille Day only in the English-speaking world, and as The 14th of July in France. Nearly all the disappointed spectators returned to the grandstand that afternoon, ready to give the air show team and the worried promoter one more chance before calling for tar and feathers.

The rain passed during the night, probably due to the transition of a cold front off the Atlantic, but the wind was still blowing. Typically, after frontal passage, the wind will blow from one direction and at one speed, without the variable gusts experienced the previous day. The Aero Club of France's wind meter read a velocity of more than 10 meters per second, over 22 miles per hour. Flying in such conditions would be foolhardy and the Aero Club advised against any attempts at aviation. However, the safety-conscious officials had little leverage over Roland Garros, who possessed no pilot's license to lose. Although confronted again with an angry crowd, the promoter, under an unfamiliar spell of good ethics, was reluctant to encourage anyone to fly, fearing bloodstains on his hands. Much to the waiting troop of aviators' surprise, Garros cranked up the Demoiselle, departed his hanger and executed a perfect take off into the wind. Not for the last time would he defy the authorities and take a chance at flying, depending on his aviation skills to avoid sudden death.

Slowly traversing the length of the straightaway into the breeze, he turned down the backstretch, turned again, and touched down lightly in front of the grandstand. Not perfectly aligned with the racecourse runway, the wind blew the landing aircraft toward the safety barriers erected between the crowd and the track. Just before his whirling propeller tore into the barrier and vulnerable people, Garros grabbed one wheel with his gloved hands, easy to do sitting between the landing gear, and stopped it from rotating, spinning the Demoiselle 180 degrees, away from the watching spectators and then killed the engine. The crown went wild.

We can only imagine how hard that flight must have been in a tiny, featherweight aircraft buffeted by the wind, close to the ground and closer to disaster. Evil-handling craft, the era's planes featured non-linear control responses and questionable stability even in calm air. Flying in high winds required fast pilot reactions to keep the Demoiselle under some semblance of control. Garros, supremely confident in his new-found skills, rolled the dice and pulled it off, even throwing in a boot-leg turn in front of the crowd for effect. Today's fighter pilots sometimes hand out business cards with an inscription proclaiming themselves as, "Masters of the Calculated Risk." A bet-the-farm mentality seems essential for the profession. Roland Garros, who would become the first fighter pilot, was already there even if he did not know it yet.

During the two days at Cholet, Garros was the only pilot to get airborne. The city council nevertheless paid all four aviators just for showing up, inviting the displeasure of the good citizens of Cholet who were still disappointed in the abbreviated display of flying. Seeing their frustration, Roland Garros volunteered to perform another air show, this time for free, on Sunday, 24 July, an offer gratefully accepted by all.

Garros returned to Cholet with his Demoiselle on 23 July having in the interim easily passed his pilot's license test. French Pilot's License #147 now belonged to Roland Garros of Paris, France. On Saturday, he flew for five minutes at an altitude of nearly 500 feet over the racetrack, testing a new engine. Sunday morning, Garros hosted a free tennis party for the young people of Cholet and arrived at the racetrack aerodrome just in time to change from his tennis outfit to his flying garb. He made two flights that day, demonstrating steep turns, climbs, shallow dives, and perfect landings, all gratis.

Garros's first sortie into the demonstration pilot's world was not an enormous success, but his second attempt was boffo show business. Seeing the potential for more good publicity, the promoter offered Garros, the "Hero of Cholet," a role in the upcoming air show at Rennes, the capital of Brittany in northwest France, and the chance to fly in yet another exhibition later in Nantes. Nantes is the 6th largest city in France, the administrative center of the Loire region, and the ancestral home of both sides of Garros's family. These air shows represented the Big Time and Roland Garros now saw a way to monetize aviation. To profit from his new avocation, he would not have to design or build airplanes, or sell them, all he would have to do is fly, get paid for doing it, and stay alive, a challenge given the poor reliability of the period's aircraft. He accepted the offered contracts, but stipulated that his fee would double. Garros's clan at Cinzano's was amazed.

CHAPTER SEVEN

FLYING IS DANGEROUS

A Crash in the Valley of the Kings

Despite its name, the *Château de Versailles* is not a castle, nor a château. It lacks stone ramparts, crenellated towers, and a drawbridge-spanned moat. It is instead a palace and rather a large one. The main building is one quarter of a mile, 400 meters, wide and contains over 700 ornate rooms. Equally grandiose, the palace gardens cover 2000 acres, 800 hectares, and feature a pool nearly 5000 feet, 1500 meters, long; big enough to stage mock naval battles. Largely built during the reign of King Louis IV, Versailles vividly illustrates the 1789 French revolution's root causes. While the King and his court flaunted lives of unbelievable luxury, the *bourgeoisie* struggled under heavy taxation and the peasants, *les paysans*, starved. Located in the southwest suburbs of Paris, the Palace of Versailles has hosted many scenes of sybaritic excess, political intrigue, sexual peccadilloes, high drama, and God-only-knows what else. But, in the 228 years of its existence prior to 1910, Versailles had never seen an airplane crash. Roland Garros remedied that situation.

The exhibition at Rennes went well the first day. Five pilots flew; three showing off larger, more sophisticated airplanes than Garros, but the crowd seemed to enjoy watching his tiny Demoiselle flit about. He logged two flights of about 5 minutes each and was preparing for a third when darkness fell. On the show's second day, the weather turned menacing with intense winds and blustery rain showers, keeping the pilots with their delicate craft sheltered inside their temporary hangers. As daylight waned and most of the disappointed crowd departed, the rain stopped, but the wind continued to blow from the west. Garros intended to fly, against other, more experienced, pilots' advice. Romain also counseled caution as well, but to little avail. You can imagine the young aviator wanted to impress his new-found peers. He aimed to demonstrate his ability to handle the Demoiselle, to show he was made of the "right stuff" as Tom Wolfe wrote much later when describing the constant competition between aviators. Probably, the other pilots thought the stuff he was made of was foolhardy stupidity.

Nevertheless, Garros took off into the teeth of the wind, the Demoiselle bouncing and rocking in the turbulence. Passing over a rank of trees lining the field, he lost control. The tiny craft dropped one wing, the other pointing at the sky, the nose fell below the horizon, and no input to the controls seemed have any effect. An updraft caused by wind blowing against the line of trees was probably the cause, tossing the Demoiselle like a falling leaf. Disoriented, Garros closed his eyes and waited for the end of the short flight and his short life. It was the first time he experienced an excessive bank angle, and without any training or practice, cluelessness reigned. Suddenly, he felt the aircraft stabilize through no action on his part, the airspeed building, and the controls again responsive. He opened his eyes to see the wings almost level, but with the nose pointed down at the rapidly approaching treetops. Back pressure on the pitch control leveled the aircraft out of its shallow dive and the shaken pilot found himself headed back toward the air field. The wind had flung the Demoiselle back where it came, preforming an uncontrolled 180-degree turn. Relived to be alive, Roland turned, using a shallow bank angle, back into the wind and landed, fighting the gale all the way, and touched down a few meters from his hanger. History does not record what the other pilots said or thought.

A large segment of a successful pilot's skill set involves the correct handling of emergencies, such as an out-of-control aircraft. Closing your eyes and hoping for the best, or the least bad, outcome is not usually a viable or survivable strategy. Roland Garros's luck held at Rennes. Good luck is also a useful quality to possess. Once an in-flight emergency has played out, a pilot must recover his or her composure and carry on without allowing a recent bit of unpleasantness to affect his current or future performance. This key attribute he displayed at Rennes; landing the Demoiselle under demanding conditions despite having just a minute earlier escaped with his life from the maelstrom. Somewhat sobered by the incident at Rennes, Garros returned to Paris and doubled down on the auto business he neglected over the summer.

Earlier during his first summer at the Issy-les-Moulineaux airfield, Garros met John Moisant, another budding aviator. The encounter changed the path of Roland's life. Moisant, although born in Illinois, USA, traced his ancestry back to Quebec, Canada. His family immigrated across the border to the States, settling initially in the mid-west and later moving to San Francisco. The Moisants spoke both Canadian French and American English fluently. John grew up an adventurer, revolutionary, soldier of fortune, rich farmer, and would-be pilot. Gregarious and talkative, he made friends easily, confirming the common stereotype of Americans and *Quebecois* alike held by most people in France.

John and his brothers bought and operated a lucrative sugarcane plantation in El Salvador, Central America, finding time on the side to lead two armed, unsuccessful insurrections against the El Salvador government's dictator. Impressed with John Moisant, the leader of neighboring Nicaragua sent him to Europe, giving him the assignment to investigate this new aviation fad and to determine if airplanes could be of any use in Central America.

Moisant attended the same exhibition at Reims in 1909 as Garros and his clan. There he caught the urge to master the new science of aviation using his considerable funds. Determined to start from the ground up, literally, Moisant set about designing his own aircraft. He intended his first sortie as a pilot to be the first flight of his scratch-built aircraft. Lack of self-confidence was not one of John Moisant's faults.

At Issy-les-Moulineaux, he hired technicians from the local aircraft factory. This area of France became known as, "*Le Berceau de l'Aviation*," the Cradle of Aviation, and skilled workers could be found there. Working through the winter of 1909-1910, Moisant designed and built the world's first and only all-metal aircraft. The Moisant Biplane, known as *l'Ecrevisse,* the Crayfish, boasted a structure of steel tubing clad with wildly expensive aluminum sheeting. On its, and Moisant's, first flight in February 1910, the craft soared to 90 feet, 25 meters, then crashed heavily. Moisant was unhurt but the Crayfish was destroyed. His next attempt at aeronautical design and construction resulted in the Moisant Monoplane, known as *Le Corbeau*, the Crow, due to its all-black color. The Crow used parts salvaged from the Crayfish wreckage. This second Moisant airplane never got airborne, fortunately. It proved to be unstable on the ground, never mind the air, and constantly tipped over. While low self-confidence was not a problem for the young Canadian-American, aeronautical engineering presented a challenge.

Recognizing at last his limitations as a self-taught aeronautical engineer, Moisant bought a two-place Blériot XI monoplane from its designer, Louis Blériot. Blériot was somewhat of a visionary, running a school for pilots in Pau, France, in the south near the border with Spain. He sold aircraft and instructed buyers on how to fly them. Moisant's flight training logbook recorded four flights in the two-place Blériot, but no solo flights.

August 1910: Back in northern France, Moisant flew his new Blériot XI from its base at Etampes to its new home at Issy-les-Moulineaux, thoughtfully bringing along his mechanic for the ride on Moisant's third-ever sortie as a pilot in command. Their flight path crossed above the city of Paris, marking the first passenger flight over a large city. It seems to be a good motivational tool bringing the person responsible for the maintenance of your aircraft along, risking his own skin, and trusting his own handiwork.

Later the same day, Moisant repeated the sight-seeing hop, this time taking his new-found friend Roland Garros up as the passenger high over the city at 2000 feet, 600 meters, on Moisant's fourth flight. Garros was visibly moved by the spectacle of Paris seen from above, although he just about froze solid. Garros always flew wearing a blue pullover sweater and flat cloth cap with the bill reversed to the back. He had never flown so high and he did not know it was cold up there. Garros later wrote this sightseeing marked his most memorable flight to date despite his intense shivering and chattering teeth. The overhead view of the City of Lights put an idea into Garros's head, one which almost killed him a few days later.

Not content with his Parisian sorties, Moisant crossed the English Channel on 17 August 1910, taking the first passenger over the Channel on his sixth flight. Again, along for the over-water journey was his mechanic, Albert Fileux, and Moisant's cat, Mademoiselle Fifi. What John Moisant lacked in engineering skills he compensated with a flair for showmanship. The cat must have been a handful for the two intrepid aeronauts in the noisy, vibrating, windy, open-cockpit airplane. Taking a fully-clawed cat aloft in a fabric-covered airplane shows a talent for the dramatic coupled with a certain lack of good judgment.

Evidently, Garros's exploits and his display of Demoiselle proficiency in the wind at Cholet and Rennes attracted attention, particularly from Santos-Dumont. On the fourth day of 1910, Santos-Dumont performed in an air show in Hungary. A bracing wire snapped on his Demoiselle at an altitude of 80 feet, 25 meters. The unsupported wing folded and the airplane spiraled to earth. Santos-Dumont suffered only bruises from the crash itself but the accident ended his flying career. During a post-crash medical examination, his doctors diagnosed Santos-Dumont with incurable, untreatable multiple sclerosis. The medics informed Santos-Dumont he could continue flying or continue living. Pick one. Aircraft of the era were hard enough to handle by an able-bodied pilot. An aviator with shaky control of his own limbs could not hope to cope. Reluctantly, Santos-Dumont retired from piloting and quit designing aircraft.

In late August, a mutual friend of Roland Garros and Santos-Dumont showed up in the auto showroom in the shadow of *l'Arc de Triomphe*. He informed Garros that Santos-Dumont intended to liquidate his aviation assets and he wanted Roland Garros to have his personal, customized Demoiselle. Visiting Santos-Dumont at his estate in Deauville just outside the city, Garros sealed the Demoiselle's purchase in less than 5 minutes. Romain and Garros drove to the Saint-Cyr airfield in Brittany to take delivery of the little bird and to modify it to fit Garros's physique. After several days of assembly, repairing the damage done in Hungary, and performing slight modifications, Garros's new Demoiselle stood ready to fly.

Saint-Cyr is location of the French army's officer training academy, founded by Napoleon. It is the French equivalent to the US Military Academy at West Point, NY, which was not founded by the Little General. At a school where marching proficiency is paramount, the Saint-Cyr grass parade ground, as at Issy-les-Moulineaux, offered a wide-open landing field. The route a crow flies from Saint-Cyr to Garros's home base in Issy-les-Moulineaux inspired Roland to execute the idea his flight over Paris suggested. He wanted an aerial view of Versailles. The flight would also be Garros's longest to date and very nearly his last.

Flying northeast from Saint-Cyr toward the French capital, Garros found the Santos-Dumont machine more advanced than his own Demoiselle with a stronger engine. He could cruise on 75% power. The craft was also more responsive, lighter on the controls, covered with lighter, expensive white silk, and built from the straightest bamboo sticks.

Approaching Versailles with Romain following along in Roland's sports car, Garros reveled in the beauty of rural

France, *La France profonde*, as it is known. Passing over the endless gardens, he cruised above the massive palace, its clusters of chimneys reaching like clay fingers for the sky. Stretching to the northeast, the wide road to Paris led from Versailles toward the Eiffel Tower barely visible on the horizon. From 600 feet, 180 meters, altitude he admired the manicured gardens, the great palace, the faux French farm village where Marie Antoinette pretended to be a common milk maid, the fountains, the mile-long pool, the forests, the whole fantastic environment constructed for King Louis XIV, the Sun King. Below Garros, stretched out like a full-sized, living Bayeux Tapestry, lay the symbol of the apogee of the kings of France, their long reign abruptly cut short by violent rebellion. From the air, the view of French history seemed to stretch on forever. Then, his engine quit.

Today, pilots of light planes practice forced landings. They are taught to be mentally prepared, to quickly identify suitable emergency landing sites: fields, beaches, roads, parking lots. Under an instructor's watchful supervision, students practice setting up a power-off approach to an unplanned landing. This essential skill is acquired even though modern piston-engined light aircraft almost never experience engine failure not caused by running out of gas. Roland Garros had never practiced emergency landings. Self-taught to fly, the subject never seemed important despite the frequent problems with his plane's engine

Garros, until his flight over Versailles, had never flown an aircraft with the engine dead. Instantly, the lack of power sent the Demoiselle descending at an alarming rate. Confronted with an urgent requirement for a landing spot, Garros thought for a moment about turning back and touching down on one of the broad, wide, smooth garden paths behind the palace. An engine-out turn is an altitude-losing maneuver. He did not have enough height left to pull it off. Wisely, he decided to land straight ahead on the broad road leading from Versailles to Paris. The wooden propeller continued to spin. Instead of powering the plane through the sky, the prop was being spun by the airflow and acting as a giant airbrake. Without power, and with the wind-milling prop's parasitic drag, the angle of descent was steeper than any normal landing, the flare at touchdown to kill the descent would have to be carefully but instantly judged. The paved, smooth road lay ahead of the rapidly descending Demoiselle's nose, leading to Paris, to safety, and to home. Roland's first-ever forced landing needed to be his best one. It almost worked.

At the last second prior to touchdown, an unseen telegraph wire strung across the boulevard caught the Demoiselle's tail. Before the single-strand of copper wire broke, it snared the plane, snatching it from the air. The tiny craft fell like a wing-shot white dove, pancaking in the middle of the road with a crump and raising a cloud of dust. Slung beneath the aircraft in the pilot's leather-strap seat, Garros's butt hit the ground first. The aircraft collapsed around him, covering him with splintered wreckage.

A nearby French army unit witnessed the crash. Soldiers ran to the crash site and began tearing away at the mess of bamboo, wood, steel tubing, and silk fabric with their bare hands. In agony and partially paralyzed, Roland Garros felt sure his back had been broken by the impact. Before the soldiers could extract him from them wreck, he called to them as they pulled at the debris.

"Ne me touchez pas!" Don't touch me! He screamed.

The soldiers, following orders from their commander and not unfamiliar with the cries of wounded men, ignored Garros's frantic objections and pulled him from the pile of wreckage. An army surgeon came running from the nearby army post and started preparing to take Garros to a military dispensary in the nearby town of Versailles. Before the litter holding Garros could be loaded onto a waiting army vehicle, Garros heard the familiar sound of his car's engine approaching, driven at breakneck speed by the flight-following Romain.

With the feeling in his legs returning and despite his excruciating pain, Roland refused the French Army's medical services, and with great difficulty climbed into the Grégoire's left bucket seat and commanded Romain to drive toward Paris. The agony of sitting upright proved to be too much. Garros turned sideways in the bucket seat into a semi-fetal position for the hour-long bumpy journey home. A journey made no easier by the primitive leaf springs of the car, which transmitted every bump and jolt directly to his aching body. It was not the best course of action to deal with a serious back injury but somehow Garros and Romain made it to Paris.

Back in Paris, Romain half-carried, half-helped Garros up the several flights of stairs to his apartment and then drove off to fetch a doctor. Then, as now, French doctors made house calls. The physician diagnosed Garros with a broken coccyx, undoubtedly from the impact with the stone-paved roadway. The coccyx is the small, useless extension of the spinal column, which leads some scientists to the conclusion that humans' ancestors in the far distant past possessed tails. It is often called in the vernacular, "the tail bone." There is no treatment for a broken coccyx save for bed rest on one's stomach.

The next day, Romain drove back out to Versailles to survey the crash scene. The troop of soldiers had dragged the wreckage off the road and kept it under guard. Romain confirmed the personal Demoiselle of Santos-Dumont was a total write-off, destroyed on its maiden flight under the command of Roland Garros. Excitement over, the soldiers returned to their primary mission, probably to protect the *Château de Versailles* against the French monarchy's return to power.

For the next two weeks, Garros was confined to his bed while his tail bone healed. It must have been a time for contemplation and decision-making. Even viewed with the invulnerability of youth, aviation was proving to be dangerous. He miraculously escaped injury in the crash before attempting his first flight, now he was in pain from damage done in the Versailles prang. More damage had been done to his bank balance. Santos-Dumont's ill-fated Demoiselle depleted his reserves, now it, and they, were gone. In less than five months, he had written off two airplanes. The car showroom was flourishing but the profits could not keep up with his flying expenses. Appearance money from air shows filled some of the deficit, but that revenue stream would soon freeze up as winter weather put an end to air shows. Even worse, his family was moving to cut off what financial aid they had been providing. His parents and extended family were less than thrilled about Roland's aviation exploits, particularly the expensive and dangerous crashes. They reduced their support, trying to force him to abandon aviation and to concentrate on his auto business.

However, Roland Garros was determined to master aviation, to keep flying. Adrenaline is highly addictive and Garros was hooked. Fortunately, a better opportunity than being a grounded car salesman presented itself.

CHAPTER EIGHT

AMERICA

LAND OF THE FREE; AIR SHOW THAT IS

Once he recovered from his crash at Versailles, Roland Garros encountered an important crossroads in his life. He needed to choose a career path to follow. He could further develop his automobile sales business and hopefully cash in on the next big wave of industrial production of the automobile age. His family support would then resume and he could continue to thrive in the upper *bourgeois* levels of Parisian society during *La Belle Epoche.* A comfortable life with money, women, sports, and his clan waited. Or, he could keep the auto showroom ticking over and focus on his aviation avocation. His financial prospects would be much more insecure; few at the time made a living in aviation without having substantial resources to invest. He could not discount the risk involved, the skies were fraught with peril—flying is inherently dangerous. His still-aching tailbone told him as much. Surviving two horrendous crashes, destroying two aircraft, what disaster might come next?

In his young life, Garros had usually taken paths less traveled. Hanging out with the Vietnamese kids in Saigon instead of his French colonial counterparts, home-schooled, refusing to learn Latin or swordsmanship, shunning a lucrative career in law for a precarious one selling automobiles, pro bike racing under an alias, it all fit the pattern of one who hears the beat of a different drummer and answers the unconventional call; a modern-day corsair sailing the seas of uncertainty. Yet, he enjoyed the trappings and the privileges possessed by the well-to-do; country homes, fine dining, long summer vacations, vintage wines, refined and sophisticated women. Accepted in those circles, no longer an outsider from Réunion Island, could he keep those contacts and pleasures while attempting to master the skies?

Sometimes opportunity comes knocking, making a life-changing, possibly life-threatening, decision easier. The promoter who put on the air shows in Cholet and Remes, needed a pilot and airplane for a one-day exhibition in Dinard, France, and Roland Garros fit the bill. Relatively inexpensive to hire, easy to work with, he flew an intriguing airplane and could rub well-to-do elbows in the right circles effortlessly. Exhibition pilots were expected to mingle with the locals, the gentry paying the bills, after the day's flying was over.

Dinard is a resort town in Brittany on France's Atlantic coast, home to several grand hotels, an elegant casino, and four wide, flat beaches. A long day's train ride from Paris and a reasonable ferry crossing from England, its position on "The Emerald Coast" made Dinard a favorite destination for both French and English holiday-makers, just the spot for an air show.

A contract for two days of flying appeared. He would be tasked to fly over two casinos, several hotels, the nearby cities of Parmé and Saint-Malo as well as Dinard, and traverse the river Rance, which separates the cities. Without hesitation, Roland Garros signed the contract, turning toward the uncharted path of aviation, choosing once again to defy convention and the wishes of his family. His decision was made, now could he make a go of it?

On 9 September 1910, Garros and Romain assembled the Demoiselle, shipped by train from Issy-les-Moulinex, on the broad sand beach of Dinard. The beach looked to be a superb flying field; flat, wide, smooth, and with no trees nearby, only a growing crowd of spectators ready for what would be for many their first time seeing a man fly. Roland had never flown off sand before and, to be precise, had never flown this exact aircraft either. It was re-assembled using some parts salvaged from the Versailles wreck. Demoiselles could be taken apart or be reassembled in two hours or so. However, the light-weight construction did not lend itself to precision assembly. The bamboo poles, metal tubes, brass ferules, and above all, the flying wires came together slightly differently each time. Exact tension drawn on the wires holding the wing in place was a judgment call by Romain. A few pounds of pull made all the difference in the aerodynamic properties of the flexible wing, profoundly affecting aircraft handling in flight. Roland would not know exactly how the bird would fly until it did.

Winds of early fall came howling across the broad, flat beach, whipping water from puddles left by the retreating tide, and lifting whispers of sand from the would-be runway. Beach takeoffs are tricky even in calm weather. Sand can hide rocks and soft spots ready to snare a wheel before lift-off. Local officials and the promoter urged Garros to wait until the wind died; even non-aviators could see the conditions were hazardous. Roland Garros would have none of it. Cross-wind takeoffs challenge even the best pilots. Some aircraft try to weathervane, to turn their noses into the wind. Other drift downwind, blown off course and off the runway. Demoiselles tended to lift their up-wind wing and tip over. But this time, the broad beach course solved some of those issues. Dinard's beach was wide enough and flat enough; he could steer the aircraft's nose directly into the teeth of the wind, crabbing across the beach, pointing toward the distant surf. His first attempt ended when a hidden stone bent a delicate spider-spoked wheel. Romain quickly changed the wheel and spun the propeller again. Demanding full power from the straining engine, Garros began another run. A gust of wind caught the featherweight bird head-on, kiting the aircraft suddenly upward. He was airborne.

Roland Garros and his tiny aircraft completed the circuit advertised by the promoter. Spectators packed the terraces outside the grand hotels and the casino in Dinard. Garros could easily discern their up-turned pale faces as he passed overhead. Crossing the river Rance, he repeated the fly-by at Parmé and Saint-Malo before heading back to Dinard. Bounced by the gusty wind, rocked by the turbulence, Garros still found time to survey the towns from which the corsairs had sailed, ancestors in spirit if not in direct lineage. Flying with the wind, the return flight went quickly. Carefully, he turned back into the wind to land on the waiting beach. With the wind speed at perhaps 40 kph, 24 mph, and the Demoiselle's landing speed, power off, at 50 kph, 30 mph, Garros approach speed over the ground was roughly 10 kph, 6 mph. He had no trouble touching down at the exact spot designated by the promoter in front of the crowd and bouncing to a stop, eschewing his trademark bootleg turn in the high crosswind. A reception that night offered many opportunities to verbally replay his flight to paying guests at the casino and they lapped it up.

The next day, Garros flew from Dinard's beach to the *l'île de Cézembre*, Cezembre Island, 15 kilometers, 9 miles, distant and returned, winning a cash prize for doing so. In two days at Dinard, he earned 11,000 francs, a considerable sum at the time, enough to buy another aircraft and equal to several months of auto sales commissions. If Roland Garros had any doubts about his recent choice of life paths, 11,000 francs easily erased them.

Aviation magazines had not been published yet; Garros's exploits at Dinard were written up in *l'Auto,* a monthly car journal, where they attracted wide notice. This public attention would solve his next problem; how to keep profitably flying with the Northern European winter bearing down. Low clouds, high winds, rain, and the snows of fall and winter would soon reduce the number of days suitable for flight and the crowds would not come out in the cold. The promoter packed up his operation for the duration of the winter of 1910-1911.

Often, when one door closes, another opens, and in the doorway stood Hart O. Berg. Berg was a wealthy American engineer, industrialist, and keen fan of advanced technology. He ran the Colt arms factory in Connecticut, went on to manage the Royal Armament Establishment in Belgium, and took time off to build and launch a flotilla of submarines for the Czar of Russia. Always interested in mechanical progress, Berg grew intrigued with the emerging field of aviation. In 1908, he and his wife witnessed a flight demonstration by the Wright brothers at the Le Mans racetrack in western France. Ester, as high-spirited as her husband was methodical, convinced Wilbur Wright to take her up for a short flight. She held her hat on with a ribbon; no self-respecting woman would go hatless, even while flying in an aircraft without a cockpit. She tied a velvet cord around her ankles to keep her long skirt from blowing up and ruining her reputation. After the two-minute-plus hop, Ester Berg strutted away from the Wright machine with her ankles still encircled by the cord. French newspaper reporters, ever fashion-conscious, noted and described her "hobble skirt." Evidently, this was hot stuff in 1908. The hobble skirt became the latest fashion fad. Ester Berg and the airplane were the source of *haute couture* excitement.

Hart O. Berg also attended the same week of aviation exhibition at Reims as Roland Garros in 1909. Berg saw the huge, enthusiastic crowds and made plans to attend a similar exposition back home in the United States the next year. During the summer of 1910, he recruited the cream of European aviation for the show, featuring French pilots and their craft. While the Wrights and Glen Curtiss were making rapid technical progress in America, they focused on sales to the US Government. That is where the money was. But the center of popular civilian aviation rested in France and everyone, including most Americans, knew it. Berg intended to bring French flying *savoir-faire* to America.

His plans hit a minor snag in the fall. Minor for Berg, but major for the Morane brothers, Robert and Léon. Both brothers were early aviators; Robert was the first pilot to fly at 100 kph, 62 mph, at the Reims meet. The brothers bought a two-place Blériot, fitted it with a 100 hp Gnome engine and an extra-large fuel tank. Their goal, a 30,000 Franc prize awarded to the first flight from Paris to circle *Le Summet du Puy de Dôme*, an extinct volcano cone on the Central Massif in south-central France, and return in less than six hours' time.

Aircraft of the day could barely lift one, or perhaps two humans (not counting Moisant's cat). As the gross weight carried aloft grows, a wing's stall speed also increases. Stall speed is the minimum speed at which a wing can sustain level fight. At heavy weights, the stall speed approaches the plane's cruising speed. On a test flight out of Issy, their over-loaded and under-powered Blériot stalled, spun, and crashed, pitching both brothers into a waiting tree and injuring both severely. In hospital, the brothers vowed to quit trusting their lives to other engineers' airplanes and to start their own aircraft company. Their paths would cross those of Roland Garros later. But now Berg needed two more flyers. In desperation, he hired Roland Garros and his friend from Issy, Swiss citizen Edmond Audemars, both Demoiselle pilots, to replace the hapless, hospitalized Morane brothers.

The French aviation performers were to leave from the Atlantic port of Cherbourg in four days for New York on a quest for American glory, not to mention American dollars. Roland Garros was about to fulfill a dream, not of flying around the Bay of Nice, but to fly in America, a country he had never visited. Shocking news, the doughty Romain could not go, he did not want to leave his wife alone in France for the weeks-long trip. Audemars and Garros hired another Issy mechanic, Jules Hue, and two assistants. Hue was not as outgoing nor as emotional as Romain, but equally, if quietly, competent. He would stick with Garros until the early days of the Great War. Frantically, two Demoiselles were dissembled, spare parts were located, bags were packed, and the whole kit transported by train to Cherbourg from Paris.

Most of the French aviators had booked in advance passage on board the *Teutonic*, a White Star Line British ship but the passenger manifest had reached max capacity. At the last minute, Garros, Audemars, and their ground crew found accommodations on the Kronprinz Wilhelm, a Norddeutscher Lloyd line boat from a German steamship company. Their aircraft, spares, tools, and equipment went along as "excess baggage." Traveling first class, Garros soon discovered he shared a four-person suite with three Germans, not unexpected on a German liner. Uncomfortable with his German roommates, why we do not know, he requested a transfer and bunked in with a ship's officer for the voyage, which passed quickly. The relatively short passage was a blessing for Garros who suffered from seasickness the entire time. The two massive ocean liners left Cherbourg on 8 October 1910. The big air show was scheduled for the 22nd across the pond in New York.

Arriving in New York, Garros made sure his ground crew was comfortably ensconced in a reasonable hotel, that the aircraft and equipment had been unloaded safely, and checked into the Hotel Knickerbocker in Manhattan. He then joined John Moisant and the rest of the French Air Show team at the top-of-the-line Hotel Astor. Never one to avoid living large, Moisant rented a palatial suite for himself, his two sisters, Matilde and Ann-Marguerite, and his new mascot, a cat named "Madame Paris." Perhaps Mademoiselle Fifi had proved herself to abhor flying in an open cockpit. Matilde, with her cherubic face, stunning smile, and hour-glass figure, did not escape the notice of Roland Garros. She later earned the second pilot's license awarded to a woman by the Aero Club of the United States, in 1911.

New York City impressed Garros with its energy, its drive, and its buildings. The place generated an electric feeling in the air. Paris, his adopted hometown, was bustling, busy, but not like New York. The French capital, long the center of European culture, had for centuries been "old money," secure in its place in the world. New York was a *nouveau riche* city on the make. With 4.8 million people, New York dwarfed Paris' population of fewer than 2 million. Newly invented skyscrapers standing 30 or 40 stories tall defined the city. Buildings in central Paris were then, and still are, limited to five or six floors, giving the elegant city a relaxed, low-rise feel quite unlike the concrete canyons lining Manhattan Island.

Waiting for the air show to begin, Garros, Audemars, Moisant, and the rest of the team sampled the best American entertainment available; restaurants, night clubs, bars, and thoroughly enjoyed them all. They particularly dug the newest fad in music, jazz. Roland later remarked on a peculiarity of

American life, segregation, which he did not understand. Born on Réunion Island, a melting pot of racial integration, spending his childhood in Saigon with his Chinese and Vietnamese friends, living in racially tolerant Paris, Roland Garros found himself in a new and restrictive environment. He observed that in the watering holes and jazz clubs of New York, most cooks, bartenders, servers, entertainers, especially the musicians, were black while all the patrons, the customers, were white. Strange stuff indeed.

At last on the 22nd of October 1910, the Franco-American air show kicked off. Where else but at Belmont Park horse racing track just outside the city? Horse racing had been outlawed by New York State at the beginning of the year due to rumors of gambling taking place and the track needed a new source of revenue. The Wright brothers, of all people, sponsored the week-long air show and tournament.

Prior to his first flight at Belmont Park, Roland Garros, now a well-paid and very well-entertained professional pilot, boasted a grand total of just over three hours flying time in his log book. To put that into perspective, a modern student pilot with average talent can expect to fly solo after seven to ten hours of dual instruction from a certified instructor. Today's standard trainer, the aforementioned Cessna 150, is an exceedingly easy airplane to fly, stable, light on its balanced controls, with adequate power, and benign stall characteristics. It can barely kill you, yet it takes seven to ten hours to solo it. Garros taught himself how to fly on an underpowered, evil-handling machine, and after three plus hours in the air, was among the premier aviators of his era. Given the horrendous accident rate among those early birdmen, perhaps having only three hours in the air was a survival advantage.

At major air shows such as at Belmont Park, pilots could make money in two ways. Their primary income came from appearance fees, fixed amounts paid for showing up and flying under contract. Additional revenue, sometimes substantial, could be had for competing in various aerial contests; max speed runs, timed events over a fixed course, point to point races, and sometimes even gimmick races such as pitting a Blériot XI against a Packard automobile in a race. Indeed, these events were covered on the local newspapers' sports pages alongside baseball, horse racing, and tennis. Aviation was a sport, a highly dangerous sport, but a sport all the same. The commercial potential for aircraft had not yet been worked out.

With the smallest, slowest aircraft in the line-up, Roland Garros and his friend Edmond Audemars flew their Demoiselles for show only, leaving the aerial contests to those with more serious airplanes. The crowds in the Belmont Park grandstands seemed to enjoy watching the dancing "dragonflies" float over the manicured grounds and sandy dirt track.

John Moisant, on the other hand, resolved to achieve glory in competition with the big boys. His air show did not start off well. Taking off on his initial flight down the main straightaway, Moisant heard the engine on his Blériot laboring and losing power. An absence of oil smoke flagged another danger sign. The engine drank its oil from a separate tank and the valve on the oil feed line was closed, starving the engine for lubrication. Use of a pre-flight checklist lay in the future. Seconds from seizure, the prudent thing to do would have been to cut the engine, land on the racetrack just below the craft, open the valve, and try again. Moisant had other ideas. He could reach the offending valve from the cockpit, open it, and continuing flying. Or so he thought. The Blériot was marginally stable at best, requiring a steady hand on the controls. In the process of leaning far out over the engine cowling, and shifting his weight in the cockpit, Moisant lost control of the airplane which crashed heavily right in front of the crowd. Moisant was unhurt and the airplane was reparable. It was not to be John Moisant's last, nor his most serious crash.

Despite some adverse late fall weather, the Belmont International Aviation Tournament was a success for Berg's Franco-American team. Moisant won a race to a tethered balloon 10 miles away and back, collecting $685, but collided with another aircraft while landing and overturned, necessitating another all-night rebuilding session by long-suffering mechanics. The main event, a timed race from Belmont Park to the Statue of Liberty, itself a gift from France, out in New York Harbor and a return leg to the improvised airfield took place on 30 October. Despite having the slowest plane, Moisant won the race, handily beating a French aristocrat and an Englishman. He bested their times by over 5 minutes, taking a short cut over the borough of Brooklyn against the Wrights' advice. The Ohioans believed heavier-than-air flight over a city to be too dangerous. Moisant was not bothered, he had already flown over Paris, twice, once with Roland Garros aboard.

The Wrights thought Moisant too clever by half and arrogant for ignoring their counsel, winning by what they felt were un-gentlemanly tactics. They found a way to disqualify Moisant, some nonsense about a late take-off, and awarded the $10,000 prize to the Count Jacques de Lesseps who needed the money even less than John Moisant.

Skullduggery aside, the Wrights proved American crowds would attend air shows in substantial numbers, the public interest was there, ticket sales and newspaper coverage proved the idea. An estimated one million people watched, for free, from the streets of Brooklyn as Moisant flew above them. With winter fast approaching, Moisant, Garros, Audemars, and the team found themselves in America and at loose ends. Moisant's next move, absent the help of Berg, but in partnership with his brother, Alfred, might have been pure genius or an unmitigated disaster. It could have gone either way.

CHAPTER NINE

THE FLYING CIRCUS

ALL ABOARD FOR RICHMOND AND POINTS SOUTH

Circuses enjoyed wide popularity in 1910, particularly in rural areas, not as popular as in the later decades of the 1800's, but still well-attended. Before electronics, TV, radio, recorded music, the internet, and the wide-spread availability of movies, mass public entertainment meant either live theatre, vaudeville shows, or circuses. Easily moving about the country on the omnipresent railways, circuses brought exotic amusement to millions. Big outfits rode on their own dedicated trains, colorfully painted and purpose-built with flat cars carrying the circus wagons. Smaller shows, often with only one performance ring and a smaller tent, chartered their trains from the railway companies.

In New York, John and Alfred Moisant hatched an idea. They would take their air show on the road, the railroad. Instead of a one-off, week-long national super-show like the Wrights put on at Belmont Park, the Moisants would travel the country by train, setting up for a one- or two-day air show and then moving on to the next town starved for entertainment. Huge attendance at Belmont Park and a million upturned faces in Brooklyn proved the premise that manned heavier-than-air flight attracted the public's attention. Most Americans had never seen a man fly and would pay, or so the Moisants hoped, to see one do just that.

Winter clamped down hard on the northern states, flying was no more possible there than over in Europe. Blessed with better weather, the American West lay at the end of a very long train ride and was anyway sparsely populated with potential viewers. So, the closest, most lucrative markets with workable weather lay in the southern states.

John and Albert hired additional "acts," pilots and their aircraft, along with a driver bringing a fast car to race planes around horse tracks where the shows tended to be held. A train was easily chartered, the railroads were used to this traveling circus plan if not with the boxcars' high-tech contents. The Moisants started scheduling gigs. Richmond, Virginia kicked off the experimental tour. John Moisant stayed behind in his luxurious Hotel Astor suite working out the tour's business aspects and future itinerary while Albert, the performers, the mechanics, and the aircraft rode the rails south to Richmond.

On 24 November 1910, the Moisant aerial show set up, ready to perform, in the state capital of Virginia. Roland Garros eagerly waited to take to the skies the next day, pleased to be able to continue living his dream of flying in America. However, he and his fellow performers encountered unexpected, serious competition for the public's attention—the President of the United States of America, William H. Taft. President Taft's long-scheduled official visit fell on the day prior to the proposed air show and the mayor of Richmond wanted to roll out an aerial red carpet. The Mayor sought to impress the entourage coming down from Washington that Richmond mattered. He requested a flyover of the President's downtown motorcade. As the mayor wielded enormous influence over local affairs, his "request" was not to be taken lightly. Albert Moisant promised His Honor a flyover and John, back in New York, agreed, welcoming the free publicity. The Moisants tapped Garros to wow the President.

Roland Garros objected to the idea of flying over Richmond in general and overhead the President in particular. Perhaps remembering his crash at Versailles, he told Albert the Demoiselle's two-cylinder engine was inherently too unreliable to risk flight above a crowded city, not to mention above President Taft. The Moisants countered with an offer for Roland to pilot John's personal Blériot XI even though Garros had never flown anything so large and sophisticated. Its wingspan reached one-third wider than the Demoiselle's and it weighed nearly twice as much, over 500 pounds, 230 kilos. Crucially, roll control on the Blériot depended on the control stick, not on leaning left and right as on the Demoiselle. The wooden stick also controlled the aircraft's pitch and yaw. Garros would have to learn an entirely new flight control system literally on the fly. He still was not on board with the risk of an engine failure while over the crowded city, but the opportunity to fly the Blériot intrigued Garros. Albert Moisant reminded Roland the Blériot had crossed the English Channel and flown over Brooklyn and Paris. John Moisant even took Garros along for one of the Parisian sorties instead of his cat, Albert emphasized. Garros's ambition for learning the Blériot overcame his caution about flight over large numbers of people with few emergency landing fields available within gliding distance. He reluctantly agreed to fly. Once more in the life of Roland Garros, the risk/reward equation skewed toward reward.

He pulled off the stunt, flying above the President's motorcade in downtown Richmond, even performing several steep turns in full view of the crowds lining the streets. In route from the show ground to the center of Richmond, Garros sampled the aircraft's controls, getting a feel for the plane, unlearning the reflexes he built up on his Demoiselle, quickly replacing them with the new muscle memory needed to fly the Blériot. Climbs and dives, turns, nose position, all had to be grasped quickly. Not for the first time and not for the last, Roland Garros laid his life on the line to learn a new aviation skill, to accomplish a new mission, to take a chance on failure and death. Awed spectators below had no idea the Frenchman was learning how to perform steep turns in the Blériot as they watched. President Taft even halted the parade to get a better view of the circling white-winged airplane. Garros flew the Blériot for the first time alone. Madam Paris, the cat, was safe with John Moisant in New York. The Mayor declared himself pleased and any remaining bureaucratic hurdles for the public air show magically disappeared.

On the next day, the 25th, attendance at the Richmond fairgrounds was sparse. Few tickets had been sold, despite the first over-flight of Richmond by Roland Garros the previous afternoon. To generate more interest and excitement, John Moisant, upon arrival from New York, led three aircraft in loose formation over the city. Still, people stayed away from the show ground in droves. In Richmond, the flaws in the Moisants' business plan became glaringly apparent. People tended to not buy tickets to see flight displays they could observe for free, whether from downtown streets or from looking up while standing just outside the venue. The Moisant brothers lost money and lots of it in Richmond, but vowed to continue their tour of the South.

Hissing steam spurted from the locomotive as it rolled to a stop, a long vaporous sigh overlaid with the screeching of iron brake shoes clamping tight on steel wheels. The din announced to the people waiting that the chartered circus train had arrived. Excited by planted articles in two daily newspapers, the public watched from neighboring platforms as the train crew prepared to unload the show. Men mostly comprised the on-looking throng but the crowd included a sprinkling of ladies. Anyone could see this was a different sort of public from the international aviators' first stop. Richmond, long a center of refined Southern culture, once the capital of a sovereign nation, represented the genteel old South and old money. This second venue appeared to be different, a hard-edged railroad hub, a hard-drinking river town, ringed with hardscrabble one-horse farms and inhospitable, forested mountains hiding moonshine stills.

Among those watching were the expected businessmen in dark suits and fedoras, accompanied by the occasional demure lady in a long dress, perhaps tripping along in a hobble skirt and wearing a fashionable hat. Rubbing elbows with the city folk also were unshaven farmers in overalls, hard-working men in brogans, their womenfolk still wearing traditional coal-scuttle bonnets tied under their chins. Shoals of small children ran underfoot. This was not the sort of fans the Moisants encountered in Richmond or Belmont Park, and certainly not in France.

Disconcertingly, Terminal Station, the scene for this action, resembled a quarter-scale imitation of the great Parisian railway stations in style. Built of red brick, it boasted of an 80-foot, 25-meter, dome with a skylight suspended over the expansive marble-floored waiting and ticketing area. Rows of dark oak benches identical to those in the numerous local churches lined the expanse. Here the congregation worshiped interstate commerce, not God. Eight platforms served seven tracks. Over 50 trains, not counting special charters such as this circus train, called there each day. A grand entrance archway, also of hand-cast brick, advertised itself as the "World's Largest Brick Arch." Doubtful, but no one questioned the locals' claim. Terminal Station, like its mentors, the *Gare de Lyon* or the *Gare d'Orsay* in the City of Light, dominated the buildings surrounding it.

Like all other circus trains unloaded at Terminal Station, this one disgorged crates, a folded tent, tent poles, personal baggage, mechanical gear of all sorts, toolboxes, and barrels of unknown contents. Roustabouts worked with haulage companies loading the items needed for an air show onto waiting trucks and horse-drawn wagons. Railroad porters, all of whom were black, watched with barely concealed amusement as white men labored to empty the train's boxcars of not exotic animals and trapezes, but of ungainly, light, strange-looking pieces of various aircraft.

Not the Barnum and Bailey, nor the Ringling Brothers' shows, John Moisant's Flying Circus hit town, and the town was not Paris, France, or any other world-class city. "Moisant's International Aviators Limited" inevitably nicknamed the "Flying Circus" from its method of transport and its deployment in tents, would be putting on a daredevil exhibition of aerial expertise in Chattanooga, Tennessee. In 1910, Chattanooga thrived as a vital link between the industrial North, the thriving Midwest, and Dixie. More important at the time than Atlanta, Georgia to the south, Chattanooga was a key railroad junction and had been since the War Between the States. Here, various railroad lines met each other, linking up with the Tennessee River and its riverboats. Perhaps due to the local emphasis on transportation, perhaps attracted by the obvious danger, the good citizens of Chattanooga, East Tennessee were curious to see if men could really fly.

After his exploits in Europe and Belmont Park, John Moisant rivaled Glenn Curtiss in American aviation fame and was even gaining on the Wrights. His flamboyant lifestyle did not detract from the marketing of his show at all. Curtiss did not fly with a cat and the Wrights were reserved Ohioans, stiff and formal. They did not even fly with each other and never rented palatial suites at the Hotel Astor.

The trip from Richmond to Chattanooga did not bode well for the next show. Cold winds and constant snow showers marked the journey. Even in the "Sunny South" winters tended towards cold and stormy. The Moisants and their performers hoped many Chattanoogans would buy tickets to the show and turn around the tour's finances. They would not stage an open display here, no free flying this time. The local horse racing track had been booked and the box office opened.

On the day of the air show, after lunching at their hotel, the best in town, the Read House, the team surveyed the show venue and doubts quickly arose among the skeptical pilots. Terrain around Chattanooga was nothing like the flat land around tidewater Virginia or tidewater France, if such a term applies. The town nestled at the bases of two imposing peaks, Lookout Mountain and Signal Mountain. Missionary Ridge bisected the city and a hill, Orchard Knob, rose nearby. Winding its way between mountains and hills, the Tennessee River coursed through the city, its fast currents flowing near the show ground. Forced landing in a winter-time river presented a danger of drowning or freezing. Hills and mountains presented a more direct challenge to the aircraft of the day. Underpowered, their maximum rate of climb measured only a few hundred feet per minute, at an angle much less than the steepness of Orchard Knob, never mind Lookout or Signal Mountains towering 1200 feet, 400 meters, over Chattanooga. Mountains and hills also funneled and shaped the brisk winter winds, the turbulence further complicating aviation.

The venue at Warner Park (then called Olympia Park) could be reached by a short trolley car ride up McCallie Avenue from downtown; the hoped-for crowds would have easy access. That was the good news. The bad news was the horse racing track, unlike the broad expanses of Belmont Park, was narrow and short. Takeoffs and landings would be difficult and tricky. Near downtown, electric wires and poles were everywhere, trees ringed the park, and the local gentry's mansions overlooked it all from a steep bluff along the river. The icy river waited on the errant aviator 1.5 miles, 2.5 km away. You could hardly imagine a riskier place for primitive air operations. The Moisant brothers booked the Warner Park location sight unseen, and no one in Chattanooga knew enough about flying to warn them of the dangers beforehand. Even worse, the fence circling the horse track lay close to the grandstand, affording an unobstructed view of the sky for free-loaders. The board barrier, minus a few knotholes, only blocked views of the track's surface. Take-offs and landings would be out of sight. But, the air space above the track was easily visible from the fence line, from McCallie Avenue, and from the surrounding public park. You would not need a ticket to see most of the air show.

Surveying the grandstand sparsely occupied by paying customers, the Moisants feared their financial goals were not about to be realized. More unwelcome news; a winter storm approached the city; passage of a cold front with attendant high winds appeared imminent. Thunder rolled off in the distance and lightning sparked on the western horizon, backlighting the tree-covered mountains. All the pilots of Moisants' Flying Circus knew Roland Garros and John Moisant were fast friends. They quickly appointed Roland as spokesperson for the group and he voiced the group's refusal to fly under the prevailing conditions. Albert Moisant, not himself a pilot, insisted on a performance. The brothers huddled. John, with the most to lose as one of the flyers, prevailed, and they made a difficult decision to announce the show's cancellation and the refund of all ticket purchases.

This news did not go down well with the thin crowd which waited all afternoon lubricated with distilled spirits, some taxed, some not. Strangely, quite a few of those who did pay to sit in the grandstand were wearing large, western-style hats. A little background is needed here. At the turn of the 20th century, circuses, while popular, did not have the greatest reputation for reliability or honesty. Scamming of customers occurred frequently, performances were faked, often much was promised and little delivered. Some shows upped sticks and left in the middle of the night to avoid paying local suppliers. Sheriffs were known to remove the axle nuts from brightly decorated wagons to prevent flight by circuses until local bills got paid, giving rise to the saying, "Making the nut." The circus-going public was very wary of traveling entertainers and quick to anger when performances did not measure up to expectations. Indeed, conflict with itinerant circus folk thrived as an underground sport in some rowdy circles. This was the unfamiliar rural American environment the Moisants encountered when they put together their "Flying Circus." The big top tent they rented for the tour as a combination hanger and personnel shelter further fostered the analogy with shady circuses. The Moisants' show hadn't yet earned the label "fly-by-night" but they were about to not fly by day.

Once loudspeakers announced the cancellation, angry, intoxicated spectators poured from the one-level wooden grandstand, ignored the offered refunds, and shouted for an air show, no matter what the weather. Pistol shots rang out, a few at first, then in such numbers to rival the distant thunder.

Evidently, numerous patrons punctuated their expressions of displeasure by firing bullets into the air. Surrounding the tent sheltering the aircraft and crew, the crowd grew more animated by the minute.

The tri-state area, the intersection of Tennessee, Georgia, and Alabama boasted for many years the largest cattle ranch east of the Mississippi River. Mountain Cove Farms operated just across the state line in nearby Chickamauga, Georgia. Rough-hewn ranch hands, identifiable by their large hats, came well armed. This explosive behavior by some Georgia cowboys took the aviators and mechanics seeking refuge in the big tent quite by surprise. Few of the Frenchmen understood the long-standing antagonism between ripped-off circus customers and offending show-business people. Fewer still grasped the cowboys' tendency toward random gunfire. Air-minded folk in Reims, France did not resort to six-shooters when severe weather cancelled a show. Yes, aggrieved spectators in Nantes chased air show sponsors through the local woods, but not with firearms.

Roland Garros later wrote he confronted two choices in Chattanooga, both bad. He could get trampled and maybe shot by the furious crowd and see his delicate aircraft trashed. Or, he could attempt to fly and maybe survive. If he crashed in the coming storm, the wreck would be away from the show ground and he could escape on foot. To the Moisants' relief, Jules Hue pushed the Demoiselle from the shelter and Garros climbed in. Hue hand-cranked the engine and his assistants pointed the craft down the makeshift runway, the propeller slowly turning. They held the craft back, steadying it against the wind. Placated, the howling mob returned to the grandstand prepared to finally see a man fly, perhaps on the final flight of his life.

Garros somehow coaxed the Demoiselle into the air without hitting the railings lining the dirt straightaway or snaring the overhead electrical cables. He flew two wide circuits of the track, the wind thankfully exhibiting the storied relative calm before the storm. For once, the surrounding obstacles prove to be beneficial. The nearby trees, mansions, and the riverside bluff shielded Garros's tiny bird from the worst of the wind's fury. Somehow, he managed to avoid the wooden railings again and touched down in front of the crowd. He executed his signature bootleg turn and killed the engine. Silence, then scattered applause came from the grandstand as the mechanics ran to recover the Demoiselle before the rain's arrival.

Calm did not prevail for long. When it became apparent Garros's slow circuits of the race track bouncing along in the rough air were to be the whole show, more triggers were pulled perforating more holes in the grandstand's tin roof. The situation seemed simple; gunfire produced flying, so why not shoot again? Despite the lightning and thunder becoming increasingly frequent, louder, and closer, Alfred Moisant leaned on another French pilot, René Simon, to take to the unsettled air. Flying for his life, whether in a stormy crash or by getting drilled by drunken ranch hands, Simon put on a dazzling exhibition of low-level aerobatics. His bird flew higher, up in the wind. Spectators neither knew nor cared if the dancing airplane they watched was being tossed around by the building storm or by piloting skill. They loved the show.

"Aerobatics" is perhaps too strong a term for Simon's display. Aircraft of 1910 were not capable of any maneuvers we associate today with true aerobatics. Low-powered, somewhat unstable, fragile, with rudimentary control systems, the planes of the time could not roll, spin, or climb vertically. An over-the-top loop would not be performed until four years later in 1914. Immelmanns, Cuban eights, split esses, inverted flight, none of these elementary aerial moves had been conceived, much less flown. Air show patrons were treated to a succession of steep (less than 45 degrees of bank) turns, shallow dives and climbs, low flight, climbing and descending turns and little else. Aircraft speed was pretty much constant, topping out around 100 kph., 60 mph. Cloth-winged craft, when flown over an air show crowd, resembled not man-made machines mastering the sky but rather giant droning white moths, or more charitably, wheeling and turning kites. Yet, people came and they marveled. When powered flight was young, any flight, however tame by today's standards, was wonderful.

Dark comes early in November in East Tennessee. When Simon landed, it was obvious to all the show was over, the makeshift airfield's only illumination flashed intermittently from cloud-to-cloud lightning bolts. Captivated by Simon's performance, the satisfied audience applauded once more and filed out from grandstand. Many more non-paying watchers outside the track piled back on streetcars and left ahead of the coming showers. Both fast learners, the Moisant brothers cancelled the next day's show, forfeiting a potential second day's ticket sales. Once the storm passed, they packed up the flying circus and departed Chattanooga for the next stop, Memphis, in far West Tennessee.

CHAPTER TEN

MEMPHIS BLUES

THE MEMPHIS BELLE TURNS OUT TO BE A BITCH

Memphis, the largest city in Tennessee at the time, lay on the southern state's far western border. At the opposite end from Chattanooga, the town sprawled along the east bank of the Mississippi River. A cultural as well as a geographic world apart from Chattanooga, Memphis occupied the opposite end of the social spectrum as well. God-fearing Chattanooga shined as the buckle on the Bible belt, even though its religious luster was sometimes dimmed by the corrosion of strong drink as is often the case in the American South. However, good times were there for the taking in unrestrained, indulgent Memphis. The town on the river birthed the Blues, the mournful music migrating up from the Mississippi delta just to the south. The town also gave its distinctive imprint to that other classic strain of black peoples' artistic expression, Jazz. Much later in the 1960's, Rock and Roll would strike its first electric guitar chords in Memphis, completing the river town's musical trifecta.

After an all-day train journey, up and over the Cumberland Plateau, the highland occupying the middle of the state, the Moisant flying circus hit town on 9 December 1910. Regardless of any financial difficulties, the troupe checked into Memphis's best hotel, the Peabody, for a week's stay. The Peabody became famous for displaying a flock of mallard ducks in the carpeted lobby's center fountain but there is no record of exactly when this tradition of hosting other vagabond aviators began.

Memphis lived two lives, on and below a bluff overlooking the wide and muddy "Father of Waters." Upper Memphis, on top of the bluff, constituted the upscale, respectable part of town. Garros and his friends encamped there in the Peabody.

97

Lower Memphis, at the foot of the bluff on the riverbank was where people went for entertainment – the domain of restaurants, bars, nightclubs, jazz joints, and women of questionable virtue.

John Moisant, Garros, the other pilots, and the mechanics found December weather in Memphis clear, but very cold. Before the invention of multi-viscosity motor oil, the lubricant in the aircraft engines would have been the consistency of molasses, or rather this being the South, like sorghum syrup. Engines were hard to crank, hard to start. As compensation, the cold, dense air would support the aircraft well. Braving the frigid sky, Roland Garros made the first flight of an airplane over Memphis on 10 December, winning a $5000 prize offered by a local newspaper. He promptly blew a large portion of the cash on wine, women, and song. The rest he spent foolishly.

Garros later wrote of the comely southern belles of Memphis, saying he found some, the ones with less make-up, attractive and available. Nights in the poorly heated Peabody hotel could be cold in the Tennessee winter. An overnight guest of the opposite gender was just the ticket to companionship, sex, and warmth, not necessarily in that order. In his memoir, he mentions the women of Memphis. Were they prettier than Parisians? Softer than the women of New York? More available than those in Richmond or Chattanooga? You can only speculate why he was so taken.

Every night in Memphis saw the airshow pilots out on the town, hosted by the city's elite. As in New York, Roland Garros remarked on the segregation of the races. At a boxing match, a jazz club, or a bar, Blacks and Whites occupied separate seating sections. Restaurants frequented by Whites did not allow Blacks in at all. Evidently, New York City held no monopoly on racial discrimination during the Gilded Age.

During one of these evening events, Garros found himself introduced by the announcer from a boxing ring as a distinguished guest, "The pilot of the world's smallest airplane." This did not sit well with him. He had flown a Blériot XI over Richmond and the President of the United States, handling the craft with skill the first time he took it into the sky. He pressured the Moisant brothers for more sorties in the larger plane. The Demoiselle, the aircraft that taught him to fly, the one he made his mark in, his signature mount, was suddenly too small, too primitive, not worthy.

As in Richmond and Chattanooga, the venue in Memphis was another harness racing track. It had been chosen for its accessibility by public transport and proximity to the city center. The pilots and mechanics staged airshows there every afternoon. Also, as at previous stops, the same problem arose. Non-paying spectators, who could observe most of the show from outside the fence, reduced the expected and hoped-for ticket sales.

Trying to generate excitement and revenue, the team staged aerial stunts designed to bring people into the fairground, paying people that is. Two aircraft flew a make-believe race against a Packard automobile around the horse track. What passed for aerobatics back then became more extreme and dangerous. Several aircraft raced from the track around two islands in the wide Mississippi and back. One show routine still stands out today. From the grandstand, the sparse crowd would see two aircraft, one approaching from the left, one from the right, level at the same altitude. The pilots appeared to be on a head-on collision course hurtling toward an impact at show center with a closing speed bordering on 100 mph, 160 kph. At the last second, each aircraft banked slightly away from the other, seemingly avoiding certain death over the backstretch. The customers could not see that one pilot flew outside the track's far railing, the other aimed inboard of the inside rail. Even with no last-second maneuvers, a collision could not have occurred. This gag was boffo show business, and has remained so for over a century. The US Air Force aerial demonstration team, the Thunderbirds, flies this show routine today in their F-16s, one demo pilot holding to the left side of the runway, the other to the right. What was exciting at a 100-mph closing velocity is spectacular at 1000 mph, but is no less safe than in Memphis in 1910.

During a show flight in his tiny Demoiselle, Garros attempted a steep-banked turn, one he had performed over Richmond in the Blériot. At 100 feet, 30 meters altitude, he stalled the aircraft which fell off into a spin. As mentioned before, when a wing stalls, the airflow separates, dissipates into turbulence, and the wing loses all lift. If an aircraft is turning during a stall, it will often spin, rotating about a vertical axis. A spin is the only inherently stable aerodynamic maneuver, it will continue unabated until positive action is taken by the pilot, or impact with the ground puts a violent stop to the spin.

Early aviators did not understand spins, did not know what caused a spin, and feared the usual outcome, a crash. Recovery technique for an auto-rotating spin is strongly counter-intuitive. First, you must break the stall, re-establishing smooth airflow over the wings. This requires pushing the aircraft's nose down, building airspeed (spins occur at very low indicated airspeed), and restoring lift. Once the wing is flying again, not falling, the rotation is stopped with rudder input against the direction of the spin. Skill at spin recovery means steepening the dive when the ground is rushing up to meet the spinning plane. Every synapse in a green pilot's brain is crying for him to stop the descent, to raise the nose, to prevent impact with terra firma. Trying to pull the nose up only makes the spin worse, a fact many early aviators learned to their very great misfortune. Even today, it is not unknown for an experienced airline pilot, who ought to know better, to attempt recovery from a stall by raising the nose of his or her rapidly descending airliner. The outcome of this ham-handed mistake is the same as it was for Roland Garros in 1910.

After about two turns in the spin, the Demoiselle and Roland Garros hit the ground with a loud crump. The aircraft lay in pieces, but Garros was miraculously unhurt, except for his pride which was bruised deeply. He vowed to concentrate on flying the Blériot, a demand the Moisants were compelled to grant until the Demoiselle could be re-built by Jules Hue, a task of some difficulty. Demoiselle parts were hard to find in

Memphis, Tennessee and bamboo was in short supply along the Mississippi. The brothers loaned Garros the oldest Blériot in the sparse fleet.

Two days later, the screaming bitch of aircraft malfunction clawed at Garros again. Flying the Blériot, he felt, rather than heard over the engine's unmuffled clatter, a crack like a rifle shot. Looking down, he saw the flying wires holding the right wing in place go limp. A main spar had cracked, the wing was about to fold up like a grounded seagull's. Fortunately, he was over the race track, an emergency landing appeared both possible and extremely necessary. Just as he touched down, the wing failed, bent backward and up. The left wing, still developing lift, flipped the Blériot over to the right. The disintegrating airplane rolled up into a ball of splintered wood, torn fabric, and hot, bent metal. Frantic ground crew members, running from the tent hangers nearby, pulled Garros from the wreck covered with blood.

One of the (paying) spectators, a doctor, ran to his car and fetched his black bag of medical tools. The doc's quick examination revealed no major injuries, just a broken nose and a scalp cut requiring two stitches which he administered on the spot, gratis. That night back in the Peabody, a hurting and sore Roland Garros was tended to by the comely Mathilde Moisant, along on the tour with her sister.

This latest prang served to spur on a discussion the circus pilots intermittently conducted with each other, usually late at night after a few drinks. Even with their macho attitudes softened by good Tennessee whisky, the subject would have been approached carefully. Among risk-takers, to seriously admit your mortality to others is to show weakness and can even serve to hasten your demise. The gods of danger demand respect. Certain norms must be obeyed.

The question before the house went something like this, "Does the public come to our performances to see us fly or to see us die?" This issue of the attraction that dangerous sports generate probably first arose in the Roman Coliseum and continues today around auto racetracks worldwide. The consensus answer is always, "It's a combination of the two motives. The crowd gets a vicarious thrill out of watching us risk our lives. If what we do were safe, fewer people would care. It is the risk, not the deaths, that sells tickets. They also come to watch us display our unique skills." From the gladiators to the Moisant Flying Circus, to Formula 1 race car drivers, to the USAF Thunderbirds, the dynamic is always the same; dangerous sports are fun to watch.

Make no mistake, aviation, particularly air show aviation, in 1910 was dangerous in the extreme. In that year alone, two Blériot pilots met their maker at air shows in Europe. Louis Blériot himself crashed through the roof of a house in Istanbul, Turkey during an air display. He promptly retired from piloting following the example of Santos-Dumont. You must wonder: With crashes so frequent, how did any early pilot live long enough to perfect his or her skills? Roland Garros, by year's end, had totaled three Demoiselles and one Blériot. One more destroyed French aircraft and he would have been a German ace, not that the concept of an ace had been conceived yet.

To be a pilot in 1910 was to crash often. How did anyone survive? Other than dumb luck, a factor not to be discounted. The answer involves those early birds, their performance, and their structures. Engineers speak of "crumple zones" in modern automobiles; metal placed to adsorb by deformation the malevolent energy of a wreck before that energy can deform the car's occupants. Stick and cloth aircraft of 1910 were flying crumple zones. Once the wooden spars, taut flying wires, bike wheels, bungee cords, and bamboo longerons crumpled, the hapless pilot's velocity was often reduced to a survivable level. Added to that was the fact that those kites did not fly very fast or very high, and dives rarely exceeded a shallow 30-degree angle. The pilots only dreamed of loops and inverted flight so crashes tended to be sedate affairs.

Their finances somewhat aided by prizes offered by the local newspapers such as Garros's $5000 score, the flying circus packed up, boarded their train, and headed southward, chasing the weak winter sun. A snowstorm was bearing down on the city by the big river, it was time to leave. Destination; Tupelo, Mississippi, another river town, whose fame lay in the future as the birthplace of Elvis Presley.

As always, the show venue in Tupelo, the local fairgrounds, proved to be a challenge. The track itself was too short, the planes had to fly off the infield. That expanse most recently served as a stockyard with all the mud and manure still in place, only the livestock had been removed.

The first day of the show the weather did not cooperate, and neither did the good citizens of Tupelo. Black clouds hovered over the show site and gusting winds make aerial operations risky. Most of the spectators gathered, for free, outside the fence. Only a handful of paying patrons scattered themselves across the small grandstand. John Moisant flew, taking off in a line calculated to miss the deepest mud and avoiding the worst cow pie piles. To the watching pilots and ground crew's growing alarm, he took out his frustrations in the air. His display of aerobatics appeared deranged and dangerous. Moisant finally landed just before the rain started, washing out any more attempts to commit aviation.

At 1400 hours the next day, a cannon shot announced the second day of the show. Again, John Moisant flew his Blériot like a madman. He vowed the night before to give customers in the grandstand their money's worth, and to perform a maneuver unable to be seen by the free-loaders mooching outside the venue. So, Moisant buzzed the grandstand, flying barely 20 feet above the wooden seats. For the price of admission, spectators got the fright of their lives, a blast of hat-scattering propwash, and a mist of burned oil sprayed on them as they ducked from the clattering contraption passing just above. Still fuming about the financial bath he was taking, Moisant landed too hot, too fast, back on the now even muddier infield/stockyard. Instead of settling gently into the mire, the Blériot's spindly wheels dug into the smelly muck, the aircraft tipped over forward, the propeller shattered itself in the swampy ground, and the aircraft's tail pointed straight up into the overcast Mississippi sky.

Somehow, John Moisant avoided being tossed out of the cockpit and forward into the muck or worse, into the disintegrating propeller. The pilot's seat belt had yet to be invented. Moisant's survival depended on his sitting position with his legs positioned straight out as if in a kayak, holding him in place under the cowling. It is inaccurate to even designate the Blériot's pilot station as a "cockpit," it was not that spacious and the term came into use later during the Great War. Moisant was lucky he was not injured and/or buried in manure and mud. This good fortune later ran out on him.

Roland Garros remarked he thought Chattanooga was bad, but Tupelo turned out to be a far less desirable air show site.

A relieved flying circus packed up and left Tupelo, Mississippi that night for New Orleans, Louisiana following the Mississippi River south across the flat delta. The Frenchmen on the team, including Roland Garros, looked forward to the Crescent City, a colonial town they anticipated replicating French culture in America. Compared to Tupelo and Memphis, New Orleans was to be both better and worse, much worse.

CHAPTER ELEVEN

LA NOUVELLE-ORLEANS

The "Big Easy" Isn't

When the Moisant Flying Circus train chugged into New Orleans, Louisiana, Roland Garros returned home to a place he had never been. He immediately recognized the French colonial architecture in the old town, *Le Vieux Carré*, the area we now call "The French Quarter." Bicycling around Saigon as a boy, he saw the floor-to-ceiling windows with louvered wooden shutters, the full-length balconies, the delicate lacework of wrought iron, and the hollow-square buildings' cozy central courtyards. It was *déjà vue* by the Mississippi River.

Linguistically, he felt equally at home. Local inhabitants of New Orleans claimed mixed racial backgrounds; French, American Indian, Black, and Caribbean. They spoke a dialect known as "Creole," a name they also called themselves as a people. Garros said he recognized a few phrases in this *patois* like those used on the far-off island of his birth. If so, those familiar words must have been buried deep in his memory. He left Réunion at age 5 and only returned for a few days once when a youth of 11.

Strolling the Old Quarter's narrow streets while speaking among themselves in Metropolitan French, European pilots of the circus were easily recognized as hailing from mainland France. Some New Orleans' white citizens took the opportunity to speak Cajun French to the bemused group, locally an act of cultural rebellion. At the time, Cajun French was suppressed, considered to be an inferior, coarse tongue banned in schools, omitted in official transactions, and not fit for high society. Speaking Cajun French in public places was not encouraged by the authorities. Despite the Cajuns' linguistic enthusiasm, the Frenchmen encountered extreme difficulty in understanding them. The branch of French spoken by the Cajuns stemmed from an obscure regional dialect used in central France 200 years prior. Isolated in the swamps of southwestern Louisiana by the Louisiana Purchase and after *Les Acadians* were expelled from British Canada, their language mutated, branched off into slang, and further diverged from the mother tongue. Without the strict supervision of *l'Academie Française*, the official French government organization charged with policing the French language, Cajun French became almost unintelligible to speakers of modern French. This heresy is now in the process of being corrected, *l'Academie Française* established an office, funded by the government in Paris, to conduct classes in classic French in Lafayette, Louisiana, the unofficial capital of Cajun country.

New Orleans' mild climate, the French Colonial-styled buildings, the Creoles and their *patois*, it all made Roland Garros homesick for Saigon. He longed to see his mother and little sister whom he missed terribly. For his father, not so much.

Edmund Audemars, another Demoiselle pilot and Swiss friend of both John Moisant and Garros, joined the tour in New Orleans. Garros was glad to be reunited with Audemars who brought word of rising European interest in aviation. Interest in not just death-defying air shows and stunts, but for commercial and military uses of aircraft, whatever those might be. Roland Garros, upon hearing Audemar's news, found himself increasingly eager to return to Paris. Their homesickness intensified as the pilots roamed the avenues of New Orleans with familiar names, such as Rue Chartes and Bourbon Street.

Another scene the pilots found familiar was the lively nightlife in the French Quarter. It was not Paris, but it tried. Every evening, they sampled a different restaurant or bar, trying cuisine unknown back home. Alligator Étouffée anyone? How about Crayfish gumbo? Fried Catfish, what is that? The seafood was spectacular, fresh, and plentiful. It did take some effort getting used to the local fiery pepper sauce, Tabasco by brand name, made in nearby Avery Island, Louisiana, and within reach on every table. Classical French cuisine can be subtly flavorful, but it is almost never spicy due to capsaicin from chili peppers. None of its five classical sauces are bright red. Garros was sufficiently impressed to mention Tabasco sauce in his memoirs. One of the few deficiencies noted was a lack of good, meaning French, wine. New Orleans drank Bourbon on Bourbon Street, not Bordeaux.

In case the troop forgot why they were there, a constant reminder was provided by posters plastered all over the city proclaiming, "See John Moisant's International Aviators Shake Hands with Death" in lurid font. These theoretical handshakes with the Grim Reaper could be observed, preferably after buying a ticket, at the abandoned racetrack in City Park, where the flying circus pitched its big tent and erected its canvas hangers.

City Park in the heart of New Orleans covered 1300 acres, 5.3 square kilometers, and represented Louisiana in miniature, with wide, slow-moving bayous, swamps, live-oak forests, open grassland, and wilderness areas, along with developed attractions such as a carousel and two golf courses.

On his practice flights out of City Park, Roland Garros marveled to see birds and animals either unknown in France or rare were in unfamiliar quantities. In 1910, before the industrialization of New Orleans, prior to the expansion of the seaport, without the oil and gas industry, minus the canal dredging, and with barely 400,000 people, the unspoiled areas in and around the city teemed with wildlife. He flew alongside formations of pelicans arranged in echelons or broad vee's, each individual coasting in the air turbulence produced by the bird in front. Garros discovered flapping pelicans can out-turn an airborne Blériot monoplane. When he attempted to join up with a flock, the birds would wheel in a tight circle, spitting the droning aircraft out to the turn's perimeter and leaving him behind. He saw elegant snowy egrets and blue herons by the score. Egrets reminded him of miniature European storks, the symbol of his future squadron, although he did not know it at the time. Hundreds of alligators sunned themselves on the bayous' muddy banks. Not the place for a forced landing. Garros and the team enjoyed flying over New Orleans, so much so that Albert Moisant instructed them to restrict their aerial displays until paying customers were in the racetrack's large grandstand

Christmas Day, 25 December 1910, the official air show kicked off as promised on the omnipresent posters. Moisant's flyers were gratified to see the grandstand full. 20,000 locals, all of them white, (Blacks and Creoles, "colored people," were banned from City Park) bought tickets, taking every available seat long before the show, scheduled from 1500 to 1800, 3 to 6 pm. To a man, the pilots vowed to give the paying public their money's worth. Forgotten instantly were the sparse crowds in Richmond and Chattanooga, the awful weather at every show venue beginning in New York, and the freeloading spectators of Tupelo. New Orleans was different in many ways, the weather being perfect with no wind and only a broken deck of high clouds. Cajun French-speaking patrons along with English-speaking Whites would see Moisant's pilots fly and fly well.

During his solo exhibition, Garros climbed higher and higher over City Park, venturing out over immense Lake Pontchartrain just to the north, higher than he had ever flown before, until his tiny craft was all but lost to view from the ground. Eventually, he climbed into the broken cloud layer, leveled off, and began weaving in and out among the puffy cotton balls. Riding the cold moist air generating the clouds, the Blériot's fabric-covered wings began icing up, Garros had never seen frost on an airborne aircraft. Worse, he was lost among the featureless clouds with no reference to solid ground, only occasional glimpses of the huge lake's wavy surface below. His wings were not the only part of the craft frosting over. The Blériot's carburetor, clogged with ice, began to starve the straining Gnome engine of fuel. With his engine dying, Garros had no choice but to descend no matter how disoriented he became. Emerging underneath the cloud deck's razor-flat bottom, he soon saw the city below him to the south

THE FIRST FIGHTER PILOT | 109

of the lake and in it City Park's broad green rectangle. Breathing the drier air below the clouds, the carb cleared itself of ice and the engine sang again until shutdown on landing during the mandatory bootleg turn

The grandstand announcer, paid to hype the show, breathlessly announced to the cheering throng Roland Garros's spiraling return down from the invisible, unknown world above the clouds. He added they just witnessed Garros setting a new world's altitude record of 7000 feet, 2133 meters. How the show barker knew this exact figure is unknown, perhaps he was told the cloud deck's estimated height and took it from there. Maybe he made it up. Garros knew this record to be bogus airshow hype. Earlier in December, another Frenchman, Georges Legagneux, ascended to 3100 meters, just over 10,000 feet, in Europe. Not able to correct the show announcer, Garros let the matter rest. Later, he would go on to set a valid world altitude record, but not over the Crescent City. The local newspaper, the Times-Picayune, never a paragon of restraint, labeled *le petit* Frenchman, "Roland Garros, the Cloud Kisser." Not the most macho of call signs, but far better than "The Pilot of the World's Smallest Airplane."

New Orleans was turning out to be a triumph, with large crowds, lots of mention in the local paper, and more social engagements than any human being, even a young Frenchman, could survive. Albert Moisant, perpetually grumpy over finances, softened a bit. John Moisant, a great friend to the air show pilots as well as their boss, lived large in his two elements; the sky and the salons of the city later called "The Big Easy."

After the hugely successful Christmas Day show, John Moisant hatched a new plan; to win the Michelin Cup. The tire company annually awarded an impressive gold trophy and 20,000 French francs, about $4000, for the longest flight by an "aeroplane" each year. In 1910, the potential winner, another Frenchman, Maurice Tabuteau, stayed aloft for 7 hours and 48 minutes, quite a feat in an era when keeping an aero engine running for more than an hour presented a stiff challenge to the mechanics.

Moisant calculated by adding an additional 130 liters, 32 gallons, of gasoline in an auxiliary tank on one of the Blériots, he could easily fly over eight hours and capture the francs, the trophy, and the worldwide publicity. John Moisant evidently did not compute the effect of the added weight of 215 pounds of fuel on an aircraft weighing a little over 500 pounds.

He would attempt the flight on the first of January to lead the next year's competition as sundown marked the end of the 1910 competition. His plan included a takeoff from City Park early on New Year's Day, a transit to an improvised field four miles outside New Orleans, yet another vacant stockyard. He would land there to top off the fuel and oil tanks. The extra fuel and oil required to set the record would prevent a heavy-weight departure from City Park. After adding more gasoline and motor oil, takeoff from the stockyard would start the timing clock. He would then circle two pylons placed 4 miles apart in a racetrack pattern, staying always in sight of the judges from the Aero Club of the United States. Garros and the other pilots reckoned boredom and the biting December cold constituted the biggest obstacles to the record-breaking flight attempt and made no plans to attend. They had better things to do.

The night of 31 December 1910, New Year's Eve, was a memorable evening in the French Quarter. Perhaps homesick for Paris, or more accurately missing authentic Parisian nightlife, Garros and the other European pilots attended an operetta at an exclusive night club and café. Not because they were fans of opera, the Moulin Rouge Review was more their style, but because the musical troop hailed from France. Female cast members had to be astonished at the appearance in the audience and at the post-performance reception of dashing French air show pilots. These young men daily shook hands with death while speaking flawless French. The showgirls were probably homesick as well after touring the frontiers of civilization in America. Somehow, the group found a stash of genuine French champagne for the after-party.

At the post-opera and New Year's Eve celebration, Garros entertained the showgirls and his fellow pilots with renditions of Chopin at a piano conveniently located in the local restaurant. French women, French champagne, and Chopin; it does not get much better than that.

Much later that night, early in the wee hours of the next morning, Roland Garros returned to his hotel, the DeSoto, with a comely singer, a young lady from Paris whose talents far exceeded mere music. The other Frenchmen found themselves equally and separately occupied. You can safely assume mutually-shared homesickness generated the impromptu sleepovers. Or, maybe it was just shear lust. Either way, the remainder of the night dissipated itself in pure, no, make that wanton Gallic passion. Around eight o'clock, Garros's door flew open. His new lady friend shrieked and clutched the covers up to her chin.

"*Roland, habille-toi et viens avec nous, dépêche-toi!* Get dressed and come with us, hurry!" one of the panicked pilots cried out.

"I hope for your sake that this is important. Is the building on fire?" was Roland's response.

"No, it's John. He has crashed at the stockyards."

"What happened? Did he survive?'

"We don't know yet, but the medical people want us there."

The pilots were to soon learn that John Moisant's Blériot crashed while landing at the stockyard and their friend, their boss, and in many ways their hero, was dead. Shaken, the four hurriedly dressed and departed for the New Orleans morgue to view the body, leaving four astonished and unclad young ladies to find a way back to their own quarters.

John Moisant died that cold morning because two key advances in aviation had not yet been invented probably coupled with a lack of understanding of the effect of an aircraft's gross weight on its stalling speed.

Modern light plane wings are built with a subtle twist from wing root to wing tip. This ensures that an aerodynamic stall, the separation of smooth airflow into turbulence and the resulting loss of lift, starts at the root and spreads outward to the tip. Turbulence produces a buffeting, a shuddering, in the airframe recognizable by the pilot as an impending stall. If not corrected by lowering the nose and/or increasing power, the vibration grows worse until the sensory message transmitted by the wing is unmistakable, "The wing is about to stall, you moron." Aircraft wings in 1910 were built straight, not twisted. This generated a sudden stall, often without warning. Lift would cease. The wing would drop with all the suddenness and often the fatal consequences of a gallows' trap door. Also absent was the cockpit seat belt, a deficiency demonstrated but not corrected in Moisant's crash in Tupelo. Earlier in the year, these same two lethal factors tossed the hapless Morane brothers into a life-saving tree in France.

Approaching the stockyard, Moisant reduced power, slowing the aircraft for landing until the stall speed, elevated by the extra fuel, equaled the Blériot's airspeed. The cloth and wooden wing stalled. It quit flying instantly and without warning. The aircraft stopped in midair, the nose pitched down, the centrifugal force hurled Moisant out of the cockpit. From 25 feet in the air, he hit the ground face first, breaking his neck. John Bevins Moisant, one of the most famous aviators of his era, died moments later. He was 42 years old.

Speculation about the fatal accident's cause consumed the surviving pilots and the US Aero Club officials for hours. It is unknown how much extra weight Moisant took on board before departing City Park, but Roland Garros smelled a strong odor of gasoline in the wrecked aircraft. He examined the flight controls; all appeared intact. Garros speculated his friend had taken his hand off the control stick to wave to the ground crew, but no one saw that happen. A consensus emerged: during a critical landing phase close to the ground, a gust of wind (the Times-Picayune called it an "air pocket," an imaginary invention) pitched the Blériot's nose down, throwing Moisant out of the cockpit. This on-the-spot analysis was almost certainly wrong, and shows how little was known about aerodynamics in 1910. From all accounts of the crash, it seems obvious now John Moisant stalled the aircraft for whatever reason; too high a gross weight, too heavy on the controls, showing off for the ground crew, or not enough airspeed. Wind gusts do not stall an airplane nor do they rotate its nose 90 degrees downward. Sudden, vicious stalls do.

Moisant's death shocked the city. Honoring him, New Orleans' main airport, built a few years later two miles from the crash site, bore the title "Moisant International Airport" until the name was updated to "Louis Armstrong International Airport" in the 1960s. Warm memories of the jazz great who loved Paris trumped, or trumpeted, the long-forgotten legacy of an aviator from the distant past. Today, the Federal Aviation Administration's three letter identifier for the airport remains "MSY" for "Moisant Stock Yards," the muddy field where the French Canadian/American pilot died so long ago.

Following the funeral, Albert Moisant left for New York City to sort out the now-tangled finances of the Moisant family. You can speculate that Albert's enthusiasm for the air show business waned when the enterprise took his younger brother. Before he left, Albert met with the pilots and ground crew to discuss the way forward. Should they abandon the tour, scheduled for Texas, Oklahoma, Mexico, and Cuba, or should they carry on? A vote was taken. The outcome was never in doubt. John Moisant lived and died for this tour, he would want them to continue. And so, they would, with John Young, an American pilot, now in charge.

Before the evening of departure from New Orleans, while the ground crew loaded the show equipment on the train, the pilots, French and American, toured the French Quarter, saying good-bye. Stopping in for a few moments in each in the places John Moisant frequented, the pilots were taken aback by the outpouring of grief expressed by the patrons and staff of the bars and restaurants. John Moisant would be missed in New Orleans.

CHAPTER TWELVE

DEEP IN THE HEART OF TEXAS

The Show Must Go On

The pilots and ground crew members were adamant. Before leaving New Orleans, they adopted "The Show Must Go On" as the motto of Moisant's flying circus. These inspiring words were inscribed on press releases, hand-outs, posters, and even painted on the airplanes. On 4 January of the new year, 1911, the first air display without the show's founder took place in Fair Park just outside Dallas, Texas. Ticket receipts exceeded any to date on the tour, surpassing even the proceeds racked up at Belmont Park in New York. Surprised to see the huge throng waiting in the grandstand for the show, the pilots probably were reluctant to ask themselves why the big crowd showed up, fearing the obvious answer. John Moisant's death received wide publicity nationwide. It was as if Glenn Curtiss or one of the Wright Brothers had met his end in a plane crash. If the public had any doubts about the dangers inherent in aviation, those were dispelled by the demise of Moisant. The colorful Canadian was perceived to be a premier pilot during the dawn of powered flight. If an "air pocket" could take John Moisant, who was safe?

The truth, as is often the case, was much more complicated. Dangers sprang from various sources known and unknown. Flight in the early 1900s posed enormous risks. The science of aerodynamics was not well understood despite, or perhaps because of, centuries of observing birds fly. If engineers suspected why a wing stalled, no one knew how to prevent this from happening or, more importantly, how to warn the pilot. Why a stalled aircraft tended to fall off into a spin and how to recover from that spin also puzzled early birdmen. True birds did not spin. This crucial knowledge remained hidden until the widespread use of airplanes in the Great War generated numerous unintended trial and error experiments.

Structural failure of feather-light wooden airframes held together by wires in tension and stretched cloth occurred frequently. Compounding the problems, aero engines were hard to keep running. Aircraft designers had two choices; the boffins could adapt existing engines from motorcycles, automobiles. or stationary power plants, or they could design new engines from a clean sheet of paper with all the uncertainties that process involved. By this time, Blériot's mounted French Gnome engines, a rotary design invented to power water pumps deep in coal mines, of all places. The Gnome offered some obvious advantages. It was well proven, used in numerous mines. It was cheap, with spare parts available. Rotary engine technology was well understood for the day. The power to weight ratio was good; the engine was light for its output. Cooling was not a problem, the spinning cylinders cooled themselves. But those whirling cylinders imparted a strong gyroscopic effect on a flying airframe, an effect un-noticed down in a coal mine. Aircraft employing a Gnome turned to the right better than they banked to the left. Carburetors presented another challenge, the fuel/air ratio in a mine never varied, but when a plane gained altitude, the pilot had to adjust the carb manually from the cockpit or risk drowning the engine with too rich a mixture. Miners loved the Gnome – set it and forget it, with no throttle, the engine ran at full speed or not at all. This all-or-nothing power scheme required pilots to plan maneuvers like landings carefully, and made formation flying difficult. With all its idiosyncrasies, the Gnome rotary engine reported for airborne duty until the Great War finally ground to a halt. It powered aircraft from both sides (the Germans built theirs under license before the war, during the conflict, they stopped paying the franchise fee). This dual-use situation, an engine supporting opposing sides, has never been duplicated in warfare.

In addition to the many technical unknowns of aviation in 1910-1911, pilot error continued to take its toll in causing crashes. Ignoring weight and balance limits; attempting flat, non-banked turns; roughly moving controls more suited to a light touch; slow flight, all these produced their share of prangs. Which unique combination of factors resulted in John Moisant's death can be and was debated, but pilot inexperience must be included, even if his pilots did not want to think about that. "If the fates of the air can take John Moisant, who was both fearless and famous, what does that mean for me?" was a line of inquiry Roland Garros and his companions loathed to take.

A packed grandstand in Dallas also weighed in on the on-going debate about whether the spectators were there to see flying or dying. If Moisant had not cashed in his chips in New Orleans in a well-publicized crash, would as many folks have bought tickets for the Dallas show? This presented another question too painful to ponder. In his mind, Garros addressed that issue and he did not like what he concluded.

During his late afternoon solo performance, thoughts of his friend's loss, his own mortality, and of ghoulish spectators ran through Garros's head. It was too much for him to bear. After takeoff from Fair Park in the Blériot, Garros climbed away, far away, departing the makeshift airfield, and disappearing from the crowd's view. A crowd who, he felt, had come to watch him crash and die. Late afternoon, the Dallas area lay covered by a broken deck of clouds like the layer which had given Garros his call sign, "The Cloud Kisser," in New Orleans. Texas clouds hung lower and denser than the ones over Louisiana. The deck was thinner, the stratiform clouds of winter rather than puffy cumulous clouds floating over Lake Pontchartrain. Garros climbed above the cloud layer and flew about aimlessly, paying tag with the wispy cloud tops. We all cope with a profound loss in our own way. Flying above the clouds, out of the thrill-seeking spectators' view, remote from the unseen earth, Roland Garros found peace. A strange sort of serenity, with a clattering engine barking just in front, propwash battering his body, a cold 55 mph, 88 kph, airstream freezing his face (no windshield on a Blériot), but peace it was. Garros, perhaps the first pilot to seek solace in the sky, unknowingly started a tradition carried on today. Whether in a Blériot at 60 miles an hour or a F-22 Raptor at ten times that speed, most pilots have learned they can temporarily outrun their internal troubles at altitude.

Illuminated by the setting sun, the cloud tops faded from gold to grey, night was falling over north-central Texas. Garros reluctantly descended below the clouds back into the real world and realized he was lost. Ranch land surrounding Dallas appeared flat and featureless in the twilight, one cattle pasture looked pretty much like any other as did the farm houses. Flying in Europe was different, each small town, river, mountain, canal meant something. Each was unique and identifiable. Dead reckoning ruled early aerial navigation. No one had yet thought to mount a compass in a cockpit. Roland Garros vowed at once never to leave the ground without a map. He knew the winter sun set in the southwest and the prevailing winds blew from west to east, carrying him with them. His position probably lay east of town and if he followed the dying sun's rays, he should spot Dallas, no matter how boring the land around it appeared.

Soon, he saw Dallas's glow on the western horizon but before he could make out the Fair Grounds, his engine sputtered, then quit, out of gas. Now, the flat grasslands provided him with a place for an emergency landing. Touching down in the rapidly gathering darkness, on unfamiliar bumpy terrain, things did not go well. The spindly, fragile landing gear collapsed and the aircraft was severely damaged. Unhurt in yet another crash landing, Roland Garros, The Cloud Kisser, hitch-hiked back to town.

John Moisant's International Aviators troop was running out of airplanes. Two more were damaged on landing at the last show in Dallas. Next stop, Fort Worth, then a small cow town 45 miles, 75 kilometers, west of Dallas. The team could field only three serviceable craft.

The budding automotive industry was just beginning to embrace high-rate production of identical cars built of interchangeable parts. Henry Ford's production lines were humming, Model Ts popping out like sausages. Airplanes were still an artisanal product, constructed one at a time to fluid specifications. During the design's lifetime, Bleriots were built in several workshops. It's a good bet no two were exactly alike. This meant parts from wrecked aircraft, of which Garros's team had plenty, could not be easily installed on other craft, or used to build a "new" plane. Jules Hue and the other mechanics performed minor miracles, but could only do so much. Despite its utter simplicity, the Demoiselle which Garros wrecked in Memphis never flew again.

The weather turned against them in Fort Worth with high winds blowing off the west Texas plains. Despite being only a few miles apart, Fort Worth is West Texas. Dallas is East Texas. Once again, a large and demanding crowd insisted on an air display and refused ticket refunds. Garros in the last operational Blériot and Audemars in his brand-new Demoiselle managed to get airborne. Both put on aerobatic displays that were half good airmanship and half wind-driven fights for survival. The crowd, perhaps sensing the risks being taken, gave the two aviators a standing ovation after the aircraft touched down.

Oklahoma City, Oklahoma, to the north, was worse. Garros flew in low clouds heavy with snow mixed with freezing fog. However, the show in Oklahoma City had far-reaching effects on the history of aviation although no one knew it at the time.

Clyde Cessna was a natural mechanic, self-taught, from Iowa. He gained a local reputation as a mechanical genius in Iowa and Oklahoma modifying farm equipment and cars. Early in 1911, Cessna earned a comfortable living as an automobile dealer in Enid, Oklahoma. Always interested in new mechanical technology, Clyde traveled to Oklahoma City on a mission. This well-to-do owner of a car store scored a temporary job unloading the Moisant Flying Circus train, then helping Jules Hue and company assembling the few remaining aircraft. The farm boy, now an auto trader, was surprised to learn how simply the planes were constructed and how rudimentary they seemed. Compared to a combine harvester or caterpillar tractor, a Blériot was nothing but sticks and cloth with a mine pump engine. Clyde Cessna vowed to build himself an airplane. Thinking perhaps there was more to learn about aeronautical engineering, Cessna hopped a train to New York City, where the Queen Aircraft Company built Blériots under license. He secured a job in the factory and in a month learned everything he thought he needed to know about aircraft construction, then returned to Oklahoma to build his airplane. Cessna's "Silverwing" was a copy of the Blériot XI. He built it from memory and powered it with a re-purposed motorboat engine.

In the then time-honored tradition, Clyde Cessna set about teaching himself how to fly. To say his flying lessons did not go smoothly would be an understatement. His first 13 attempts at flight ended in crashes before he even got airborne. Either Cessna was not as natural a pilot as he was a mechanic or his design omitted some key features of the successful but tricky Blériot XI. Now the laughingstock of Oklahoma, Cessna angrily vowed to make the Silverwing fly. He went on to say that once it flew, he would torch it, set it on fire, and never attempt aviation again. On his 14th attempt in June of 1911, he took off. His first try at a turn ended up with him and the airplane snared by a tree. But Clyde Cessna was hooked. Forgetting his incendiary vow, he improved the design and named his second airplane "The Comet." At the end of 1911, Cessna was flying five-mile round trips and his nickname became "The Birdman of Enid." The next two years saw him make a lucrative living putting on flying exhibitions at county fairs, an activity halted by World War One. Following WWI, Clyde Cessna, along with Walter Beech and Lloyd Stearman, founded the Travel Air Airplane Company. Later, he left Travel Air to start Cessna Aircraft, a company building airplanes today with hundreds of thousands of Cessnas flying throughout the world.

Clyde Cessna's story is unique; few spectators at the Moisant flying exhibitions went on to start aircraft companies. But the air shows undoubtedly inspired many people who had never seen a human being fly. It would be hard to exaggerate the impact of the flying circuses, of which the Moisant team was but one and the most famous, but there were others. The romance, the danger, the thrills of taking to the sky, all took hold in the public's consciousness. Aviation quickly matured from a foolhardy stunt to something real, something the ground-bound public could understand and embrace. They saw intrepid pilots in their flimsy craft take off, circle the improvised flying fields, perform a few stunts, and return to earth. If these Europeans could fly, why couldn't anyone? The inevitable social gatherings convened in the evenings after the performances proved that while these young men spoke with funny accents, they were regular guys, not supermen.

Shows in Temple and Waco, Texas followed, then it was on to Houston. In south Texas, the paying public's darker side almost produced a disaster. Two days of flying went well, but on the third, the weather turned adverse. Late in the day, Garros got airborne in a stiff breeze flew a few circuits and landed with some difficulty. The show announcer told the large crowd that, due to the winds, flying was done for the day. Enraged, the crowd poured from the grandstand carrying torches made from rolled-up newspapers and threatened to burn the three remaining airplanes on the spot. John Young begged Roland Garros and René Simon to fly, to do anything to placate the cloud. Garros and Simon weighed two bad alternatives; fly in the wind storm and maybe crash, destroying their precious aircraft, or watch the drunken mob burn those same planes. They reluctantly agreed to take off.

Loudspeakers announced to the crowd that there would be flying after all, and would the spectators please return to the stands. Nothing doing; sensing a trick, the mob with its torches refused to move. The situation was rapidly deteriorating into anarchy. Mechanics attempted to clear a path through the throng for takeoff, with limited success. Simon went first, fearful his wing tips would decapitate someone standing too close or a drunk would fall in front of his propeller. He made it and then it was Garros's turn in the Blériot. The ground crew released the airplane, but the way forward was not clear.

Garros rolled, gathering speed and scattering spectators like autumn leaves. Once airborne, Garros followed Simon away from the fairgrounds in the gathering twilight. The frightened two pilots landed safely in a pasture outside of town and hitch-hiked back.

As they approached the show venue, they saw flames from burning structures licking the horizon. Simon and Garros feared the show season was finished. If the crowd had torched the tents and hangers, there would be nothing left to support the remaining two airplanes spending the night with the cows behind them. When the accommodating driver dropped them off at the fairgrounds, they realized the mob had instead burned down the grandstand. Leaving Houston and its violent spectators behind, the Flying Circus headed north to another Texas city, to an unplanned rendezvous with military overtones.

CHAPTER THIRTEEN

THE TOUR CONTINUES

FLYING CLOSER TO WAR

Next stop on the tour, San Antonio, Texas, lay 190 miles west of Houston. Unlike Houston, the town gained fame through a rich military heritage. In the early 1800s, San Antonio and Texas itself was a province of the country of Mexico. However, migration from the United States, primarily from the American South, rapidly turned the population mix from predominately Hispanic to Anglo. English-speaking Texans, all US citizens, revolted, intending to found an independent, Anglo-dominated country. The Mexican government, during its rather clumsy attempt to put down the separation movement, surrounded a small band of Texans in the old Spanish mission at San Antonio, "The Alamo." William Travis of Alabama, Jim Bowie, inventor of the famous Bowie knife, from Louisiana, and legendary Indian-fighter and frontiersman Davy Crockett from Tennessee were the leaders of the resistance. The new Texans hoped to hold out until the rebel army led by Sam Houston, also of Tennessee, came to their rescue. The hastily-fortified church and its 200+ desperate defenders survived for 11 days against the much larger Mexican force. On 6 March 1836, the Alamo fell and the few rebels remaining alive, including Crockett, were put to the sword. Eventually, Texas gained its independence from Mexico and existed as a sovereign nation for ten years until annexed by the USA in a friendly take-over. After the War Between the States, the US Army established a major base in San Antonio, naming it after the Texas rebellion's leader, Sam Houston.

Following an air show on 4 February 1911 in San Antonio, the Moisant troop's aviators were invited to participate in war games conducted by the US Army at Fort Sam Houston. It is not known who generated this aerial idea, but whoever extended the invitation was slightly ahead of his time by including fixed-wing aircraft in a war game. More of a military exhibition than actual training, the maneuvers were to be conducted in front of a grandstand. The stands faced an open field with artillery pieces deployed in front facing a line of rounded, forested hills. These hills hid the imaginary enemy, but the simulated soldiers' location was unknown to the gunners. Finding them fell to an aviator, a civilian Frenchman.

Roland Garros, the only pilot taking the invitation to participate seriously, took off from in front of the grandstand and flew off in the direction of the nearby hills, peering below for the simulated enemy. This classic reconnaissance role typically belonged to the horse Cavalry. From time immemorial, the equestrians' mission involved scouting out the opposing forces' location then reporting back to the command authority, who would then devise an engagement plan. The time required for a troop of horses to find the enemy and return to headquarters stretched out to hours and sometimes days, far too long for the observers to wait in the grandstand. Some free-thinking officer, probably of junior rank, came up with the idea of using Moisant's aircraft to replace the horses as scouts and sold the idea to the senior brass.

Hydrogen-filled balloons had been used to spot enemy forces since the 1850's, but use of fixed-wing aircraft was a revolutionary concept untried by the hide-bound military and naturally unwelcomed by the Cavalry. How could these fragile, unreliable flying machines be relied on in time of war? How could one pilot replace the eyes of hundreds of cavalrymen? Garros later wrote he thought about the possible utility of aircraft in battle but kept his ideas to himself. Learning to fly at the French army base at Issy, he saw at once how easily troops could be spotted from above.

Flying over low, scrub-covered hills of south-central Texas, he soon spied what he assumed to be an infantry platoon hiding in the brush. Descent to a lower altitude revealed the "enemy" to be a herd of wild goats. Nevertheless, Roland

Garros landed back at Headquarters and reported as if he had fixed the opposing forces' position. Like cavalrymen, airborne scouts reported what they saw in person. Use of radio equipment in a 1911 cockpit strained bounds of technical credulity. Following the show script, the big guns opened with a roar, not at the goats, but at a pre-planned impact zone. The show was a considerable success and if anyone questioned the propriety of a Frenchman, even one speaking good English, serving as an advance scout for the American Army, they did not mention it and neither did the local papers.

Using aircraft to determine the positions of enemy troop formations represented an idea whose time had come and was soon simultaneously adopted by armed forces in Europe and the USA. Roland Garros may have been the first airborne scout, maybe not, but his performance for numerous US Army dignitaries in San Antonio contributed to the acceptance of the concept that clattering, fluttering aircraft could replace horse soldiers as advance scouts. Four years later during the Great War, French aerial reconnaissance would save Paris from a German invasion and turn the tide of battle from a war of maneuver to a dreadful slog of trench warfare, but none of this was foreseen on the dusty fields of Fort Sam Houston.

Roland Garros's scouting expedition for the US Army, while a dress rehearsal for the real thing, was not the first use of aircraft in an actual war simulated or real. Later in 1911, Italy invaded the Turkish colony immediately across the Mediterranean from the boot of Italy, a place eventually known as Libya. Late to the establishment of colonies, Italy found all the good places taken. The Italo-Turkish war resulted. It was a war fought primarily by incompetents. The Ottoman Turkish empire was crumbling from within, riven by factions, old and decrepit, poorly led, and saddled with an army which had forgotten centuries earlier how to fight. The Kingdom of Italy, united for a scant 40 years, was still learning how to field a modern military.

Feeling their way, the Italians did establish an Air Service flying Taube monoplanes like the French Blériots. Of what use these smoking contraptions would be was anyone's guess. Once the Italian Army established a beachhead in Libya and pushed the Turks out into the surrounding desert, of which there was plenty, the Air Service was ferried across, set up an airfield and began looking for something to do.

On 23 October 1911, Captain Carlo Piazza flew the world's first combat mission in a fixed-wing, heavier-than-air aircraft while scouting for the Italian Army. Unused to being observed from above, the Turks were easy to spot and tended to be camped in isolated desert oases. On 1 November of the same year, things became more serious. Lt. Giulio Gavotti took to the air armed and looking for trouble. He carried with him four grapefruit-sized grenades in a leather satchel like those used by mail carriers. He circled at low altitude over grove of palm trees clustered around a muddy watering hole. Turkish troops camped among the trees watched, looking up in curiosity. Gavotti hurled the grenades, one by one, down on the Turks. Without a bombsight or any calculations on ballistics, the Italian used the TLAR method of bomb aiming, i.e., That Looks About Right. Surprised, the Turks took cover and no damage or casualties were reported. An inauspicious start to aerial warfare.

Two weeks later, another Italian pilot achieved another first. He was shot down. Firing bolt-action, single shot rifles up into the air, the Turks got lucky. However comical these engagements seem now, they set the stage for the carnage to come.

Leaving the simulated war games behind, the circus members boarded their train for the long, boring ride across the semi-desert of west Texas. Arrival in El Paso, unbeknownst to the aviators, would land them near an actual war zone where the bullets flew in earnest and the enemy was not goats.

El Paso sits on the far western tip of Texas, perched like an accusatory finger pointed at Arizona with New Mexico a few miles north and west, and Old Mexico just across the Rio Grande River to the south.

In 1911, Mexico was in the midst of a revolution, led not by renegade Texans, but by Mexican citizens sick of the dictatorial and corrupt rule of El Presidenté Portfino Diaz. Francisco Madero, the rebels' leader, deputized the powerful governor of a relatively prosperous northern state as his military commander for the region bordering the USA. That man was Pancho Villa, and he brought much to the revolution. Thousands of men along with their horses and guns reported to Pancho Villa. Villa played the part well, with an impressive bushy mustache, sporting a wide sombrero, with ammunition belts crossing his chest. Often pictured in photos astride a white horse, he was known as a "Caudillo," which translates to "An owner of a large ranch" or "A military strongman." Today, Pancho Villa would be labeled a "warlord." While publicly supporting Madero, Villa participated in the revolution mostly for his own gain, increasing his personal wealth and power over northern Mexico.

Mid-February 1911, Pancho Villa's men laid siege to the government forces occupying Ciudad Juarez, the Mexican city on the south bank of the Rio Grande across from El Paso, Texas. Madero, anxious about fighting so close to the US border and fearful of provoking an intervention by the American government, which supported Diaz, ordered Villa to abandon the attack and retreat southward. To Pancho Villa, the line between a revolutionary political objective and apolitical banditry appeared fuzzy and ultimately immaterial. You can surmise Pancho Villa's goals did not include establishing a Jeffersonian democracy in Mexico. Sensing victory over the isolated and dispirited "Federales" holed up in Juarez and smelling the opportunity to loot the city, Villa ignored his erstwhile boss and pressed home his attack.

Albert Moisant, Roland Garros, and their fellow aviators, if they knew of the Mexican revolution at all, failed to anticipate how the shadows cast by a war just across a shallow, muddy river from El Paso would affect their air show plans. After checking in to their hotel, setting up their tents and hangers, and assembling their aircraft, the troop found half the population of El Paso perching on the city's highest roofs watching the action across the border. Despite the desert mountains just to the north in New Mexico, El Paso is relatively flat. It was difficult to observe the fighting from street level, hence the roof climbing. Garros and the others soon joined the Texans atop the buildings, not knowing who to root for; Villa's banditos/rebels or the Federales. The scheduled show the next day turned out to be a financial disaster, the grandstand was nearly empty. Why pay to see some Frenchmen risk their lives flying when you can watch actual ground combat and cavalry charges? Later that day, an American aviator, C. K. Hamilton, took off, flying down the Rio Grande's course, being careful to stay over the north bank and in the USA in case of engine failure. He checked out the skirmishes. Hamilton, who did see a cavalry charge, was probably the first pilot to witness war from the air. He would not be the last. Giving up on preoccupied El Paso, Albert Moisant ordered the circus to pack up and board the train. The destination, which involved a detour eastward to avoid the fighting, was Monterrey, Mexico, revolution, or no revolution.

Meanwhile, back in Europe, another ambitious man with a magnificent mustache, a wide, waxed handle-bar as opposed to Pancho Villa's drooping brush, prepared for a war yet to be fought. Kaiser Wilhelm II, Emperor of Germany (Kaiser is German for "Caesar"), an erratic and narcissistic man, was simultaneously in charge of and captive to the German Army's High Command. The generals, all of Prussian heritage, knew war with France loomed on the horizon. They did not know exactly when or where it would start, only that they would start it.

Germany emerged as a unified country in the 1860s and 70s with the merger of numerous semi-independent German-speaking states, including Bavaria but not Austria, under the tight control of a Prussian cadre. Prussians played the militant Spartans to Bavaria's life-loving Athenians in the new German state. Now finally, the Teutonic elite believed Germany should take its place in the first rank of nations, not only in Europe, but worldwide. Germany felt itself geographically hemmed in, surrounded by nation-states viewing German ambition with considerable alarm. France, traditionally the principal power on the continent, lay to the west, the Russian super-state to the east, the Alps to the south. Beyond the mountains was Italy, itself newly unified. The Austro-Hungarian Empire, an ally, blocked expansion to the southeast. Britain's Royal Navy ruled the high seas. Germany's ocean access, on the Baltic Sea in the north, could be easily blockaded. Furthermore, the German economy did not greatly benefit from trade and wealth generated by overseas possessions; all the lucrative colonies had been grabbed centuries earlier by other Europeans. Germans felt, rightly or wrongly, the other European powers were conspiring to keep *Der Fatherland* under thumb, forever constrained to the second tier of nations, weak, and inconsequential.

The architect of German unification, Prince Otto von Bismarck, the "Iron Chancellor" and political leader of Germany, announced, "We are satiated," meaning German expansion was complete under Kaiser Wilhelm I. Following Wilhelm I's death, his grandson, Wilhelm II, assumed the throne in Berlin. Ambitious Prussians conspired with the young Kaiser, himself half-Prussian, half English (due to his English mother), telling him greatness was within his royal grasp. He could be the leader of Europe's strongest country, be a modern Teutonic Caesar. Wilhelm II, a vain, insecure man easily swayed by flattery, dismissed Bismarck from office in 1890. The High Command began preparing for the invasion of France. Why France? Invading France was what Prussians did. A short war with Paris during unification in1870 easily captured the formerly French departments of Alsace and Lorraine. Aggression and annexation generated intense Germanophobia in France; the people wanted the two rich provinces back. In Berlin, they knew the preeminent power on the continent and the largest country in Europe, France, must be defeated to fulfill German, read Prussian, ambitions.

Germany's thirst for expansion and influence did not go unnoticed in Europe. France, knowing the Prussian tendency toward invasion and conquest, built a series of fortresses, many along the border with Germany and others in northeastern France, all facing east. Britain, not a continental power, jealously guarded her naval superiority and embarked on a rapid shipbuilding program, churning out Dreadnought-class battleships and cruisers like so many armored sausages. Russia, with no natural geographical barriers for defense on the flat north German plain, organized itself and its huge army for rapid mobilization. The Austro-Hungarian Empire, belittled by the Turks on the southern border and coping with restive, captive Balkan states, sharpened its swords. Europe in 1911 resembled a jumble of matches rubbing against each other in a too-small box. An ignition spark seemed inevitable. The fire would quickly spread through an entangling system of alliances and treaties. Europe was spoiling for war. But when and where would the killing begin?

For the Moisant circus, Mexico paid off. Grandstands in Monterrey filled for each performance and pesos rolled in despite the inevitable presence of freeloaders outside the gates and the disappearance of revenues to corrupt local officials.

Moisant's pilots were nevertheless unhappy, their aircraft were wearing out and becoming even more hazardous to fly. Use of wing warping for lateral control demanded the wings be flexible and lightly built. Repeated flights with constant warping action loosened the wooden joints and the frequent assembly and dis-assembly of the aircraft took its toll on the spruce structures. Dedicated mechanics worked wonders, but fatigue set in, the airplanes were tired. During an emotional meeting with Albert Moisant, the pilots convinced the show director, who never flew, to invest in new sets of wings, ordered from the licensed Blériot factory in New York City and paid for out of the Mexican box office bonanza.

The air shows were such a success El Presidenté himself, Diaz, requested and received a private showing, the troop remaining in Monterrey an extra day. It is unknown if the visiting aviators discussed watching Pancho Villa attacking Diaz's Federales in Juarez. Diaz asked if a flight could be arranged over Mexico City, the capital, which had never seen a fixed-wing aircraft fly. There existed a sound reason no aviator had ever flown there. Mexico City sits at an elevation of over 7350 feet, 2370 meters, above sea level, near the maximum altitude attainable by a Blériot. The take-off roll would be long in the thin air.

Roland Garros, perhaps foolishly, accepted the challenge and somehow coaxed his craft into flight from a large city square, the old wings clawing for lift, the engine straining to breathe. Early engines were fed by a carburetor, which mixes fuel and air for combustion in a fixed ratio. At higher altitude, the air is much thinner and the ratio is too rich with too much gasoline for the available oxygen. Garros managed to climb and circled the dormant volcano, Chaputelpec, overlooking the city. His engine running increasingly rough and misfiring, Garros set up for landing back in the square when the engine quit, the propeller continuing to windmill. A row of trees lined the square, waiting for the Blériot. Garros lacked enough altitude to glide to a dead-stick landing, but at the last instant, the engine caught with one last gasp and lifted the aircraft over the trees.

Now local heroes, Garros and the other pilots were entertained by the French Ambassador at his palatial mansion in the city. The French invasion of Mexico in 1861 had been forgiven, and the American invasion of Northern Mexico, to capture Pancho Villa, lay five years in the future. French and

American pilots of the Moisant Circus were the toast of the town and many were the toasts raised in their honor.

With his flight over Chaputelpec, Garros inadvertently set a world attitude record for fixed wing aircraft, reaching almost 10,000 feet. He knew he scored the record, but with no official witnesses and no certification by any aero club, the honor was purely informal. Garros vowed to someday set an official record for high altitude flight, a promise he was to keep.

Traveling to Veracruz, Mexico on the Caribbean coast, the circus put on one last series of shows, all well attended and all profitable. Engines liked the dense sea level air much more than the wispy gases of Mexico City. Moisant booked passage on a packet steamer for the next and last stop on the tour. The French pilots were homesick, eager to return to the Paris they knew and loved, to French food, French wine, French nightlife, and French women. They had been traveling in the Americas since November of the previous year, it was now March of 1911. One last stop, a few more shows, and then it would be time to return home. Perhaps symbolically, before they boarded the ship, the mechanics made a bonfire out of the old, worn-out wings. New wings, built in New York, would be fitted at the next venue, Havana, Cuba.

Roland Garros saved most of the money he made with the circus, wiring it to Paris. He commissioned the construction of a new Blériot, a two-seat model, larger than the one he was now flying in air shows and identical to the craft his much-missed friend John Moisant flew across the English Channel. Garros remembered fondly his aerial tour over Paris in such a craft with John. Delivery of the new bird was delayed, it never caught up with the tour until Havana, shipped there directly from France. Disassembled, it represented the aviation state of the art and it cost roughly three times as much as his previously-owned craft, the tiny Demoiselle.

After disembarking at the port and clearing customs, Garros and the troop arrived at their hotel in Havana. There, in the lobby, suspended by wires from the ceiling, was his new Blériot! The airplane arrived in Havana a few days prior; the crates containing the bird were forwarded on to the hotel. Hotel management, sensing a public relations and advertising coup, ordered the aircraft to be assembled by local mechanics who probably had never seen an airplane, much less put one together.

Roland Garros's reputation among his compatriots was one of a calm, relaxed personality, very slow to anger and capable of tolerating numerous slights. Seeing the aircraft, his dream bird, slapped together, on vulgar display like a stuffed gull, he lost it. Angry to the point of violence, Garros's frustrations with the tour boiled over. Long, boring train trips, unfamiliar food, miserable flying weather, constantly changing hotels, risking his life for half-empty grandstands and freeloaders, all had taken a toll. His new, expensive Blériot would have to be taken completely apart, each separate piece examined for damage, and reassembled. Who knew what damage could be hidden? The wings, delicate as always, might be fatally compromised.

Garros demanded the team change hotels. Albert Moisant, usually the epitome of financial prudence, agreed. Seeing Garros was in no mood to be denied, he rebooked the circus into a luxury hotel on the promenade facing Havana Bay. Good revenues from the shows in Mexico helped salve the monetary burn. The new Blériot was rescued, taken down, and carried in pieces to the hangers at the show site, a low, swampy field near town. It would be several days until the new craft would be ready. Until then, Garros would carry on flying John Moisant's old plane, now fitted with new wings from New York.

The Mayor of Havana suggested to Albert Moisant attendance at the shows would be enhanced if the aviators were to set an aviation world record. Moisant agreed and "volunteered" Garros, aiming to establish a world altitude mark. The aero club of Cuba installed a barograph in the old/new Blériot. It would record the lowest atmospheric air pressure encountered during the ascent, thus the maximum altitude attained could be calculated.

But something was wrong. The new wings were not a good fit for the older airframe, making the craft unstable, hard to control. Flying an unstable airplane is like balancing a broom stick vertically in the palm of your hand with the bristles pointing skyward. It can be done, but the process is exhausting and a crash is always one bad move away. Aircraft of the time were delicate things, easily upset. Perhaps the wing attachment points were incorrect, too far aft. Maybe the wing profile was wrong or the warping mechanism too sloppy. For whatever reason, the bird was a handful to fly safely.

Still, Garros coaxed the unstable bird up to 2200 meters, 6800 feet, before the instability became almost too difficult to counter. If the aircraft were to depart from controlled flight, to fall off on a wing, a spin would result. In 1911, despite advances in aviation, spin recovery remained a mystery. Also, spinning down from high altitude, the bird would turn faster and faster until the light structure broke up and fluttered to earth in fragments. Without a parachute, the little Frenchman would be doomed. 6800 feet was far from a world record and much lower than he achieved over Mexico City. The failed attempt at an altitude record whetted Garros's desire to succeed at high flight. Albert Moisant, ever the showman, declared in the press Roland Garros had set an altitude record, for Cuba.

At last the new Blériot was reassembled and checked out. Garros took Jules Hue, his personal mechanic, with him on the first flight. It is not known whether the airplane ride, Hue's first, was a reward for faithful service or an inducement for quality work on Hue's part. Landing back on the soft ground, Garros misjudged his approach and damaged the landing gear. Hue repaired the undercarriage in time for Garros to take the leader of the National Assembly of Cuba for a flight. At an altitude of three or four feet, Garros let a wing drop. The wingtip caught the ground and brought the craft down in a vicious, tight circle, a maneuver later named a "ground loop," which wiped out the landing gear once again. Unperturbed, the Cuban politician declared his short flight a success.

After a free display of aerobatics over Havana Bay, the Cuban stop ended. Later, Roland Garros would write his fond memories of Havana included the first flights in his new airplane and a tropical drink concoction made of rum, coconut juice, lime, and sugar—the Piña Colada. Finally, it was time to go home.

CHAPTER FOURTEEN

BACK IN FRANCE

HOME AT LAST

The return to France for Roland Garros was not to be as simple or as direct as he hoped. After the final, free show over Havana Bay, Jules Hue and the mechanics disassembled the aircraft for the last time, packed their tools, struck the tents, crated the pieces, and had the lot carried to the Port of Havana for shipment by sea to Key West, Florida, not Europe. Non-stop steamship connections from the island to France did not exist. The tired team would have to sail from New York after yet another long, boring train journey up the US East Coast.

Garros charged Hue with carefully packing and preserving the broken pieces of the Demoiselle Roland crashed in Memphis and toted along during the subsequent stops on the tour. This wreckage never flew again, but it held significance as the last aircraft built and flown by his hero, Santos-Dumont. Roland told Hue he intended to treat the wreckage like some religious artifact, the bones of an airborne saint, and to keep the pieces safe in storage at Issy in France.

Once in New York, Garros and his Swiss friend, Edmund Audemars, encountered unexpected problems with US Customs and with Albert Moisant. Both disputes involved money. Before the issues could be resolved, they missed their scheduled steamship across the Atlantic. The argument with Moisant sprang from the amount due the two pilots from the air show tour's profits. Eventually, after much haggling, a sum was agreed; Moisant promised to wire the cash to Paris once all outstanding bills were paid. The aviators kept to themselves their doubts as to whether Albert would indeed pay up or when he would do so. They had no alternative but to trust him. As for the second problem, US Customs officers wanted an export fee for the disassembled aircraft or a bribe. It was hard to tell the difference. The distinction arose from the question as to where the fee would end up, in the US treasury or the officers' pockets. New York Police officers got involved, which did not help the situation at all and probably raised the tab on possible bribes. Garros and Audemars sent their crates and luggage to be loaded on the *Bretagne*, the next boat to France, at the last minute. They evaded the Police and the Customs agents, boarded the ship, and hid in the Captain's cabin until departure. It is hard to imagine all this happening under the authorities' watchful eyes without money changing hands under the table and palms being greased, but bribes or no bribes, they were off for home.

After ten, long, stormy days and the usual seasickness, the voyage arrived at Le Havre, where they left from almost seven months prior. The two friends, relieved to be homeward bound, treated themselves to an expensive first-class train carriage; destination – Paris. The bustling but grimy port of Le Havre was certainly in France, but it was not Paris, not even close geographically nor culturally. They would not feel truly home until they saw the Eiffel Tower.

Arrival at the train station in northern Paris hit the two homesick Frenchmen like a *baguette* between the eyes. The immense, vaulted entry hall teemed with real Parisians chattering in metropolitan French. Members of the crowd laughed. They sported fashionable clothes – beautiful women in hobble skirts, dapper men in what the English called "Bowler" hats and the French knew as *"Chapeaux Melons."* An air of sophistication hovered over the crowd like the aroma of broiling *escargots* in garlic butter. They were home.

The train from Le Havre chugged into *Le Gare Saint-Lazare* at 1300, One o'clock. By the time the many crates, trunks, tools, and various aircraft components were loaded on trucks bound for Issy, it was mid-afternoon, too late for lunch and too early for dinner. The French normally insist on eating meals on schedule. Dining is normally too serious an activity to indulge impulsively or to put off until later. One of the city's best restaurants, *Le Mollard,* waited near the station and despite the odd time of day, the grateful and hungry returnees hurried there. Garros and Audemars commandeered a table, demanded service, and placed an elaborate and long-planned order, one they discussed and debated on the train. They did not crave Southern-fried chicken, Creole seafood, Texas steaks, Mexican food, Bourbon, nor Piña Coladas.

Accustomed to light business during quiet mid-afternoons, the typically grumpy waitstaff managed to serve an elevated platter of fresh, raw oysters from Marennes, France on ice along with a chilled bottle of white Burgundy, an elegant *Pouilly-Fuissé*. The shellfish *entrée* led to a roast young chicken, *Poulet,* with truffles and pan juices, *au jus*, then filet of beef, rare. History does not record which bottle of wine they enjoyed with the beef, but you can bet it was not white. An elaborate pastry creation found only in Paris, perhaps a Napoleon, a *mille-feuille*, finished off the long-awaited meal. Satisfied, Garros left the service staff a generous tip, a technique he learned in the USA. Tipping is usually not done in French restaurants. The suddenly-friendly waiters did not object to this decadent American vice.

The next stop, the office of Moisant's lawyer, served to see if they would get paid for the months spent risking their lives and endlessly enduring what passed for civilization in North America. It is instructive to note their priorities here, a long, gourmet French meal, then vital business dealings. To the two aviators' mutual astonishment, the agent handed them each bundles of 1000-franc notes. Moisant paid off to the last *sou,* or penny. Financial issues settled for the remainder of 1911, Roland Garros arrived back at his apartment, where all was in order. He immediately began to think about his next step, his next challenge, while he unpacked his steamer trunks and planned his evening. That night, he dined with the group of friends he missed terribly while on tour, regaling them with tales of his many adventures in the New World.

On the long train journeys across the USA and Mexico, Garros and Audemars discussed and conceived a business plan for their future aviation interests, a plan to be executed upon their return to France. Albert Moisant's honest payoff gave them the working capital to start. Using the "bones" of Santos-Dumont's personal Demoiselle as a pattern, they intended to improve the badly underpowered airplane by modifying the design to accept a Gnome engine, the same power-plant installed in the far more numerous and popular Blériots. As pilots, they now ranked among the most experienced in Europe. As aeronautical engineers, not so much. Their idea had to be one of the worst since John Moisant's "*Ecrevisse.*" Demoiselles weighed practically nothing, the Gnome engine was over twice as heavy as any installed to date on a Demoiselle airframe. The mill had twice the power output. Also, as a rotary, with the cylinders whirling around the crankshaft, the Gnome would put considerable torque loads on the aircraft's structure. All this increased weight, power, and torque was to be imposed on a flimsy structure consisting of bamboo poles held together with knotted twine. With the confidence of the clueless, they rented a hanger and workshop on the airfield at Issy, retained once again the services of doughty Romain along with Jules Hue and several other mechanics. The team began work on the Frankenstein-monster Demoiselle.

Roland Garros soon found himself torn between various career choices. He could focus on his neglected auto sales business, make more money, and certainly enjoy a safe, comfortable life as a Parisian playboy, a *Boulevardier.* He knew how to do that. Or, he could devote more time to the new aircraft design, getting his hands dirty. What really piqued his interest was the upcoming summer aviation season. It featured two long, cross-country air races, Paris-Madrid, and Paris-Rome. Long-distance air racing was coming into vogue, aircraft were becoming reliable enough to complete the flights, and public interest was high. Sponsorship money flowed into the aero clubs managing the races, particularly from newspapers. Still, flights of many hundreds of miles while crossing mountain ranges such as the Pyrenees and the Alps presented non-trivial challenges. The aircraft of 1911 were getting better, but they were not that good, yet. Engine failure over, say, Mont Blanc would result in almost certain death. But, as noted before, adrenalin is highly addictive, and Roland Garros was hooked. Audemars, not an adrenalin junkie, volunteered to oversee the aircraft modification scheme at Issy, freeing Garros to pursue his dream of air racing, a dream which almost became a nightmare during his first race.

CHAPTER FIFTEEN

OFF TO THE RACES

Not as Easy as It Looks

Roland Garros traded his new, almost unused, two-seat Blériot in on an even newer single-seat version, the latest model, and joined the Blériot factory's air-racing team. Slightly smaller, the new aircraft presented a sleeker profile to the slipstream, added a few knots of airspeed, and tended to be more maneuverable. A race from Paris to Madrid, Spain kicked off the summer racing season. *Le Petit Parisian* newspaper sponsored and bankrolled the race, a natural fit for someone of Garros's diminutive size.

On Sunday, 21 May 1911, the competitors left Issy airfield at five-minute intervals, the first taking off at 0500, just after Spring's early-breaking dawn in the northern latitudes. Garros departed, eventual destination Madrid, at 0516, as recorded by the Aero Club of France. Lowest total elapsed time over three stages would determine the winner at the Spanish finish line.

Publicized in numerous articles by the sponsoring paper, the race drew enormous public attention in Paris and in the surrounding federal Department, the *Ile-de-France*, Island of France. This capital region corresponds to the District of Columbia, DC, in the USA. *Le Petit Parisian*, reflecting the era's loose journalistic ethics, reported the attendance of 250,000 people at its own event at Issy. Cooler heads in the *Gendarmerie Nationale*, National Police, estimated the crowd at "only" 100,000 strong. Whatever the true number, it is astonishing that legions of people would arise before dawn on a rainy Spring Sunday and journey out to a muddy suburban airfield. They came to watch primitive aircraft struggle into the air one-by-one from the military parade ground and then disappear into the grey mist, all heading southwest. Misty it was, with rain showers pelting the local area and reduced visibility in all four quadrants of the dark sky. Still, the crowds came and stood in the dripping rain, demonstrating intense interest in early aviation by the French people.

The night before the race, Garros, as was his habit, dined with friends in Paris, but left the restaurant very early in the evening, much to the surprise of his companions. No late hours for a professional pilot. Garros intended to leave for the airfield between 0300 and 0330. He would need his wits about him during a long, stressful day.

A racing pilot's chief stressor in 1911 involved aerial navigation. Flying point-to-point over the French countryside challenged the best sense of direction. The few available maps were almost useless. Compiled by the military to facilitate army ground maneuvers, the maps offered scant information for a pilot. It was very difficult to consult an un-folded paper map in an open cockpit while buffeted by the slipstream and trying to fly an unstable the aircraft at the same time. The transparent windscreen waited to be invented. To navigate, a pilot would have to memorize a stage's ground checkpoints as well as the compass course to each.

When transportation depended on horses or on human feet, maps were unnecessary, the traveler merely asked for directions as he or she slowly passed through town after town. Trains and canal boats did not need maps either, their operators' choices were obviously constrained. You cannot get lost in a canal. When motorcars became common, the need for reliable maps grew. Who wanted to stop for directions every few miles? The Michelin rubber company, seeing a need and an opportunity to promote auto use and to wear out tires in the process, began publishing road maps of France early in the 20th century, adding commentary on sights to see along the way, and inspecting road-side restaurants for the hungry traveler. This publication later grew into the world-famous Michelin Guide with its multiple star ratings of eateries. However, the rudimentary Michelin Guide of 1911 was of little help to the aviator, no one knew what the noteworthy physical features mentioned in the book, the churches, the towns, the bridges, the roads, looked like from the air.

Cross-country air racers could follow the many railway lines linking the country, these were highly visible and easy to fly along, except for the tunnels. But trains tracks took the routes with the gentlest gradients, not the ones most direct as the crow, or the Blériot, flies. Rivers were even less helpful, meandering all over the place. Canals were worse guides than even railroads, dug along the lowest water level. Fortunately, before the racing season, someone thought to mount compasses in aircraft. Prior to take-off, the pilot laid out a course to his destination on a military map with a ruler and then followed the derived compass course when airborne. Given a known airspeed, plus or minus a wind effect, and a known distance to go, a pilot could fly a compass heading. When the calculated time elapsed, he looked for prominent landmarks to pin-point his position. This technique is called "dead-reckoning" navigation. If the pilot did not reckon right, he might be dead.

The first cross-country air races were all about who could navigate the most efficiently over the shortest distance as much as they were about raw aircraft speed. Indeed, the contending airplanes' maximum speeds were very similar, about 60 mph or 100 kph. Competitors with the most reliable airplanes and the best flight plans enjoyed the best chances of winning, not the ones slightly faster in the air.

After a wet departure from Issy, his wooden propeller throwing up a cloud of back wash from the soggy grass, Roland Garros turned the nose of his monoplane to the southwest, dodging rain showers, and peering through the early morning mist for the railroad he intended to follow to the city of Orleans. He deviated from and returned to his desired compass heading repeatedly while avoiding the worst weather. It was a miserable day to be flying and Madrid lay 655 miles, 1050 kilometers, ahead.

Just before Paris disappeared in the squalls behind him, Garros turned, looked back over his shoulder seeking the Eiffel

Tower's familiar outline. There the grey lady stood, barely visible, her upper decks lost in the ragged overcast, but still the symbol of home. Next stop, the city of Angoulême, the Nouvelle-Aquitaine region's capital. Garros planned to follow the main rail line to Orleans, then fly along the Loire River until he reached the city of Tours. Out of Tours, he would find and track another mainline railroad to Angoulême. Angoulême, a city he never visited, should be easy to recognize. It is perched on an escarpment overlooking the Charante River. Since Roman times, the town has been a transportation hub; all local roads and eventually all railroads led to Angoulême. Once his dead-reckoning time expired, any line of transport visible below would lead him to the city on the bluff and to the finish line for Stage One. All the racers and their support staffs would spend the night there.

Garros's Gnome engine had other ideas. After he passed Tours, it started running rough, missing beats, and losing power. Unable to maintain level flight with the sick engine, he was forced to land in a field of budding rye, the new shoots of grain not yet long enough to hide obstacles such as ditches and rocks in the damp earth. The problem—fouled spark plugs. Rotary engines were notorious for loading up their spark plugs with unburnt oil. Castor oil was sucked into the crankcase with the gasoline/air mixture feeding the engine. As the cylinders spun, the plugs, at the engine's circumference, could be drenched by excess oil slung radially out by the rotation. Long before platinum-tipped, non-fouling plugs, oiled plugs were a common problem plaguing long-distance flight if the pilot was not diligent at adjusting the fuel/oil mixture. Garros carried with him a spark plug wrench, which he set about using, removing the seven plugs in turn, drying them with a rag, and re-installing each. The whole operation consumed 45 precious minutes of elapsed time.

The forced landing drew a group of local people, *paysans* in French, from which we get the English word "peasants." Peasants or farmers, the locals were eager to help, one went to find more gasoline while Garros worked. When the engine was ready and the gas tank refilled, they carefully pushed his airplane back to a take-off position facing into the light wind. Roland coached a strong-looking young man on how to start the engine by spinning the propeller, which he did, oblivious to the danger of being sucked into the rotating blade. Garros, lugging aloft extra liters of fuel, just managed to get airborne, the Blériot clattering, bouncing over the rough ground. With his engine straining, his wheels clipped the hedgerow lining the field. The aircraft continued to climb, slowly, while the helpful *paysans* watched as the first airplane they ever saw, much less touched, disappeared into the hazy air. Hopefully the field's owner was among them, to send a bill to *Le Petit Parisian* for his trampled crop.

Delayed by the emergency landing and the hasty tune-up in the rye field, Garros expected to be trailing the pack when he touched down in Angoulême five hours and 15 minutes after take-off. To his great surprise, he was in first place. Several pilots and planes were scattered around the French countryside like so many outsized fallen leaves grounded by mechanical problems and the rotten weather. Others never left Issy. Crowds of spectators, whatever their true numbers, spilled over onto the flying field, to get a better look at the aerial operations. A troop of foot soldiers was charged with clearing a path through the throng, a task at which they were inept. Crowd control in France at the time, particularly with a sizeable multitude, usually fell to the Cavalry. Horses, however well-trained, would have been panicked by noisy, unfamiliar flying machines, so the ground troops did what they could.

One racer, flying an untested, all-metal aircraft, encountered severe stability problems probably due to the extra weight of additional fuel and a passenger/navigator. He turned back to land with the crowd still scattered on the field. In the confusion, several people, including two dignitaries, were injured by the returning, barely controllable aircraft. This accident shut down race operations for the day.

In Angoulême, things were no better. Locals bought tickets to see an air race. What they saw was individual landings spaced hours apart. Furious ticket-holders rioted, trashing the flags and decorations marking the improvised airfield. The race's second stage was postponed for a day due to a combination of bad weather, forced landings, and rampaging spectators at both the takeoff and landing airfields. Not an auspicious start to an air race.

Stage Two, Angoulême to San Sebastian in Spain, began in the usual rainy spring weather. Roland Garros, the surprised race leader, took off first, the few remaining spectators saw him disappear once again into the grey mist. He climbed to 3300 feet, 1000 meters, to get above the low clouds and followed his compass blindly, with little reference to unseen check points below. Garros took a calculated risk in climbing though a layer of fog and mist. In 1911, flight into an overcast, thick clouds, or fog, usually resulted in a loss of control, followed by a spin or tightening spiral. The result often involved a fatal crash, unless sight of mother earth could be re-established with enough altitude for recovery without pulling the wings off the aircraft. With no artificial horizon, no turn-and-bank indicator, no blind-flying instruments of any kind in the cockpit, a pilot's inner ear, the source of his sense of balance, lied to his brain. Vertigo and complete disorientation stemmed from the internal conflict between what he saw with what he felt. Garros managed to keep upright by treating the underlying cloud deck as the horizon. Cold, saturated air soaked him to the bone and coated what instruments he did have with condensation. He continually wiped the glass faces of his compass and altimeter dry with a chamois skin.

The further south he flew, the better the weather, the under-cast broken, until he spotted the town of Bourg, where the Dordogne and the Garonne rivers merge to form the Gironde. Seeing the Gulf of Gascony on the horizon and knowing if he kept the Atlantic Ocean on his right wing, he would not be too far off course. This plan led him on to Bordeaux, on the Gironde River where the famous vineyards stretched inland to the hazy horizon.

Only one thing now lay between Roland Garros and his second stop in San Sebastian, Spain. The Pyrénées Mountains, their peaks lost in the clouds, blocked the shortest route to San Sebastian. He would have to go around them to the west. Mountain flying requires an aircraft which can climb faster than the slopes ascend, one which can turn around in a canyon, and which can top the lowest passes. Aircraft of 1911 could do none of these aerial maneuvers.

Garros decided to continue flying along the coast, passing over the posh resort town of Biarritz, almost on the Spanish border. San Sebastian beckoned 20 kilometers, 12 miles, south of the frontier. Shortly after crossing the invisible border, he consulted his tightly folded map, looking for the shortest route, holding the map low in the cockpit sheltered from the slipstream.

Before turning toward San Sebastian, he checked his fuel level and found it dangerously low. Another forced landing could not be avoided. Aircraft of the time employed no electrically powered gauges. The primary means of determining the amount of fuel remaining involved a marked glass tube mounted on the rudimentary instrument panel and connected to the fuel tank with copper pipes. The level of fluid in the glass supposedly reflected the level of fuel in the tank. An alternate method required sticking a graduated stick into the copper tank and seeing how wet it got. But, this fool-proof manual technique was difficult to accomplish in flight. Garros's sight glass indicated he was soon about to run dry. He needed to get on the ground, soon.

Garros spotted a sloped pasture, thankfully devoid of sheep, on a bluff overlooking the Atlantic Ocean and set the Blériot down, dodging rocks. He killed the engine on touchdown, the aircraft bouncing to a stop. Once his ears recovered from the engine's din, he heard nothing but the squawks of circling gulls and the crash of surf on the beach below the bluff. Near the shore sailed a Spanish navy ship stationed there to rescue aviators forced down at sea. Looking for assistance in the form of more fuel, Garros jogged down a steep dirt path leading to the coastal road and the beach. Shouting and waving his arms, he attempted to catch the Navy's attention, but to no avail. Evidently, the *Armada* was tasked to aid wet aviators, not ones on land, or perhaps those sailors on watch were not watching. The grey ship steamed away leaving Garros even more alone. After waiting equally in vain for a motorist on the coast road, he returned uphill to his airplane, where he found a dozen Christian monks in brown robes from a nearby monastery examining his craft as if were a grounded white angel. Garros knew the Spanish word for gasoline, *benzina,* but the monks, thunderstruck by the apparition from the sky standing in front of them, could only make the sign of the cross and offer up prayers in answer to his pleas for help. Anyway, their vows of poverty precluded the use of anything burning *benzina.*

An hour slowly passed during which a group of local farmers slowly gathered around the downed plane and its distraught pilot. With nothing to do but wait, Garros checked once again the cockpit sight glass. It indicated plenty of fuel, enough to reach San Sebastian. He assumed the erroneous reading resulted from the slope under the aircraft's wheels and continued to wait.

Waiting, he spotted another racer following the coastline south. The other pilot, seeing the white Blériot parked on the green hillside, buzzed Garros and the spectators, passing less than 300 feet overhead, taunting the downed pilot. Eventually, one of the team's mechanics assigned to shadow the flight arrived with a police escort and five liters of gas. Refueling and a downhill take-off were routine and accompanied by cheers from the small crowd including the monks. Roland Garros threaded his way through the low costal hills and landed in San Sebastian less than a half-hour later.

In their canvas hanger, the Blériot team's chief heard the story of Garros's forced landing, a delay costing him two precious hours of elapsed time. A dipstick probed into the gas tank on Roland's airplane revealed it to be over half full. He could have easily made San Sebastian non-stop without the extra five liters, as calculated. The cockpit sight glass must have burped an air bubble, giving him the bogus low-level indication, which then corrected itself with the bouncy landing. If Garros had manually gauged the tank while on the ground, he would have immediately retaken to the sky and would still be in first place instead of relegated to second. A hard lesson learned.

That night at the hotel in San Sebastian, Roland Garros found himself in a strange new land, the Basque country. San Sebastian, a major tourist destination then and now, sits on the coast, framing the beautiful La Concha harbor, itself opening into the Bay of Biscay. Over dinner, the team enjoyed a meal of unfamiliar Basque food while seated communally at a long wooden table, as is the local custom. They were probably too involved debriefing the day's events to appreciate the fine Basque cuisine for which San Sebastian is rightly famous. One thing they could not do is speak to the locals in their own tongue. Roland was fluent in Creole, English, French (of course), and knew some Spanish, but in the border country, they speak Basque. This language, not a dialect of Spanish, is not related in the smallest way to any other language world-wide. A modern, unproved, and unprovable theory, holds that Basque descended from the language of the Neanderthal race of humanoids. Modern humans, *Homo sapiens*, displaced the Neanderthals on the Iberian Peninsula around 22,000 BCE. The last Neanderthals in Europe died out in the region less than a few hundred years later, going extinct around the Rock of Gibraltar further south. From genetic research, we know modern humans interbred with their stronger cousins and lived alongside them for thousands of years. Perhaps, isolated in the mountainous Basque region, modern people adopted the Neanderthals' language, which was probably as complex as any of ours in the dawn of humankind.

Whatever language they used, the Blériot team vowed to regain the race lead the next day and swore an oath to not make any more Neanderthal-type mistakes.

Roland Garros became increasingly distrustful of the Gnome engine mounted in his plane. Even after cleaning the spark plugs, he did not feel it developed full power, particularly at altitude. This would present a real problem on the race's last leg to Madrid. From San Sebastian, he would have to fly over the southern Pyrénées, then the Guadarrama Mountains, and climb up to the Iberian central plateau to land at Madrid. Madrid is the second highest national capital in Europe, second only to Berne, Switzerland. Some of the city's neighborhoods are over 2700 feet, 800 meters, in elevation.

The team mechanics tested the engine at Garros's request and reported it to be sound, achieving 900 rpm, on the low side of a Gnome's operation range of 900-1100 rpm, but within limits.

The race's third and final leg was flown on 24 May 1911. Only three entries remained, the rest having failed to make San Sebastian for various reasons. Garros took off first and once airborne and climbing, knew his engine was still sick and too weak to surmount the coming mountains. Carburetor trouble probably played a part in his troubles. These primitive units included no way of compensating for the thinner air at altitude and could not be properly tested on the ground. In addition, the weather was again marginal with low clouds and a thin overcast.

Roland Garros could have turned back to land at San Sebastian, disqualifying himself from the race. He elected to press on, hoping to be able to follow valleys through the mountains then coax enough power out of his sick mill to make it up to the Madrid airfield. Flying in the mountains in bad weather is not the safest idea in aviation, but if he was to win the race, he would have to chance it. Things were about to get dangerous, more so than he expected.

After a few minutes of following a narrow valley to the southeast, his engine began running rougher and rougher until level flight became impossible. His sole choice was to set the plane down. Only one open field lay within gliding distance and it was tight and crescent-shaped. He managed to land but on the short roll-out with the engine dead, his right wing clipped a barn, breaking some of the light wooden structure, of the aircraft, not the barn.

Garros borrowed a bicycle from the farm's astonished owner and set out for the nearest town. His past cycling exploits came in handy and he made good time. He phoned the team hotel in San Sebastian with an assessment of the damage and his location. Soon, a motorcar with the team manager and two mechanics met him on the road. They picked up Garros and his borrowed bike, proceeding to the scene of the emergency landing.

One mechanic repaired the damaged wing while the other cleaned the fouled spark plugs. The process took over an hour. Surveying the small, *croissant*-shaped field, the team manager doubted if Garros could be airborne again, but he pulled it off, using the skills he learned operating out of tight, hemmed-in race tracks in America. While Garros waited on the repairs he questioned the local farmers and shepherds on the route forward, men who gathered to watch the show from the sky.

Locals told Garros the valley continued southeast and he could follow either the high-tension electrical cables and pylons lining the valley or the fast-running river to an electrical sub-station powered by a dam at the valley's mouth. There the terrain would open. As if things were not dicey enough, now high-tension lines entered the mix of hazards. A braided steel electrical cable stretched tightly between two tall pylons would snatch a fragile wood and cloth monoplane out of the sky like a spider web catches a fly. Garros learned this painful lesson at Versailles.

Wanting no part of the mist-obscured valley with its spider web of transmission lines, Garros climbed laboriously through the thin overcast until he was skimming the cloud tops. From on top, the puffy clouds looked like a cottony river in the sky constrained on each side by the mountains forming the valley. All he had to do was fly along the sky-river until he could spot the flatter terrain ahead. He allowed himself the hope he might finish the race after all and stay alive.

It was not to be; finishing the race that is. His cranky engine once again began losing power forcing him to descend back down into the clouds floating above the valley floor. How far above the ground was the bottom of the clouds? He broke out underneath the wispy overcast in time to spot the waiting electrical lines and the river. Plan B was to follow these features, but that idea was cancelled by the Gnome. Another force landing loomed. He saw the transformer yard of the power station, all the electrical cable led to it, beside the raging river. Without enough power to clear the cables, he set the Blériot down on the river bank where its skinny bicycle-type tires instantly sank into the mud, wiping out the landing gear and skidding the dying aircraft into the water. Once again, things were very quiet with only the water's rush marring the silence. He climbed out of the wreck and waded to the shore in the freezing water and began trudging back up the valley road.

For the second time that day, he met the car with the mechanics and the manager on the road. They dropped off the technicians to salvage the wreck and drove back to San Sebastian, beaten. At the hotel they learned the two other entries also dropped out. One made it as far as Getafé, on the same plateau as Madrid but no further. His engine seized up. The third pilot returned to San Sebastian after, he said, an airborne fight to the death with a Pyrénées eagle. The press and race officials believed him. For all, the Paris-Madrid race was over, not one pilot completed the course.

Roland Garros took the train back to Paris, not in the best of spirits. However, the Paris-Rome race offered a chance for redemption and it kicked off in just a few days.

Chapter Sixteen

Another Race, Another Chance

This Time, It is Rome or Bust

Following the Paris-Madrid race fiasco, Roland Garros expected to be let go by the Blériot air racing team. Louis Blériot would have none of that. He announced his admiration for Garros's perseverance in coping with a sick engine and his demonstrated ability to fly his way out of difficulties. All those successful forced landings in tiny fields counted for something, despite Garros hitting a barn during one landing and parking his aircraft partially in a river in another. Blériot presented Garros with a new, factory-owned model XI, a two-place craft, replacing the airplane drowned in the Pyrénées Mountains' icy torrent. The mechanics installed their best brand-new Gnome in the pristine bird and Garros took it aloft for two test flights to check out the new mill. On the second hop, he landed at Buc, an airfield near the Palace of Versailles and the departure point for the upcoming Paris-Rome race.

Evidently, clean living does not pay off, judging by the bad luck he encountered during Paris-Madrid, thought Garros. The night before Paris-Rome, he partied with his usual crowd, male and female, until 0300, or as the French refer to this time of day, *les bonnes heures*, the good hours. After less than two hours of sleep, he left his apartment for Buc airfield and his next big adventure.

The Paris-Rome race was sponsored by another Parisian newspaper, *Le Petit Journal,* which, in competition with *Le Petit Parisian*, publicized the second air race to be run in less than a week. 100,000 spectators, as estimated again by the Chief of Police, showed up at the Buc aerodrome to see the aircraft depart at 0600. Fighting a hangover and lack of sleep, Garros ate his breakfast and gulped hot coffee, *café au lait avec croissants*, standing beside his plane.

For this competition, the organizers did not separate the course into fixed stages. The published requirement specified the racers must overfly the French cities of Dijon, Lyon, Avignon, Nice, and Pisa in Italy in route to Rome. Between these checkpoints, the pilots were free to choose their own routes and stopping points. Instead of individually timed departures, the pilots would take off in what would later be known as a "Le Mans Start" in the auto racing world. First pilot to reach Rome would be the victor. French military units cleared the aerodrome of spectators and the ground crews positioned the 12 entrants line abreast with each pilot standing beside his craft. As each man's name was announced on the public address system, he mounted his cockpit. A small explosion detonated by the dignitary serving as the official starter signaled the start. Working quickly, the mechanics spun up their engines and scurried out of the way as the aircraft began rolling across the wide parade ground.

Garros broke ground rising into the dawn air following another plane but soon found himself alone in the sky. Each pilot charted his own course to the southeast. For once, the weather remained reasonable and flying was smooth. Determined not to repeat the mistakes of Paris-Madrid, Garros monitored his fuel supply carefully. Before the tank ran dry, he set the monoplane down in a field near the town of Tonnerre 125 kilometers, 78 miles, short of Dijon. Perhaps alerted by pre-race publicity, a crowd soon gathered. Guarding his fragile aircraft, Garros sent some of the spectators into Tonnerre for more fuel. The helpful locals returned in short order. Garros filled his fuel tank and took off again after an hour's delay, headed east to Dijon, city of mustard fame.

Landing at Dijon, Garros was in second place, an hour behind the race leader, the hour he spent on his improvised pit stop. There was no way to quickly trouble-shoot the excessive fuel consumption he experienced. He should have been able to reach Dijon non-stop. After another hour spent refueling at

Dijon, he took off for Lyon to the south following his compass, the instrument given to him by John Moisant. He followed the designated heading a little too intensely and overflew the river he intended to follow to Lyon.

Lost, he landed in a large field and asked two *paysans* where he was and inquired as to the direction of Lyon. Oriented and airborne once again, he found Lyon and landed at the check point in front of a large crowd of spectators. His rival for the race lead, another Blériot pilot named Beaumont, landed a few minutes prior and was eating his lunch. Beaumont invited Garros to join him in the Blériot team's hanger to relax, for the wind was picking up. Roland insisted he and his teammate should leave immediately for Avignon and not squander the lead they built over the other competitors. The wind strengthened; it was on Garros's nose, holding him back and reducing his speed over the ground. Again, his lack of experience in long-distance navigation betrayed him and he followed a too-long route to Avignon. Touring in America, Garros traveled from point to point by train, never honing his dead-reckoning skills. He finally reached Avignon just before midnight, landing in the extended spring twilight between two rows of fires lighting the runway. He was no longer in second place. At the airfield, he recognized his old friend, Edmond Audemars, from the Moisant circus tour. Audemars and his Demoiselle were in Avignon for an airshow in conjunction with the race along with another pilot in an older Blériot.

Every *bistro* and *brassiere* closed for the night in Avignon, an ancient city which hosted one of two rival Popes during the middle ages. Garros slept hungry at a local hotel for three hours and departed at 0330 in the dim light of dawn. Tracing the Rhone river south, he sensed something was wrong with his Gnome. Losing power, he returned to Avignon. The team's technicians replaced the spark plugs and cleaned fouled valves, taking a precious hour to do so. The engine quit again 35 miles, 55 kilometers, south of Avignon, this time for good.

Without power, he glided to the nearest suitable landing spot, a wheat field. Planted during the winter, the wheat was already waist high and hiding rough ground. On touchdown, Garros heard a loud crack when the aircraft bounced off an unseen hummock. Rattling to a bumpy stop, he deplaned to survey the situation. The Gnome's cylinders were stained dark blue, a sure sign of overheating. It had seized, freezing the propeller. Either the new engine had not been broken in properly or the fuel/oil ratio was maladjusted. Worse, each wing bent upward, signaling cracked or broken wing spars. Roland Garros's race was over in this bird. Two *paysans* came running up as he consulted his map. According to the farmers, the nearest town was called Mallenmort, which loosely translates to "bad in death." A fitting omen for a snake-bit race plane. Borrowing a bike, Garros pedaled into Mallenmort. He placed a phone call to a hotel back in Avignon where he reached Audemars. The Swiss friend drove down to Mallenmort and returned Garros to Avignon, dropping off the borrowed bike along the way.

Garros need a plane and he needed one quickly. The rules awarded prize money to the first pilot to arrive in Rome regardless of which, or how many, aircraft he used. Additionally, there was an intermediate prize of 50,000 francs given to the first arrival at the next stop, Nice, France. At the airport, a well-worn Blériot's avaricious pilot wanted 25,000 francs for his craft, a price higher than a new plane commanded. Garros informed the enterprising gentleman he was not in the habit of carrying that much cash while flying and offered a promissory note. No, came back the reply, the seller was hesitant to accept a note from a man whose chances of living to make the necessary deposit were uncertain. Desperate, Garros consulted a train schedule and determined the team manager, Albert LeBlanc, would be arriving at the train station in Nice shortly. He called the station, found LeBlanc, and the manager wired the required sum to Avignon. Garros fired up the tired, old Blériot and set off for Nice.

His most recent Gnome burned itself up, probably from too-tight machining clearances or oil starvation. The older mill in his just-purchased craft suffered from exactly the opposite problem. The rotary leaked like a sieve and the 60 mph propwash soon covered Garros's head and face with a thin coating of castor oil. He was forced to wipe his goggles' glass lenses frequently with his handkerchief to have any visibility through the scum. Garros also fought the tendency to lick his lips, no matter how cold or saturated with oil they became. Gnome engines were lubricated with castor oil because it is insoluble in gasoline and is not diluted by the fuel/air mixture in a crankcase. However, castor oil is a powerful, fast-acting laxative for humans. Swallowing castor oil while flying in a cramped cockpit would prove to be uncomfortably problematic.

To make matters worse, the weather deteriorated. Garros encountered buffeting winds and driving rain showers – harder and harder as he flew south. The pelting rain smeared the film of oil on his owl-like goggles; soon he could barely see through the rainbow of colors hampering his vision. In a desperate attempt to wipe away the gunk, he broke one lens. Now, he could only see out of one eye, poorly. Problems were stacking up; he could barely see, the rain was coming down harder, and he was lost. Time for another emergency landing, this time in a reed field beside a dirt road turned into a shallow creek by the storm.

There was no one around. He splashed south on foot down the road until he came on a bicycle leaning up against a stone wall, no owner visible. Garros "borrowed" the bike and pedaled furiously along the wet road toward what he hoped was the town of Fréjus, the next refueling stop. He encountered a *paysan* who looked at Garros as if he just landed from Mars. Garros wore a leather coat, pants, and boots, was muddy, soaking wet, and smeared with oil except for one white circle around his good eye. The compatriot confirmed he was indeed on the road to Fréjus and added he saw an aircraft land there a few minutes ago, ahead of the storm.

Garros rode the bicycle into Fréjus, probably unaware of the irony. Flying was supposed to eliminate the need to continually ask for directions from locals as in the age of horses, but he found himself often doing just that. Finding his ground team in Fréjus, Garros and two mechanics jumped into a waiting auto, lashing the stolen two-wheeler on the rear, and drove back to the downed craft, stopping to replace the bike where he found it.

While the crew members worked to clean the spark plugs and find the oil leak, Garros stomped out a takeoff path in the tall reeds as the rain let up. After what seemed to be an eternity, the Gnome was pronounced ready for flight. Garros took off on the short hop to Fréjus with the ground crew following in the car. The rain finally stopped, but twilight approached. Refueled, Garros launched again, wearing new goggles, destination; Nice.

The approach to Nice was shadowed by gathering darkness. The city is built on and surrounded by hills, their slopes falling into the Mediterranean Sea, their contours invisible in the dark. Garros flew out over the bay looking landward for the airfield, a gutsy move in the dark with a suspect engine. Engine failure would mean a night in the water, if he was lucky enough to survive the crash and to not drown in his heavy leather clothes. The city's lights shown bright on the hills and he spotted lighted boats bobbing on the wine-dark sea, but where was the airport?

The airport at Nice was constructed for air races in 1910 and occupied a mud flat between the famous boulevard, *Les Promenade des Anglais,* paralleling the coast and the ocean. For some unknown reason, the airport gained the name "*Nice-Californie*" and kept the Franco-American moniker for many years. The present-day Nice-Côte d'Azur Airport occupies the same reclaimed land between the city and the sea after expansion made possible by filling in the bay.

In the night, Garros spotted a line of fires outlining the runway, fires lit by the French army to identify the airfield for the racers. With the ocean off his right wing and the Promenade on his left, he touched down at Nice-Californie just before midnight only to learn Beamount arrived 20 minutes earlier. Roland Garros lost the 50,000-franc prize by a quarter of an hour.

Once again, no eating places were open, nor were any hotels along the *Promenade.* He hired a room in the hotel across from the railway station and fell into bed, exhausted.

It had been a long, hard day filled with miserable weather, punctuated by perilous forced landings, frantic bike rides, and a hazardous recovery after dark on an unfamiliar, seaside airfield. Yet, even with the lack of sleep for the past two days and meals grabbed on the run, rest did not come quickly or easily for Roland Garros in Nice. He must have been discouraged by his air racing results. Despite his dogged perseverance, his risk-taking, his flights into marginal weather, his attempts at cross-country navigation, his forced landings, he had nothing to show for his efforts. His first race was no better, he wrecked an airplane and logged a DNF, Did Not Finish, placing in the Paris-Madrid race. His prospects for finishing, much less winning, the Paris-Rome event with an old, tired airframe and a highly suspect engine did not look good either. He had already written off another new Blériot in the current fracas. How could this go on? He could be booted off the team for incompetence, he could die in a crash landing somewhere out in the sticks, or he could be lost at sea.

When under stress, and Garros certainly felt it, a mind tends to look back on happier times. Laying in his bed, the memories of his happy adolescence there in Nice came flooding back. He saw himself bike racing in the surrounding hills, dining and drinking with his friends, playing on sports teams, and ditching boring classes at school. Those warm, sunlit days seemed so long ago. Even further back in his memories, images of exotic Saigon remained vivid. He missed his family, now broken up, missing intensely his mother and younger sister whom he had not seen in years. Even his distant and demanding father seemed not so unpleasant. Roland Garros was 22 years old and he wondered if his best years were behind him as he pondered his future, assuming he had one. Aviation in 1911, as proven by his friend John Moisant, was dangerous in the extreme. Sleep finally came, washing away his fatigue and his rosy memories. Tomorrow would see him try for Rome.

Early on the morning of Tuesday, the 30th of May 1911, Roland Garros learned from the team manager that the race leader, Beaumont, suffered an engine which, despite the mechanics' best efforts, would not start. Worse yet, a pursuing pilot flying a Morane, André Frey, had already landed at Nice following a before-dawn take-off and was preparing to leave for the next stop, Pisa, Italy. Albert LeBlanc, the manager, *le Chef d'Equipe*, saw the race lead slipping away. He urged Garros to leave for Pisa, regardless of the disturbing noises emanating from his elderly Gnome.

Garros took-off, trying to ignore the clattering and leaking engine, and flew east along the coast, *Le Côte d'Azur*, which was anything but azure, covered by a gray overcast and buffeted by high winds. He overflew the harbor at Villefranche, passed Cap Ferret, then saw Monaco off his left wing, the tiny principality covered by gloomy clouds. He was welcomed into Italian airspace by fierce winds rocking his featherweight bird. Most Italian mountains run parallel to the coast breaking up East-West air flow, but near the French border, the canyons point to the coast, funneling the tempest out to sea over low sand hills. At very low altitude. Garros flew just above the wave tops, to escape the howling wind's worst effects, and turned south following the coast.

If his geriatric power plant failed, or if he lost control in the wind, he would pancake the plane into the ocean where his survival in the high waves, assuming he lived through the impact, would be doubtful. The lower he flew, the less turbulence to ride out; but the limited sanctuary came with a reduced margin of error. Modern-day pilots who have flown a vintage Blériot, such as legendary movie air-stuntman Frank Tallman, remarked on how little roll control the aircraft exhibited. Wing warping worked considerably better for birds, from which it was copied, than it did for fixed-wing aircraft. Tallman estimated a Blériot XI exercised about 10-20% of the roll authority of a modern light plane. If a random gust upset the craft and a wing dropped too far, it could not be picked up with the application of opposite control stick. The pilot needed to dive in the direction of the bank to generate enough lift to level the wings. This would have been suicide at low altitude. Garros found himself at the waves' mercy, the foamy crests reaching upward for his puttering white bird. Waves whose lacey tops were blown off by the wind.

Tired of fighting with the elements and struggling to stay airborne, Garros was relieved to see his refueling stop of Genoa, birthplace of Christopher Columbus. The city hugged the coast of the Ligurian Sea, as the ocean is called on the Italian Riviera.

Landing, Garros located LeBlanc and the mechanics standing ready to service the aircraft. They told him he had beaten André Frey to Genoa and was now in first place. Garros grabbed the breakfast he had not had time for in Nice while the technicians again cleaned his engine's oiled-fouled valves. Would it last until Rome? No one knew. Anxious to preserve his lead, he took off, following the coastline as it turned south to form the boot of Italy. Around One o'clock, 1300, he spotted, what else, the leaning tower of Pisa, no fancy navigation required. Nursing his sick Gnome, which was losing power by the minute, he touched down in Pisa at a temporary airfield marked by a captive balloon. He was still in first place. The mechanics needed hours to work on the engine and the telegraph reported Rome was enduring a violent thunderstorm, so the decision was taken to overnight in Pisa. Frey had stopped in Genoa and Beaumont was stuck in Nice. As the race leader, Garros was feted, wined, and dined by the local dignitaries. He relaxed, enjoying a classic dinner of Northern Italian cuisine at one of the town's most luxurious hotels. Rome could wait.

Up before dawn on Wednesday, the last day of May 1911, Roland Garros's mechanics reported that while he dined, they fixed his engine without a doubt. He left at first light. The storm passed Rome during the night, sweeping away the clouds and leaving a clear, blue sky. He overflew Livorno with its picturesque harbor and proceeded southward down the Tuscan coast. It was a beautiful day for flying with no turbulence to rock the aircraft and no rain. Garros enjoyed the view, illuminated by the radiant Tuscan sunlight, light which inspired painters since the first artist put brush to canvas. It would be a smooth cruise to Rome and victory.

A sudden loud clank shattered his revelry. It sounded as if an internal part of the Gnome had broken loose and was rattling around inside the spinning engine. With power failing, yet another forced landing loomed. The rolling Tuscan hills afforded no unobstructed fields, all he saw was vineyards marching up and down the slopes. He spotted an accessible area unoccupied by wine grapes and aimed for the rugged patch of land. Just prior to touchdown, he saw a deep pit waiting to swallow the aircraft and tried to bank hard right, too far right. His right wingtip drug the ground, slewing the plane to the right. The spindly landing gear collapsed, the Blériot fell over to the left, the other wing caught earth, and the ship spun back to the left before it folded like a bad Vaudeville act. Without a seatbelt, Garros was thrown from the cockpit and ended up under the crumpled wreck. With barely a half-hour of flying time elapsed, the fuel tank with its almost full load of gasoline could ignite at any moment. Garros scrambled from the pile of debris that used to be an airplane and put some distance between himself and the possible explosion.

Catching his breath and taking inventory, a wave of intense pain hit. His shoulder felt like his clavicle was broken. While looking for a landing spot, he noticed a railway line less than a kilometer, perhaps a half-mile, away. Struggling with his pain, he walked to the right-of-way and trudged along the tracks, back toward Livorno. Soon, a steam engine appeared, chugging northward. He waved it down with one arm. The engineer and fireman pulled him up into the cab and hearing the tale of his crash, adjusted the johnson bar (the throttle on a steam locomotive) to churn the train up tracks in a cloud of white vapor and black smoke to the next town, Cecina. It was better than riding a bike. At the station, Garros telephoned LeBlanc who, when he learned Garros was not in mortal danger, told him to return to Pisa by train.

Garros checked back in to his hotel in Pisa around 1400, 2 PM, and fell into bed. An ex-flyhalf on the French national rugby squad, he was un-familiar with the pain of a knocked-about body. To his relief, his shoulder did not appear to be broken, just wrenched. LeBlanc looked in on him later that night with news, some good and some bad. Beaumont's engine had been revived. He overflew Pisa and landed in Rome, winning the race. The good news was yet another replacement Blériot XI arrived in pieces from the factory. The mechanics intended to work all night to assemble it and to wake up the engine. Second place was within grasp if Roland Garros was in good enough physical shape to fly.

The next day, Garros dragged his aching body out of bed, thanked the technicians for their all-nighter and after a short test hop took off for Rome at 1030. This day did not start as pleasantly as the previous one. Frank Tallman wrote these early crates lacked the ability to trim out their control surfaces to reduce parasitic aerodynamic loads. Blériots were invariably tail-heavy, requiring constant forward pressure on the cockpit control stick to hold the tail up. It must have been agony for Garros to muscle the aircraft along in level flight with an aching body and a barking shoulder.

The new XI came directly from the production line configured for a customer. It was not modified for long-distance racing and carried only enough fuel in its smaller, lighter tank for about an hour of flight. Rome waited two hours away, a refueling stop would be necessary, but where.

Still, the flight went well. After logging less than an hour of uneventful flight, the engine began sputtering and coughing, indicating a lack of fuel. Northwest of the town of Castiglione, one of many bearing the same name in Italy, which translates to "Little Castle," Garros spied a group of peasants, *campagnards,* working in an open field. To their amazement, he set the aircraft down among them and with his limited Italian, announced his need for gasoline. Two farmers set off in a horse-drawn cart in search for fuel.

Waiting for the gas seekers to return, the *campagnards* took the opportunity to share their meager lunch with Garros; hard-boiled eggs and rustic red wine. Post-lunch, an impromptu party broke out, with a band of local musicians drawn to the scene around the aircraft, the first they had seen up close. More wine flowed as folk music livened up the growing crowd. Garros finally broke ground, destination Rome, accompanied by the sound of Mandolins, Accordions, and cries of, *"Buona giornata!"* Good journey!

After an hour of flight, the engine began missing. Garros landed once more in a cleared field, cleaned the spark plugs, and took off, losing only a few precious minutes.

At last, the Italian capital appeared on the horizon. Roland Garros flew over the Eternal City and the Tiber river, admiring the Coliseum, the Roman Forum, the Piazza Navona, and Saint Peter's Basilica across the river in the Vatican. His initial look at these famous and spectacular landmarks was tainted by the knowledge he would finish second due to numerous mechanical problems with his various aircraft, several of which were now scattered across France and Italy in broken pieces. However, his stay in Rome turned out to be not at all bad.

Chapter Seventeen

THE TOUR OF EUROPE

Racing the Grim Reaper

At the awards ceremony in Rome for the Paris-Rome race, Garros spotted an old friend of his father, Jean Ajalbert, whom he met at home in Saigon. Roland introduced himself as his mother's grown-up son and omitted any mention of his estranged father. A Frenchman, Ajalbert was a well-known and respected lawyer, a poet, a prolific writer, and a human rights activist who often visited the Garros household in Vietnam. In a famous *cause célèbre*, Ajalbert publicly defended a French army captain, Albert Dreyfus, convicted of passing military secrets to the German General Staff through the German embassy in Paris. The innocent Dreyfus was railroaded by the sensationalistic press and by rabid anti-Semitic public opinion. He was a Jew from Alsace who spoke German. Many people asked where his true loyalties lay. Other officers were jealous of his superior abilities and wanted to eliminate professional competition. After a secret trial, Dreyfus was exiled to Devil's Island, French Guiana. In what became known as *Le Affair Dreyfus*, Jean Ajalbert, along with many other members of the French intelligentsia, gained reputations as fierce proponents of tolerance and humanity, not to mention simple justice. The ease with which Dreyfus was framed and convicted indicated the widespread belief that Germany operated a spy ring inside France. In Germany, people suspected a mirror-image French intelligence network existed. Both parties were probably right in their suspicions and that the bilingual provinces of Alsace and Lorraine provided a ready supply of spies. Ajalbert operated on a more interpersonal level as well. He knew the history of conflict between Roland and his father. He also learned of the elder Garros's dream of reconciliation, but

Georges did not know how to approach his resentful and rebellious son. Perhaps Ajalbert could be a helpful intermediary.

Uncharacteristically, Jean Ajalbert invited Roland Garros to dinner at the *Castello di Constantino*, the Castle of the Emperor Constantine, perhaps the best-known restaurant in Rome at the time. Its colonnaded dining room overlooked the city from one of Rome's famous seven hills. Ajalbert was much impressed but also deeply saddened by his dinner guest. Roland seemed pre-occupied and remote. He paid little attention to the numerous, elegant Italian ladies at adjoining tables, each subtly eager to meet the dashing young French aviator. Garros picked at the well-prepared Northern Italian cuisine and appeared unimpressed by the spectacular city view. The last two behaviors Ajalbert chalked up to a bout of homesickness and to the memories of Saigon, which the dinner with an old friend summoned. But, ignoring the pride of Roman womanhood, *Sacré Bleu! Quel horror!* Such behavior is rare at age 21. It was obvious to Ajalbert that Roland Garros was deeply troubled by the perceived loss of his family; his mother and sister due to distance and his father due to deeply-felt and long-lasting conflict. Garros conversed somewhat superficially about aviation and air racing but avoided any sort of dialog concerning his family.   Uncharacteristically,   Jean Ajalbert was at a loss for words, unable to reach his younger friend. Before parting, the two men promised to meet in Paris. Intrigued by the young Frenchman and his aviation avocation, Ajalbert would later write an account of Garros's life in an essay published after World War I. Contemplating the sad situation, Ajalbert vowed to find a way to reconcile Roland and Georges Garros. It would not be an easy task.

Back in the City of Lights, Roland Garros discovered he was becoming famous. The elite club of nationally-known French aviators welcomed its newest and youngest member. This clan of flyers rarely met as a group and did not socialize among themselves, but they all knew who was in and who was not and how each pilot earned his wings. The informal club of aviators was limited to the professionals, those who risked their lives often and for money. Garros was featured in a supplement of *Le Petit Parisian* on Sunday, 12 June 1911, which told in breathless purple prose of his first-place finish on the initial stage of Paris-Madrid and his second-place ribbon in the Paris-Rome event. That he was young, handsome, and a member of Parisian café society did not hurt his public image at all.

Recognizing an opportunity for good publicity, Louis Blériot announced to the Parisian press corps that Roland Garros would participate in the upcoming European Circuit race, the longest event yet at 1500 kilometers, over 900 miles. The circuit would start outside Paris at Chateau Vincennes, a French military base, and the last station on a Paris Metro line. The itinerary would include a mandatory first stop in Reims to commemorate the seminal week of aviation held there in 1909. The race would then proceed on to Liège, Utrecht, and Brussels in Belgium, then to Roubaix and Calais back in France. The racers would cross the Channel to Dover, return to Calais, and finish back in Paris. Seizing the intense popular interest in flying, *Le Petit Parisian* would sponsor the contest.

Louis Blériot provided Garros with another new model XI from a seemingly endless supply of aircraft. Indeed, between 1909 and the onset of the Great War, various Blériot factories churned out over 1000 airplanes, making the Blériot XI the world's first mass-produced aircraft. That is, if a device assembled individually by artisans can be labeled massed-produced.

Inclusion of England on the race route proved an interesting move. At the time, the island of Great Britain floated in an aviation back-water with little substantial aerial activity underway. France lead in all things aero followed by the USA in distant second place. Across the Atlantic, aeronautical developments were held back by the litigious Wright brothers, who seemed to believe they owned the patent on the airplane. The Wrights demanded, but rarely received, a $1000 royalty payment for every aircraft produced, world-wide. A thousand dollars represented serious money in 1911 and the French, among others, ignored the Wrights' demands. Did *Le Petit Parisian* include a stop in the United Kingdom to spark English interest in aviation or to rub British faces in French aerial superiority? It was not to sell newspapers in the United Kingdom. No proper Englishman would read anything but the Times of London. Given the centuries-old rivalry between the French and the English, you must assume the Circuit of Europe involved one-upmanship and a well-thumbed, prominent Gallic nose at *Les Anglos Saxons.*

Lack of much British success in the emerging field of aviation perplexed the famous polymath and futurist H. G. Wells, a patriotic Englishman, who took pen in hand as he was often wont to do. He wrote well in various genres but is best known as one of the three fathers of science fiction. Wells's popular books predicted the invention of aerial bombardment, spaceships, communication satellites, the internet, death rays (lasers), and amazingly, nuclear weapons. He is best-known for a device he alone foresaw, but which has not yet been realized, the time machine, which he featured in a book of the same name. H. G. Wells railed against what he saw as the indolence and sloth of British youth. Young, well-bred men played Cricket instead of building aeroplanes. Following Louis Blériot's first flight across the English Channel, Wells predicted, quite accurately, an aerial attack would eventually come from the continent and the United Kingdom could no longer count on the Royal Navy for the defense of its home islands. In 1897, H. G. Wells described in vivid detail a defenseless London under aerial bombardment, the populace panicked by the death raining from the sky, the city aflame, the authorities powerless, and civil society breaking down. He chronicled these future events in his book, "The War of the Worlds," but his fictional attackers came from Mars, not Munich. Wells made his point but no one took him seriously, categorizing the book as "Science Romance." His dire predictions came true earlier than he feared. The real carnage originated not from Mars but from Germany. The horrific Zeppelin night bombing raids of the Great War produced the terrible effects he predicted. During

London's Golden Age, H. G. Wells was a prophet without honors is his own land. Across the Channel, the French ignored him. Meanwhile in Berlin, the German High Command continued polishing and perfecting the Schlieffen Plan detailing the coming invasion of France. In Southern Germany, Count Ferdinand von Zeppelin worked on his dirigibles.

The Circuit of Europe race was scheduled to begin on 18 June 1911, and things did not go well. Strong windstorms were blowing over most of northern Europe but the race organizers insisted on starting anyway. Having little knowledge of flying, newspaper officials saw no problem in taking off in a strong, direct crosswind. Aircraft of 1911 had no means of steering on the ground until flight was imminent and there was enough airflow for the aerodynamic controls to take effect. These craft needed to take off and land directly into the wind. A crosswind could have several possible effects, all of them bad. Some planes could weathervane uncontrollably, aligning with the wind, and heading toward the crowd lining the runway. Other types of airplanes tended to drift downwind, also toward the spectators. A gust could lift the upwind wing and flip the plane over on its back. This happened to race pilot Léon Lemartin. The wind inverted him just before lift-off and rolled his spindly craft up into a ball of sticks, cloth, and wires. Lemartin died in hospital a few hours later.

Garros successfully took off on time, no doubt aided somewhat by the Blériot's pivoting wheels which allowed a crab angle into the crosswind. However, his new Gnome seemed down on power and he returned to Vincennes. He landed with the aid of those swiveling wheels and the mechanics changed the spark plugs. He launched again into the gale after being penalized an hour by the race committee for his unauthorized return to the starting line.

Enroute to the first refueling stop at Bethany, France, wind-generated turbulence buffeted Garros, his wings shaking and flexing alarmingly. Roll control by wing warping required a flexible structure to allow control cables to change the wing's contours. Flexibility was dangerous in high winds; the wings

172 | ED COBLEIGH

could fold up or even separate from the airframe. During refueling, Garros instructed the mechanics to stiffen his wings by splicing on reinforcing braces. The strengthened structure was safer in turbulence, but degraded the Blériot's already marginal roll control. While the technicians worked, Garros's friend Edmund Audemars, who was following the race in his fast, six-cylinder Grégoire sports car, informed Roland of more pilot losses. Pierre Landron crashed and died outside Paris when forced to land at Issy in the crosswind. Naval Lieutenant Princetreau was incinerated when his landing gear collapsed during yet another crosswind landing. His fuel tank ruptured, spraying gasoline over the crumpled wreck, its pilot, and the red-hot engine with fatal results. One day of racing, three deaths, the clan of aviators, Garros's newly-adopted extended family, was growing smaller rapidly.

Despite the tragic losses, the race continued. Garros held his position during the various stages, encountering the usual emergency landings and unplanned stops. On the first of July, approaching Calais on the coast a strong wind blew off the English Channel. With a troublesome engine, his Blériot struggled to make headway so he set the monoplane down in a field only 20 kilometers, 12 miles, short of the port city. Usually wind intensity decreases near the ground, but not this time, it continued to howl across the impromptu aerodrome. Only the actions of a group of villagers saved the aircraft from destruction. They held the plane down while it bucked and flapped its wings like a raptor held down on a perch by jesses knotted around its talons. A Blériot left the ground at about 30-35 mph, 50-55 kph, with a full load of fuel. A 30-mph head wind will lift the aircraft into the air regardless of whether the engine is running or not. The doughty peasants restrained the aircraft while they watched Garros clean the spark plugs; then the villagers pointed the craft into the wind and a brave volunteer spun the propeller. Released by the amateur ground crew into the teeth of the gale, the bird leapt from the ground, halving the normal 200-foot, 60-meter, takeoff roll.

In Calais, all flying was suspended for two days, allowing the participants to journey by chartered ship across to County Kent in England to take part in and to observe the Gordon-Bennett Cup air races of 1911 at Eastchurch. An Englishman earned a rare British victory in the 1910 races at Belmont Park, New York, so England boasted the honor of hosting the 1911 event. Garros did not fly in the Gordon-Bennett closed-course race, which was won by an American, Charley Weymann, flying a French Nieuport. Weymann's victory foreshadowed an American contribution to air combat during the Great War when the US Army Air Corps flew the graceful but fragile Nieuport fighters built in France.

The band of racers traveled together to England by sea and you can speculate on the inevitable conversations about the high fatality rate they experienced, with the race's most hazardous leg, the Channel crossing, yet to come. People in dangerous situations; wars, mountain climbing, bull-fighting, auto or air races, assume a certain *laissez-faire* attitude toward deaths, even the loss of close companions. Self preservation produces a line of thinking that tells a risk-taker that he or she is too careful, or lucky, or skillful for the Grim Reaper. "Yes, poor Pierre got the chop, what a pity, but I can't be killed because I'm me," always seems to be the prevalent attitude. This human dynamic is part avoidance, part self-preservation, and part coping mechanism. It allows the survivors to carry on, to function, and to not be paralyzed by the acknowledgement of extreme risk and of life's temporal nature. There are no records of these conversations between the pilots. But, among risk-takers, the verbal process is always the same and it is certain the talks took place, maybe in a hanger, perhaps over dinner, or most probably with brandy and cigars late at night.

Back in Calais, the race resumed on 3 July with a stage over the English Channel which for some reason the French call "*La Manche.*" Two flights; one to Dover and a return trip to Calais. Droning above the ocean, Roland Garros could not help but remember how less than a year earlier, his hero and friend John Moisant made the same journey along with his cat and mechanic. The race's last stage ran from Calais to Amiens, a mandatory refueling stop, and then back to Vincennes.

Garros refueled in Amiens within sight of the tallest Gothic cathedral in France and left immediately for Paris, 75 miles, 120 kilometers away. He flew low over the watershed of the Somme River, the stream flowing through Amiens. Beneath him, the French countryside slept under the late morning fog blissfully unaware of the horrors to come along the Somme's banks, carnage wrought by the Great War. The land would be churned into a morass by artillery fire, farmer's fields would be crisscrossed by muddy trenches, and the air defiled by decaying bodies of men and horses. Nearly-finished in Berlin, the German invasion plan called for a rapid advance across the countryside drained by the Somme, destination Paris. The battle for the French capital would be fought along the Somme's banks. On this misty summer day, the filthy clouds of war were not yet covering the green patchwork of farms and villages, only the soft, white fog of summer. No one French knew what lay in store for them.

Garros soon discovered the railway line he intended to follow to Paris and Vincennes disappearing under a fog bank, forcing him to continue on a compass heading while attempting to read his map in the wind-swept cockpit. Up ahead, he saw the forest of Vincennes. He would eventually be able to find the airfield in the green expanse laced with mist, but for a racer, every minute counts. For once his Gnome hummed on tune, and he climbed to 3000 feet, 900 meters, to get his navigational bearings and to ensure he could glide to the aerodrome in the not unlikely case of sudden engine failure. Attempting an emergency landing in a dense forest with few clearings could prove fatal in a flimsy Blériot. Three pilots had already died during the race, no need to make it four. Ahead in the haze he spotted the central tower of *Le Chateau de Vincennes* poking up through the fog like a square lighthouse. The castle's keep, which in French goes by the slightly ridiculous name of *jonjon,* is the tallest in Europe at 51 meters,

175 feet; height which paid off, serving as a signpost marking the nearby military airfield.

As he set up his landing approach, he saw no other aircraft on the field. He would be the first plane to land. Also visible was a sea of spectators lining the grass runway. The sponsoring newspaper touted the crowd at over 200,000, which is unlikely. Later, Garros wrote he remembered wishing the triumphal moment could last longer. After three hazardous races and deaths of several fellow pilots, he was about to touch down a winner.

The Blériot bounced to a halt on the uneven grass and the propeller sputtered to a standstill. Instantly Garros and his craft were surrounded by a multitude of people. The press of humanity left him without space to climb down from the cockpit. Everyone wanted to shake his hand. The celebration soon dissipated when another aircraft, also a Blériot, appeared on the horizon. Garros's teammate, Beaumont, departed Amiens barely 20 minutes after him and he found the Vincennes airfield straightaway. Once again, Roland Garros finished in second place, defeated by the hour penalty awarded by the race committee at the start for his return to the field for better spark plugs. He made up 40 minutes on Beaumont over the course, but not the full 60. *Le Petit Parisian's* next edition labeled Roland Garros, "The Eternal Second" after his runner-up placing in both Paris-Rome and the Circuit of Europe. The moniker stuck, to his chagrin, but the nickname made him famous among the aviation-crazed public and guaranteed him a reservation in any Parisian restaurant.

CHAPTER EIGHTEEN

SECOND ISN'T GOOD ENOUGH

NEW PLANE, NEW TEAM

Roland Garros hated not winning, detested being "The Eternal Second" the newspapers labeled him. In bicycle racing, track and field, and rugby, he enjoyed winning, placing first, not second. No more major air races were scheduled for 1911. He would have to find another prize to pursue and hopefully win thereby shaking the stigma of second place. One obvious goal was the world altitude record. He already flew higher than any other human, but unofficially in Mexico. Record-setting flights required the aircraft to carry aloft a calibrated, recording altimeter. The French Aero Club did not recognize his mark and indeed Garros's maximum altitude had been surpassed since his tour of the Americas with the Moisant Flying Circus. His mount that day, a standard Blériot, was not optimized for high-altitude flight, the airframe possessed more potential, but required modifications to extract maximum performance. He would need longer wings, a different propeller, and a high-altitude engine. He would also need much warmer clothing. Garros pressed Louis Blériot to build a dedicated plane, one which could set a new record, not just a few hundred feet or meters higher but one which could put the record out of reach for some time. Blériot, busy with manufacturing his eponymous airplanes and running his flying school, promised Garros he would investigate the project, but reaction at the factory was slow, too slow for Roland Garros. Far slower than Parisian night life.

After the Circuit of Europe race, Garros's young urban friends entertained him night after night at trendy watering holes. Cinzano's, l'Opera, and the famous bistro, Le Coupole, saw the "in" crowd drinking and dining. Once, he would have been content, even pleased, to be the center of such attention. But the Parisian playboy of two short years prior no longer existed. Competition in a dangerous sport, aviation, and the deaths of people he knew and knew well, had matured the young man from Réunion Island by way of Saigon. In addition to his discontent and boredom, other problems loomed beyond what to order from an upscale menu.

The joint venture with Edmund Audemars and Albert Moisant to upgrade the Demoiselle aircraft with a more powerful engine was not going well. Jules Hue and old friend Romain had been instructed to make the necessary modifications at Issy but no one bothered to ask the question, "Will this work?" from an engineering standpoint. As testing was soon to show, it was not a good idea to mount an engine twice as heavy and twice as powerful in the delicate bamboo-braced Demoiselle. This "cut-and-try" approach to aircraft design was typical of the era. Few people knew how to scientifically design or modify an aircraft and those who thought they knew were not about to share information with a competitive world. The mechanics lopped 80 cm, nearly three feet, off the plane's tail. This shortened the lever arm at the rear and raised the bird's nose for the Le Rhône's longer propeller to clear the ground. No one thought to examine what effect this ad hoc modification would have on the plane's weight and balance equations. Aircraft, particularly aircraft weighing around 300 pounds, 135 kilos, are very sensitive to where in the structure the center of gravity falls in relation to the wings.

On the monster Demoiselle's first test flight, Hue started the engine and Romain released the bird for flight. The aircraft fairly leapt off the ground with the engine pointed at the sky. The nose rose and kept coming up. Full forward on the pitch control stick produced no effect. The nose continued to climb, a power-on stall was imminent. Alertly, Garros sensed things were not going well and were unlikely to improve in the short term. He quickly hit the ignition cut-off switch, killing the berserk engine. Without power, the aircraft stalled and the nose fell even faster than it climbed. The doomed Demoiselle, after having ascended only a few feet, hit nose first and both wings broke off. Garros was somehow unhurt. It was back to the non-existent drawing board for the team.

A week later, Audemars experienced another crash which again destroyed the aircraft and its engine. A spark plug managed to escape the whirling cylinders and conked Audemars on his leather flying helmet, leaving a nasty gash. Seeing real potential for getting someone killed, Albert Moisant pulled the plug on the project, probably saving either Garros's or Audemars' life. Restless, Garros looked for some other outlet for his flying urge.

He modified his own personal Blériot to carry two people by adding an additional bucket seat behind the pilot. Standard two-seat Blériots mounted their occupants side-by-side. Perhaps learning from the Demoiselle re-reengining fiasco, Garros proceeded cautiously. He flew with progressively heavier sandbags in the aft seat until he could hoist aloft 100 kg, 220 pounds without degrading the aircraft's handling characteristics.

In late July, promoter Albert Barré planned another flying exhibition at Dinard on the Atlantic coast. Bored with the relentless Parisian nightlife, and with everyone who was anyone leaving Paris for their August vacations, Garros agreed to fly again at Dinard, for a sum. He enjoyed flying off the beach, the sand was smoother than the lumpy grass at Issy and the runway stretched for miles. The main problem was the strand ran north and south and the prevailing winds were from the west necessitating cross-wind takeoffs and landings. Garros's first flight over the town and the casino was uneventful and he invited Barré along in the rear seat for his second exhibition. While they were airborne, the wind picked up, a fact Garros failed to realize.

Recreational beaches of France and England were lined with tiny shacks, called "Chalets" in England and "*Cabines*" in France. These were, and still are, windowless wooden huts about the size of a roomy walk-in closet allowing modest beach-goers a place to change into their swim suits in private. Landing on the beach in front of a line of *cabines*, Garros's Blériot drifted across the landing zone propelled by the strong crosswind and headed for the watching spectators. Fleeing in terror at the sight of the approaching aircraft, parents picked up their children and ran. Before the plane's wheels could be stopped by the sand, a wingtip caught the corner of a *cabine* and the aircraft pivoted into the wood hut. Garros cut the engine to land so the propeller was stationary. Both the *cabine* and the aircraft disappeared in a cloud of debris during the ensuing crash. Rescuers came running to separate crumpled aircraft debris from the hut's weathered boards, and found Garros and Barré sandwiched together in the tangled mess. Both were unhurt beyond cuts, bruises, and damaged egos.

Once it was determined no one suffered a serious injury, the festival committee's Chief addressed the crowd. He reminded the spectators of the hazards of aviation and organized a cheer for the two shaken aviators. Roland Garros tasked Jules Hue to salvage the wreckage and to return the wrecked aircraft back to the Blériot factory to be re-built. Later that night, Garros received a telegram requesting his participation in an air show on 12 August 1911 in the town of Saint-Etienne, France. All he needed was an airplane. Returning to Paris, Garros signed the contract for the air display and ordered yet another aircraft from Louis Blériot.

Sainte-Etienne is a coal-mining town located in south-eastern France on the edge of the *Massif Central*, the rolling plateau occupying the center of France. The airshow proved to be a financial bust as the airfield was surrounded by low hills allowing the spectators to watch for free. Still, Roland Garros got paid to fly, and during the meet took possession of his new Blériot, the one he intended to use to set the altitude record. He also received from the factory his rebuilt aircraft, which he loaned to his friend Edmund Audemars to fly during the show. The air show at Sainte-Etienne proved to be routine, without drama, but while there Garros met several important, interesting people who would influence his immediate future.

Charles and Gabriel Voisin were known as "Industrialists," an English word. Today they would be "Entrepreneurs," a French term. Together the brothers established the world's first commercial aircraft manufacturing plant in 1905 in Billancourt, a suburb of Paris. They built aircraft to their customer's specifications some of which could fly, a little. They used the proceeds from the sales to finance their own aeronautical developments. From 1905 until about 1909, Voisin-built aircraft set numerous "world" records in France for duration and speed. The Wright brothers' exploits across the Atlantic were widely believed to be hoaxes among Europeans. How could unknown bicycle mechanics from nowhere, or Ohio, invent the airplane? As a result of this disbelief, the Voisin brothers gained a reputation for developing state-of-the-art aircraft. This misconception was corrected by the Wrights' flying exhibition in Paris in 1908 which showed how far ahead the Americans were. The Voisins persevered, building biplanes and monoplanes for several customers.

One such customer was Léon Delagrange, a famous sculptor who turned from the esoteric world of fine art to practical domain of aviation. Delagrange was the first to put a Le Rhône engine in a Blériot, doubling its horsepower and making the Blériot XI a viable aircraft. One of Delagrange's sculpture models and one of his mistresses was the actress and singer Elise-Raymonde Deroche. In polite French society, actresses and female stage entertainers were barely one step above street whores in social standing. However, a shady past was not the insurmountable barrier to advancement it was in uptight Anglo-Saxon countries. Indeed, in the 1940s, Edith Piaf, a streetwalker who could sing like a bird and was named after one (*piaf* is French slang for Sparrow), became the toast of France. But in 1909, what respectable woman would display herself on a stage, or on the movie screen, to strangers? From working in music halls to posing in the nude was a small step for Ms. Deroche and she became Delagrange's constant companion and model.

Delagrange, along with the voluptuous Ms. Deroche, attended the Wright brothers' exhibition and the artist/aviator vowed to step up his flying game as a result. Also bitten by the aviation bug, Elise-Raymonde contacted Charles Voisin and asked him to teach her how to fly. Like Roland Garros, she received no dual-control instruction. She taxied faster and faster until she was able to lift off and fly for over 300 yards, 270 meters, alone in a Voisin biplane. Evidently impressed by more than her new-found piloting skills, Charles Voisin persuaded Elise-Raymonde to leave Delagrange and become his lover instead. Not for the last time would a woman of easy virtue be attracted to the exciting world of aviation, its dashing pilots, and rich industrialists. A fast learner, in March of 1909, Elise-Raymonde earned the first French pilot's license given to a woman. Probably sensing her flying career would be enhanced by more social prestige, Elise-Raymonde assumed the title "Baroness Raymonde de la Roche" despite having no royal blood. She was the daughter of a plumber.

Elise-Raymonde Deroche flew in the famous air meet at Reims in1910 where anyone and everyone in aviation attended, except the Wrights. She suffered a tremendous crash, breaking an arm and a leg and was still recovering, not flying, at Saint-Etienne a year later. Her return to the cockpit was later interrupted by the Great War, when women were prohibited from flying for some dubious reason. She volunteered for service as a military chauffeur, driving senior officers around. Not content to stagnate behind the wheel, Deroche studied aircraft engineering during the war, a remarkable feat in a time when very few women entered the professions. They encountered biting chauvinistic discrimination when they did. Her goal was to become the world's first female test pilot when peace resumed. On her first test flight in an experimental aircraft in 1919, she crashed, dying in the wreck. A statue honoring Elise-Raymonde Deroche, Baroness or not, can be seen today at the French national air and space museum at Le Bourget airfield outside Paris.

Prior to flying at Sainte-Etienne, Roland Garros met the Voisin brothers and the "Baroness de la Roche." Impressed by the resources and organization displayed at the show by the Voisins, Garros asked to join their team thereby gaining access to their excellent mechanics and well-equipped shop. He briefed the brothers on his plan to set the altitude record and Charles accepted his offer to join the organization. This change allowed Garros to focus on flying and the necessary socializing and let Jules Hue work with the Voisin team to make it all happen in the air.

After the show at Sainte-Etienne, the Voisin circus traveled north to Le Mans for a late August exhibition. Attendance at Le Mans was slightly better, but the flying was substandard with numerous crashes. A Farman biplane broke in half, impacting the ground among the crowd of spectators. Unbelievably, no one was hurt, perhaps due to the absence of a densely packed crowd. Municipal good luck ran out in 1955 at the 24 Hours of Le Mans auto race, when a Mercedes racing car tumbled through the crowd killing 84 people. In 1910, no one died; no pilots and no paying customers, a relative rarity.

Pre-war aviation was not a vocation for the timid. In France alone prior to 1910, over 40 pilots died in crashes. No less an expert than Louis Blériot, who certainly witnessed his share of mishaps, said that survival in a prang was not due to the cleverness of the aviator but rather resulted from the elasticity of the airframe. A pilot's primary fear was getting hit by the heavy engine or the still-turning propeller. Léon Delagrange, the aforementioned sculptor, aviator, and womanizer, died in a crash with his skull crushed by a Le Rhône crankcase in 1910.

With Autumn and its unsettled weather rapidly approaching, Garros determined to make his assault on the world altitude record before the winds of fall arrived to make flying even more hazardous. He shipped his new, purpose-built Blériot by rail to the beaches of Dinard. Rather than return to Paris, he rode with Charles Voisin and the "Baroness" to the North Sea town in their touring car. There he would attempt to enter the record books as a Number One, not an Eternal Second.

CHAPTER NINETEEN

NUMBER ONE AT LAST

On Top of the World

Cold. Cold which sluices through flesh and swirls around bones like Artic Ocean waves breaking around pilings of a pier. Cold that freezes exposed skin, plunges icy daggers into the lungs, turns fingers and toes into inert stubs and starts uncontrollable shivering. Cold that drains energy out of the body like blood from a mortal wound. Roland Garros was slowly freezing to death.

He took off from a smooth beach near Dinard at 8:20 on the morning of 4 September 1911. Officials from the Aero Club of France arrived at 7:00, just after dawn, to install a recording altimeter, called a "Barograph," in the open cockpit of his Blériot XI. Sealed from tampering, the unit would record on paper the highest altitude reached on today's record-challenging flight. Peering through a small glass window on the barograph, Garros could determine his exact altitude. Would it be high enough to set a world record?

Early morning and the wind remained calm. A thin, ragged cloud layer at medium altitude filtered the rising sun giving an aura of unreality to the flight. Garros climbed through the hazy deck easily, the aircraft seemed to know what was expected of it and the new but often troublesome Le Rhône engine sang, pulling the white aircraft higher and higher. Despite the filmy stratus beneath him, he saw enough of the sea, beach, and estuary to navigate. Keeping station over Dinard in a racetrack pattern, he turned the aircraft slowly, banking the aircraft only slightly. Energy spent and lift lost while turning was energy not dedicated to climbing. In anticipation of the extreme cold encountered at high altitude, Garros had pulled an extra knit sweater on under his leather flying coat. It was not enough.

★★★

Air temperature falls according to a fixed formula as an aircraft climbs. For each 1000 feet, 300 meters, of altitude gained, the ambient temperature drops about 5.4 degrees F, or 3 degrees C. Assuming a sea-level temperature of 60 degrees F, a reasonable assumption for an early fall dawn on France's Atlantic coast. At his target altitude of 4000 meters, 12,500 feet, Garros would feel the air temperature rushing past his face to be less than -5 degrees F, 5 degrees below zero or -20-degrees C. With a 50 mph, 80 kph, prop blast lashing his face and sapping heat from his body, he was miserable. Still, he climbed. He would not be denied the record.

Medical opinion at the time warned that at high altitude, the heart could malfunction and the circulatory system might slow down delivery of blood to the body. Human life at altitude was uncommon in 1911. The highest alpine peaks had only been climbed as recently as 1855 to 1865, peaks which reached up into the sky as far as Garros intended to fly. Few people outside Tibet had ever lived at these altitudes. Of course, alpinists knew the energy-sapping effects of low air pressure and thus low oxygen levels. Breath comes in labored gulps, exertion is painful, energy levels fall as the altitude experienced climbs and the air gets progressively thinner. But humans had survived and functioned at those heights, the climbers did summit the peaks. However, the mountaineers spent days if not weeks acclimatizing themselves as they inched their way skyward handhold by handhold. Roland Garros would reach alpine height in a little over an hour.

4000 meters, 12,500 feet; the barograph's thin needle told him he now held the record but he wanted more. Despite the aircraft hovering on the verge of a stall in the thin air, barely hanging on the propeller, it seemed to have a little more climb in it. Garros handled the controls gently, as you would touch an ailing but dangerous animal, coaxing the Blériot ever higher. If a wing stalled, the bird would flip over into a spin. Spin recovery was dicey under the best of circumstances at lower altitude. No one really knew for certain which techniques worked. The few pilots who recovered from a spin rarely remembered what they did and the ones who did not recover were not around to say what did not work. They were dead. Complicating matters was the fact that a spin-recovery technique effective in one type of plane would not necessarily work with a much different craft. Bottom line; a spin at this altitude would almost certainly be fatal. Before the spin's rotation could be stopped, the aircraft would probably break up under the higher air speed resulting from lessened drag.

His feet and hands were numb, wooden appendices, his face iced. He continued to climb, evermore slowly now. Finally, the bird stopped climbing; the barograph read 4200 meters, 13,000 feet, a new record.

Garros felt his heart racing. Was this the dreaded coronary malfunction the doctors wrote about? He did not know; maybe it was the excitement of reaching the pinnacle of his vocation, long sought-after. Thinking was hard up here.

Descent would not be easy. The rotary engine operated either full on or completely off. He killed the motor with the cockpit switch and its bark died instantly. Only the rushing of the slipstream could be heard, along with the propeller's hum while being spun by the airflow. Garros, as much as he wanted to return quickly to the warmer lower air, could not just put the nose down into a dive. The stick and cloth airframe would come apart if the airspeed got out of control. He would have to glide back down, slowly, and coldly.

Roland heard and felt a sharp ping, a note struck from somewhere in the airplane. Was it a guide wire breaking? His warp-able wings were held rigid by tightly stretched wires. If one broke, which one was it? From the cockpit, he could verify all the wing-top wires were intact. Wires underneath the fuselage which prevented the wing from folding upward were invisible from his view. Could it be one of them? Another ping rang out, what was that? Why was it so difficult to think clearly, so hard to focus?

The brain is an oxygen hog, requiring constant enrichment from red blood cells. Even a slight deficiency in oxygenation will slow down the thinking process. Now, we know cognitive decline can begin as low as 5000 feet, 1600 meters. By 10,000 feet, 3200 meters, decision-making ability starts to degrade. Higher is worse. Alpinists never noticed this effect, as the mental slowdown is gradual as one climbs a mountain and the brain adjusts as much as it can to the new environment.

The second ping literally rang a bell in Garros's head. It was the engine cooling. Overheated from the relentless climb, the below-zero air flow was freezing the cylinders, contracting them, the metal was shrinking, the pieces rubbing against each other. If the engine froze, he would not be able to choose his landing site. Garros turned the contact switch back on and the engine roared back into life. He let the mill warm up and then killed it again. The long, slow, gliding descent was punctuated by periodic engine blasts until finally he touched down gently on the sandy beach in view of the Dinard Casino's terrace. The waiting public, having paid to see him land and to meet and greet the new world altitude record holder, erupted in applause as the Blériot rattled to a stop.

At last he did it, he was the best, the highest-flying pilot in the short history of aviation. Later, Roland Garros wrote that the rapid heartbeats he experienced during the record-setting climb did not result from a lack of oxygen but rather from an excess of excitement. His record would stand, a least for a while, as winter shut down most flying in Europe. After schmoozing with the paying customers that night at the casino, Garros returned to Paris by train to spend the winter there. For the first time in his life, he wondered what there was to do, what pleasures waited in the City of Lights.

CHAPTER TWENTY

DOWN RIO WAY

TROPICAL ADVENTURES

Boredom stalked Roland Garros. His re-immersion into Parisian café society had been seamless; it was as if he never left. Except for the adulation, that is. Pioneering aviators, particularly one who now held the world's record for high altitude flight, were the toast of the town. France's self-assumed superiority in aviation, the Wright brothers and Glenn Curtiss notwithstanding, reinforced the nation's pride in its collective technical and artistic ability. The Eiffel Tower, Suez Canal, Paris Métro system, Grand Palace, fanciful bridges such as the *Pont Alexandre III* across the Seine in Paris, all these engineering marvels fed French hubris. Not that the superior attitude needed much assistance. Young, handsome pilots, while they lived, became famous and featured in the popular press much like American test pilots came to be in the 1950's. Before there was Chuck Yeager, Scott Crossfield, Joe Engle, and "Fish" Salmon, there was Louis Blériot, Léon Delagrange, Santos-Dumont, and yes, Roland Garros.

Garros's life consisted of short business days followed by long convivial dinners with the same group of friends, some of whom were other aviators, but most of whom were not. Parisians at the time, and to a certain extent today, used bistros, restaurants, and bars as communal living rooms. There was nothing to do at home, no TV, so why not go out and socialize. Garros was not a culture vulture. The art scene held no interest. He only occasionally took in a play or a movie.

Reading bored him. He did find time for sports, focusing on rugby with the occasional tennis match. The auto sales showroom demanded little attention. However, the Grégriore car company's management was changing their business model. Instead of building the sports cars Garros loved to drive and could sell, the factory's new output concentrated on family sedans which he did not and could not. The new autos left him figuratively cold in the Parisian winter.

His long-time companions also verged on being boring. He had grown apart from them. After risking his life numerous times, flying over much of Western Europe and vast parts of North America, and competing against the best aviators in the world, conversations about social matters seemed trivial. For someone who faced death daily, questions of who was sleeping with whom held few interesting answers. The young pilot succumbed to a syndrome common among pilots. Once he or she has seen the world from on high, has entered the domain of the air, terrestrial life with its picayune problems tends to be beneath consideration, mentally and physically. Another major factor in his discontent must have been the financial aspects of his life. Money to be made as an aviator, if he survived the experience, far exceeded any possible income from the somnolent car business, particularly the selling of boring cars.

Mid-Fall, Charles Voisin proposed another tour over the winter through the southern United States, like the series of shows staged by the Moisant Flying Circus. Garros declined, telling Voisin he was not interested in again encountering drunken cowboys armed with pistols who burned down the grandstands when the weather prevented flying. He also experienced quite enough of the revolution in Mexico.

Voisin countered with an idea for an airshow in Rio de Janeiro, Brazil followed by others in Sao Paulo, Brazil and in Buenos Aires, Argentina. Now, that was more like it. Roland had never been to Brazil, but Rio enjoyed the international reputation of being a city on the make. Soon, Garros and his Swiss friend Edmund Audemars signed a contract to fly in Latin America with aircraft furnished by the Queen Aircraft Company of the Bronx, New York City. Queen would furnish three new Blériots from the factory, and Garros would bring over his record-setting Model XI from France. Jules Hue, ever ready for a trip, was onboard with the plan. Charles Voisin would organize it all. A wild and crazy American, Willis McCormick would be another pilot. Leaving Le Havre on a cold day, 2 December 1911, the team sailed for Rio where the Southern Hemisphere summer waited.

After a long, five-stop, seasick voyage, the team finally set foot on the quay in Rio de Janeirio. Jules Hue and the Voisin mechanics erected their canvas hangers at, what else, the local horse racing track and waited for the aircraft, shipped separately from New York, to arrive. With nothing better to do the team set about exploring Rio.

They arrived at an optimum time in Latin American and Brazilian history. Economies of countries of the continent's southern cone were booming. Enriched by agricultural exports to Europe, Argentina ranked in the top ten of the most prosperous countries on earth. Chile was shipping copper to feed rapid global electrification. Costal Brazil was shaking off its jungle image and the fertile Brazilian heartland was growing crops year-round. The capitals, Buenos Aires, Santiago, and Rio were rapidly re-built in the hope of replicating Europe's great cities. The mayor of Rio, an admitted francophile, in 1902 started converting what had been a disease-ridden, slum-filled mess into an imitation of the City of Lights. Shantytowns were cleared; streets were opened to wide boulevards; electricity, water, and sewer systems were installed; swamps were drained. Rio's entire population was inoculated against tropical diseases whether the inhabitants wanted to be or not. To complete the makeover, buildings sprung up in the then-current Modern Baroque style. The Municipal Theatre rivaled the Opera Garnier in Paris in pretentious grandeur. Photos from around 1910 show a city whose structures would not look out of place on Boulevard Haussmann near that Parisian opera house.

The politics driving of all this modernization was tabbed *"café com leité society."* *"Café com leité"* in Portuguese translates to *"café au lait"* in French and "coffee with milk" in English. This moniker represented a coded description of how Brazil was governed by rich men who sipped coffee in cafés and a reference as to how the country was financed: by lucrative sales of coffee and sugar to Europe and America. An underlying comment about Brazilian society also hid in the moniker. White people in charge and black people not. The country was run by and for people from two provinces producing coffee and sugar. Revenues poured in from abroad. Parisian café society financially supported its analog in Rio. As previously mentioned, Santos-Dumont's extensive aeronautical experiments found their funding from Brazilian coffee exports.

Roland Garros said Rio reminded him of the island of his birth, Réunion, with more than a little of his hometown, Saigon, thrown into the mix. The summer steamed hot and humid, warm water lay all around, tropical plants rioted in their fecundity, and the multi-race population tended to be outgoing and friendly. At first, the little Frenchman suffered from homesickness, his sad longing for home triggered by a place he had never seen before. Missing his estranged family on the other side of the globe exacerbated the malady. Even the spectacular town could not cheer him; that would come later.

Rio occupies one of the world's most beautiful places for a city. Rounded, jungle-clad mountains march down to the sea where sparkling, scimitar-shaped beaches await. The well-protected harbor and salt-water "lake" provide shelter for pleasure craft as well as commercial boats.

The city faces southeast, protected from the South Atlantic's rolling swells by a distant headland to the north. Corcovado Mountain at 2300 feet, 720 meters, towers over the city. Atop it a huge statue, 125 feet, 38 meters, tall of "Christ the Redeemer" with outstretched arms welcomes everyone. Sugar Loaf, a much smaller hill shaped like a lump of Brazil's lucrative export, guards the harbor entrance. The problem is that all this wonderful topography and all those pristine beaches leave little flat, buildable space for an actual city. Rio's light-colored buildings are scattered amongst the green hills like piles of pale, dead leaves in the narrow crannies between moss-covered boulders. Even today, Santos-Dumont airport occupies an island in the harbor, its runway pointed directly at Sugar Loaf.

Inhabitants of Rio were, and still are, called *"Cariocas."* Carioca means "white house" or "white man's house" in the regional American Indian dialect and indeed most local buildings are white. The Frenchmen there for airshows in 1912 discovered the Cariocas carefully cultivated an aura of good times and a laid-back attitude, a meme surviving in spades today. Fighting his homesickness, Roland Garros and his companions took full advantage of Rio's pleasures, splashing on the beaches, and journeying to the top of Corcovado. It is not recorded whether they hiked up or took the cog railway, but from on top, the spectacular view of the city impressed. Life was good in Rio and the more Cariocas they met, the better it got, particularly if those Cariocas were female and pretty. They undoubtedly encountered some of these comely lasses in a spectacular coffee shop in the central business district. *Confeitaria Colombo* was and is today a two-story restaurant, coffee shop, and bakery whose décor would have been familiar to denizens of Parisian café society.

At last, the aircraft arrived from New York; but when Hue and the Voisin mechanics unpacked the crates, they were shocked. Instead of a trio of new Blériots, laying there in pieces were one old, tired Blériot which had seen better days, a two-place model XI which had been hastily repaired after a major crash, and a Nieuport biplane with several important components missing. The Queen Aircraft Company was out of aircraft.

Roland's own record-setting Model XI remained enroute from France, arrival date unknown. Garros wanted to wait until a serviceable aircraft, namely his, showed up before flying but the promoter demanded some aviation take place and soon. The promoter paid considerable sums upfront and to date collected no revenues. Jules Hue and his team tried to make something airworthy. They assembled the old bird, patching as necessary. Conversion of the rickety two-place aircraft to a single-seat plane would increase its structural integrity and provide a reason not to give local dignitaries airplane rides. A crash with a VIP on board would generate adverse publicity. Bad for politics, but perhaps good for ticket sales.

On his first flight in Rio, Garros found the "experienced" Blériot more responsive and agile than he expected. He flew several circuits over the city showing the flag and building interest among the public in the coming aerial exhibition. This venture was not without danger; who knew how long the worn engine would last and there were few open places suitable for an emergency landing in the crowded city. Feeling the danger, Garros decided to fly outside of town over the personal residence of the President of Brazil, Marshal Hermes Rodriques da Fonseca. There he saw the President, who despite being a military man, was chosen in the first free election in Brazil's history. El Presidenté was holding some sort of social event on his mansion's spacious patio. Even from altitude, Garros could spot numerous colorful uniforms among the gathering, uniforms which demonstrated the Latin American propensity for gaudy military garb.

Seeing the sea of up-turned faces, most with impressive mustaches, Garros seized the moment. He banked the old Blériot into a spiral, rotating around the patio's center and descending lower and lower until the impromptu audience began to head for the exits fearing a crash amongst them. Just before impact, he straightened the wings, pulled out of the shallow dive, and tossed a handful of his business cards over the side which fluttered down on the presidential retreat like so many tiny white leaves. Garros waggled his wings in salute as he left the scene to return for landing at the race course/aerodrome. A prank to be sure, but one which would pay off in a few days.

Once Garros's Blériot arrived and was assembled, it was possible to complete the air show contract signed between the Queen Aircraft Company and the local promoter. After the last well-attended show, he completed a round trip flight between Rio and the city of Nitero, across Guanabara Bay. At the time,

Nitero was a separate city in a separate Brazilian state. Today, it is a well-to-do suburb of Rio connected by a 13-kilometer, 8-mile bridge. For a pilot who flew in pan-European air races, the hop over to Nitero and back must have been easy. Regardless, Garros pocketed the 80,000 French francs on offer.

Upon returning to his hotel, Garros was approached by two Brazilian army officers bearing one of his air-delivered business cards. They informed him they were assigned to study the feasibility and desirability of establishing an air arm for the Brazilian military. They needed Garros's help and advice. Roland was initially reluctant to get involved, even for monetary compensation, as he did not consider himself a mercenary. The proposed pay was good and without any immediate prospects for employment, he accepted. But not before asking the two staff officers why they had not contacted Santos-Dumont instead. After all, Santos-Dumont was a world-famous aviator, a pioneer of flight, and he was Brazilian. Their reply recounted the many years since Santos-Dumont visited Brazil. All his aviating occurred in Europe. He was hardly considered a native son anymore. This attitude turned around over the intervening years. Now, Santos-Dumont is a national hero in Brazil, no matter where he flew or how long he lived abroad.

Garros's duties for the military fell into three categories. There were flights over a nearby jungle-covered mountain range to determine the practicality of aerial scouting in that environment, a flight over an army base (and Marshal de Fonseca again), and an evaluation of thirty volunteers, all candidates for pilot training. In the newly repaired and once again two-place Blériot, Garros took each of the thirty up and let them handle the controls over the Bay to determine their aptitude for piloting. Following his report to the army, eight young men were selected and promptly sent off to France to train as pilots. Aerial scouting a jungle-covered mountain range proved to be possible but futile. Winds whipping through the passes prevented him from flying low enough to see beneath the canopy of trees. Flight over the President, now his paymaster, included neither aerobatics nor aerial advertising.

Roland Garros thoroughly enjoyed his stay in Rio and much to his surprise, his consulting work with the army. On his last flight there, he went aloft for his own pleasure to see the beautiful city from the air one last time. To document the view and to record his fond memories, he took along a camera. It was a bulky view camera using glass plates for film. Each shot required sliding out a delicate plate and re-inserting an un-exposed one into the device's back. It must have been a handful, flying the unstable aircraft while operating the heavy but fragile camera.

To show their appreciation for the cooperation and support shown by the Brazilian army toward the airshow pilots, the Queen Aircraft Company representative laid on a grand gourmet dinner. The menu featured classic French cuisine and the best French wines available in Rio. Invited were most of the army's senior generals and their wives. The evening could have gone better. Used to the more relaxed Brazilian civilian social schedule and not familiar with military protocol, the pilots arrived very late to find their guests well into the cocktail hour. Generals were resplendent in their fanciest formal uniforms, their spouses in elegant ball gowns. The airshow team showed up in smoking jackets instead of the expected formal dress, i.e. tuxedos. It was a major *faux pas*; late to a military function and underdressed to boot. The atmosphere relaxed a bit at the dining tables. It looked as if relations were improving. The evening concluded with a champagne toast by Willis McCormick, the lone American on the team.

In the upper reaches of Latin American society, particularly in military circles, after-dinner toasts were an art form and a long form at that. Guests were expected to wax poetic, at length. 5-10-minute speeches were common before glasses were gratefully emptied. McCormick rose, champagne flute in hand, and ended the *soirée* with, *"A Votre Santé,"* to your health. It was not a landmark in good Brazilian/French/American relations.

As Roland Garros surveyed the grumpy Brazilian generals, he could only have been impressed by their splendiferous uniforms. Acres of gold braid, fringed epaulets, dozens of medals (awarded for what?), gleaming boots, and elaborate fore-and-aft hats were everywhere. The popinjays around him illustrated the principle stating the less there is for an armed service to do, the more elaborate their uniforms

Armies in Latin America were more of a social network than a lethal force. Military men exercised political control, fought the occasional inconclusive border skirmish, put down and/or fomented rebellions, and dressed up for every occasion. These clotheshorses never fought real wars.

Of course, Latins claimed no corner on the gold braid market. Back in Europe, uniforms shown like the sun. with officers of European armed forces seemingly competing in splendor. Why? They did not fight real wars either. Europe had been essentially at peace for over two generations. But not for long. War was coming, everyone knew it, and no one knew what, or who, would touch it off. Germany, despite unheard-of prosperity, felt hemmed in by the old powers, denied its place in the rank of nations. France desired Alsace-Lorraine back. The Ottoman Empire was crumbling. The Austro-Hungarian Empire faced a succession problem. An old Emperor was competent and loved. His heir was not. Russian nobility partied on, oblivious to the communist rebellion fermenting beneath them. The matchbox was full, waiting on a spark.

An arms race broke out with the launching of HMS Dreadnought by the Royal Navy in 1906. This state-of-the-art battleship instantly rendered obsolete every capital ship in every other navy. Germany knew the Dreadnought class of ships would ensure Britannia would continue to rule the waves unless countered. Kaiser Wilhelm II ordered his shipyards into frantic action and a continent-wide naval arms race ensued. Between 1905 and 1910, the average military budget doubled across Europe and continued to rise in following years. While they polished their brass, shined their boots, and honed their ceremonial swords, Europe's military leaders were convinced the coming conflict would be short, decisive, and glorious and their side would win easily. This was not to be.

Oblivious to the war clouds gathering in Europe, Roland Garros and the team left Rio on a costal steamer, headed further south. He wrote later he left behind new friends and beautiful ladies, weeping.

CHAPTER TWENTY-ONE

BACK TO EUROPE

First Place in France

The final two stops on the Queen Aircraft Company tour proved to be slowly-paced with lots of spare time enabling the team to enjoy Latin American life and to recharge their notional batteries for re-entry into Europe. After a short costal steamer cruise and a landing at the port of Santos, Brazil; the team journeyed to Sao Paulo, Brazil, a quick ride inland by rail. Sao Paulo is in southeast Brazil, a short distance from the coast. It was then and it is now the largest city in Brazil and the largest Portuguese-speaking city in the world. There, after a test run, Jules Hue informed Garros his Blériot's motor had broken a vital part and destroyed itself, not to be repaired. Ordering a new engine from Rio, Garros cooled his heels in Sao Paulo for three weeks waiting on the new power-plant.

Once the new Le Rhône was installed, Garros collected another pot of easy prize money for the first flight between Santos and Sao Paulo. Money pools had been established by local newspapers in Rio and Sao Paulo in previous years when flying was in its infancy but the prizes were never claimed and were never updated to consider the rapid advances in aviation. This oversight did not prevent Roland Garros from pocketing the award after a flight of less than half an hour.

Crowds attending the airshows in Sao Paulo were large and enthusiastic, enough to make the trip financially worthwhile, but Garros chaffed to move on and return to Paris. Three plus weeks in chaotic Sao Paulo did not compare to 21 days in sedate, urbane Paris. Perhaps the three inactive weeks reminded him of what he was missing back in the City of Lights. Never mind, it was time to move on.

Buenos Aires, Argentina hosted the last exhibition flights on the tour. The Argentine capital was a different city entirely from the exuberant Brazilian metropolises. BA, as the locals called it, possessed pretentions to be one of the world's most sophisticated cities. The country's agriculture-based economy was booming, drawing migrants in from all over the world to take advantage of the opportunities for advancement. Italian workers and Spanish managers made up most of the newcomers adding to the city's multi-cultural mix. At the turn of the 20th century, BA boasted of having rudimentary skyscrapers, a metro system, elegant public buildings, and wide boulevards. Whereas Brazilians imitated France in their urban construction, the Argentines looked to London for inspiration although broad thoroughfares are nowhere to be found in the English capital except for Pall Mall. *Casa Rosado,* a magnificent, ornate building, the President's official residence, would not look out of place next to Buckingham Palace. Locals imitated the British in their social aspirations as well. Word among the chattering classes of Latin America held the Argentines, "Spoke Spanish, had Italian names, acted like the French, and wished they were English."

Instead of the usual horseracing track, the airshow team operated out of a venue built for Latin American rodeos, which offered much more open space for takeoffs and landings. However, advanced sales of tickets only trickled in. It seems the *uber*-sophisticated citizens of BA were *blasé* about aviation and picked up the English upper classes' studied indifference to things aeronautical. Garros took to the sky in his Blériot and overflew the city to drum up interest, including the obligatory flight over the Presidential Palace. Attendance picked up, but the pilots felt compelled to demonstrate risky aerobatics to give the crowd their money's worth and to sell more tickets for the next show.

At last, the tour was over, the bills paid, bags packed, and the aircraft crated for shipment back to France, loaded on the boat ready for departure. Garros was anxious to return to Paris, it was almost Spring there. Just before the ocean liner sailed, he stood dockside by the *Rio de la Plata,* the river flowing on the city's northeast shore. A frantic call, in French, stopped Garros's from boarding. Marcel Paillette, a French pilot resident in BA approached Garros with an offer to buy his personal Blériot. Garros was hesitant, he became attached to the airplane which set the world's altitude record and one he logged many hours in. With Charles Voisin's help in negotiating, Paillette made his fellow Frenchman an offer he could not turn down. Garros sealed the deal with a handshake and while grasping the younger man's hand, told him to take good care of the old girl.

The steamship liner pulled away from the quay, leaving the crated aircraft back on the dock. Garros watched from the rail as the city and his bird disappeared into the horizon. He headed home, but to what? He owned no aircraft, signed no contract to fly, and saw no clearly defined future.

Twenty-four long, miserable days at sea later, the ship reached Europe, assuming one considers London, England to be in Europe, which many English people would not. A newspaper headline from the era proclaimed, "Storms Lash Channel, Europe Isolated." A boat trip across that Channel and a four-hour train ride to Paris took Roland Garros home. He wrote in his memoir he was ecstatic to sleep in his own bed, in his own apartment, and to be able to look outside at dawn and see his favorite tree. Its leaves would once again announce with their movement or stillness whether the coming day would be fit for flying. All he needed was an airplane.

Charles Voisin, no stranger to living large, organized an elegant dinner to wrap up and to celebrate the South American tour. Voisin chose the Ritz hotel, then as now perhaps the most luxurious in Europe, if not the world. Finished in 1898, by 1912 the Ritz reached the pinnacle of prestige and prices. The dinner took place in the hotel's dining room, with a meal prepared by the kitchen of Chef Georges Escoffier, the father of French *haute cuisine*, known as *le roi des cuisiniers et le cuisinier des rois*, the King of chefs and the chef of kings. The food did not disappoint. During the tour, the American Willis McCormick had embarrassed Garros with his uninhibited antics and rough-around-the-edges manners. Few beachgoers in Rio plunged into the surf wearing a white silk business suit. To mend fences and to show that he, Willis McCormick, recognized the stabilizing, unifying role Garros played on the team, decided to surprise Roland with a gift. When Garros picked up his brocaded linen napkin to dine, under it he found an expensive Cartier watch presented with the team's thanks. In contrast to his *faux pas* of a toast in Rio, Willis waxed poetic, his eyes sparkling like the bubbles in his champagne flute. The wild American's address, not a mere *"A Votre Santé,"* expressed hope Roland would remember the Voisin team each time he looked at the watch, no matter if their paths never crossed again.

It had been a dizzying climb, literally and figuratively, in aviation for Roland Garros from selling automobiles and drinking at Cinzano's bar to being toasted in the Ritz's golden-domed dining room. Charles Voisin's chartered dinner at the magnificent edifice on *Place de la Concorde* was perhaps the first time the Ritz hosted famous, or infamous, aviators, but would not be the last. During World War II, the German Luftwaffe took over the entire building for use as its Parisian headquarters. Commandant Herman Goring spent many nights there, most of them in a morphine-induced haze after spending all day looting Parisian art collections owned by Jews. The Nazi air force was considerably less welcome in the gilded halls, the fine restaurant, and the Ritz's bars than the Voisin Flying Circus had been thirty years previously.

Roland Garros, eager to continue his aeronautical career but at a loss as to how, scanned French newspapers for the coming summer's aviation events. No major point-to-point races appeared scheduled but there was a new kind of race on the agenda. The *Circuit d'Anjou* would be run in June over two days around a triangular course for a total of 1100 kilometers, 700 miles. The course's turning points were to be three ancient cities in the Anjou region, Angers, Cholet, and Saumur located

300 kilometers, 190 miles, southwest of Paris. Racers would fly three circuits one day and four the next.

After the fiasco involving the Queen Aircraft Company when Garros and Jules Hue pieced together aircraft from junk parts until Roland's own Blériot arrived in Rio, Garros vowed never to fly in competition or exhibitions with an airplane he did not own. So, he ordered another Blériot from the factory. The bird arrived in time for a few test flights, but he got to know the bird well, flying it from Paris to Angers the day before the race, 15 June 1912.

Also arriving in Angers, much to Roland's surprise, was his father, whom he had not seen since years ago in Marseille. Garros senior was the epitome of congeniality, smiling, shaking everyone's hand, laughing, buying drinks. Georges Garros also informed his prodigal son that his ex-wife, Roland's mother, had re-married the previous week in Saigon. That this event was news to Roland is indicative of how estranged he had become from his scattered family. Georges' attempt to re-insert himself in his now-famous son's life gathered mixed reviews. The air race crowd accepted Georges, but Roland remained coolly distant.

Most French aircraft factories entered the *Circuit d'Anjou* race hoping to gain favorable publicity and to highlight their designs for French military personnel who were expected to monitor the long race. Pelterie, Bréguet, Deperdussin, and of course Blériot, were there. Touring the temporary hangers on the airfield at Avrille, the starting point, Garros quickly learned the disadvantages of being a privateer not on a factory team. Most sponsored pilots sported the newest 70 horsepower le Rhône engine while his race plane, despite being brand-new, mounted the earlier, 50 horsepower mill. Aircraft of the day were limited in their top speeds by aerodynamic drag, the extra 20 horsepower would probably produce at most a 5-10 knot, 3-6 mph, speed advantage, but that would be enough to outrun Garros in his Mark XI over the long course.

Sunday, 16 June 1912 dawned dark, windy, and rainy. Thunderstorms lurked in the area and a cold wind from the west warned of an approaching Atlantic storm. Dismayed by the lousy weather and not wanting to risk their aircraft, their pilots, and more importantly, their reputations, the factory teams' leaders refused to compete until conditions improved. They banded together trying to force the race organizers to delay the start and levied a fine of 20,000 francs on any factory team which defied the pact and flew.

Roland Garros realized this bad-tempered boycott opened the field to him and represented his only chance to defeat the better-funded and better-equipped factory teams. He and a few other private entries agreed to fly, no matter what the weather, despite intense pressure from the factory pilots to join the boycott. Five minutes after 9 o'clock Garros took off from Avrille and headed east for nearby Angers under a 300-meter, 1000-foot, overcast, with a freshening wind at his back.

Angers, Cholet, and Saumur are in relatively flat terrain where wandering streams meet the Loire River. The Romans fought over each town, as did the Gauls, the English, and the French. Consequently, each city is graced by distinctive castles of various provenance. In each town, a pylon marked the race's turning points. The level land, the obvious rivers, and the castles allowed easy navigation on the race's first lap. Garros could dodge the many rain squalls without worrying about hitting a hill or getting lost.

Dodge he did. The weather began the day badly and steadily deteriorated with driving rain, gusting wind, and biting cold. His Blériot, never easy to fly under the best conditions, seemed to fight him every second of flight. By the late 1930s, aircraft used the forces generated by the airflow over the control surfaces to move those surfaces. A pilot could tip the balance of forces acting on an aileron and the slipstream itself would deflect the aileron in the desired direction which would in turn bank the aircraft. Only enough strength to move the control stick a few inches, a few tens of pounds, was required. For example, at 400 miles an hour, 650 kph, the aerodynamic forces exerted on a Spitfire's wing and on its ailerons were enormous. Yet, the Spitfire was famous for "being light on the controls." A 19-year old Royal Air Force pilot, weighing maybe 130 pounds, 52 kilos, 9 stone 4, could easily control a Spitfire.

In 1912, this aerodynamic servo effect had yet to be invented. Pilots of Roland Garros's era were compelled to muscle the controls, constantly fighting the aero forces. In turbulence, the job got harder. A gust would dip a wing and the pilot would pick it up, warping the wing structure to do so. It must have felt like Garros was holding the Blériot up with his arms.

During the required three laps of the race course on Sunday, Garros fought the wind and the rain, still without a windscreen to deflect the slipstream. At 60 mph, 100 kph, raindrops hit his goggles like wet bullets. He wiped the rivulets off with his leather-gloved left hand. He dared not let go of the dancing wooden control stick in his right. Jules Hue's ground crew massaged Garros aching arms while refueling the aircraft and exchanged wet gloves for dry at the same time.

Monday was worse. The threatened cold front moved through the Anjou region, and while the rain relented a bit, the wind was stronger behind the moving front. Garros landed after completing four miserable laps just before five o'clock. Exhausted and soaked to the skin, he had to be lifted out of the cockpit by the loyal Jules Hue. Roland's spirits returned when the race ended at 6 pm. He won. His was a display of gritty determination more than an exhibition of raw speed.

Louis Blériot was ecstatic. A privateer beat the factory teams, who declined to even take to the air. Garros made the point to anyone who would listen, that his victory proved the Blériot XI's utility for military operations despite it 50-hp engine. He buttonholed spectators, assuming some were military evaluators *incognito*, pointing out that wars are not fought solely during good weather. No one at the time could predict how useful aircraft would be in an armed conflict, if all. But they certainly would not be handy if they could not fly in the rain. And rain it would during what became known as the

Great War. But, on Monday, 17 June 1912, war was still distant and Roland Garros won his first air race.

20,000 francs richer, Garros publicly offered to sell his race-winning Blériot to the French military but received no word that anyone in uniform would be interested. Interviewed by the press after the awards ceremony, he was told the "ink-stained wretches of the fourth estate" would no longer refer to him as "The Eternal Second," since he won the summer's most prestigious race and he also held the world altitude record. Asked about why he flew when the factory pilots would not, Garros gave a detailed reply revealing his state of mind and displayed an attitude recognizable by today's pilots.

He told the reporter that when you are a professional pilot, you are obliged to behave professionally. This means learning all you can about your aircraft, what it can and cannot do. One must know what the risks are, what are the limits of good judgment, how far you can push into bad weather. A professional pilot must know when to stop taking chances and stop for the day, he went on. Garros finished with the admission he realized each flight could be his last and this knowledge generated fear in his mind. Overcoming fear, mastering the risks involved, and performing under pressure are what separates a real pilot from a dilettante. This exact philosophy was articulated years later by legendary test pilot Chuck Yeager, and became known as "The Right Stuff." Either a pilot has the right stuff or he or she does not. The legendary 8th Fighter Wing's pilots during the Vietnam War called this approach to hazardous aviation, in their case air combat, as being "Masters of the calculated risk." Whatever it is, Roland Garros showed it in 1912.

CHAPTER TWENTY-TWO

THE SUMMER OF DISCONTENT

No Longer the Record Holder

Summer in 1912 passed quickly, too quickly for Roland Garros. Following his triumph at the *Circuit d'Anjou*, few enticing aeronautical adventures immediately presented themselves, at least none worth the valuable if vacant time of a leading aviator, the world altitude record holder, and a champion air racer. At Angers, after the awards ceremony, he again offered his race-winning Blériot to the French military, but no offers came in. Garros parked the bird in his hanger at Issy and waited for a response from the Ministry of War and waited and waited. All summer.

Bored with the lack of serious aerial competition and with Fall rapidly approaching, Garros and two pilot friends, Audemars and Barrier, along with the ever-present Charles Voisin, gave up on France and decided to participate in an exhibition held in Vienna, Austria. Naturally, this offered an excuse to order two new aircraft and Louis Brériot's factory obliged. One plane was identical to the used, unsold craft hangered at Issy, but the second mounted the newer 70 horsepower engine. In early September, the new planes were disassembled and loaded on a fast train to far eastern Austria. The air show team was again on the move.

Disembarking from their train in Vienna, the Frenchmen found themselves in a different but still very European world. If Paris boasted of being the epicenter of Western pop culture, fashion, entertainment, and engineering, and it did so boast, then Vienna had to be the leading city in classical music and deep intellectual thought. Led by composers such as Brahms and Strauss, the "Vienna School" of music turned out music still enjoyed today. Who has not heard the "Vienna Waltz?" On a more somber note, psychiatric treatment of mental illness, coupled with psychoanalysis as a pseudo-science, began in Vienna during the era, a movement led by Sigmund Freud.

The largest German-speaking city in the world, with more people than Berlin, Vienna harbored political exiles from all over central Europe, including a contingent from Russia. If Berlin was the brains of the Teutonic empire, in Vienna beat its heart and soul. Intellectual ferment and a tolerance for weird ideas flourished in the Austrian capital unlike in buttoned-down, Prussian-dominated Berlin. Socialism and other disturbing forms of political/economic organization were debated at great length in the city's famous coffee houses. At one time, Adolf Hitler, Leon Trotsky, "Marshal" Joseph Tito, Sigmund Freud, and Joseph Stalin lived within a mile of each other in Vienna and frequented the same coffee houses. It is not known if any of them ever met or if they did, what they discussed.

The Austro-Hungarian Empire's ornate capital looked the part, with Baroque public buildings, broad squares and parks, and elegant hotels. Roland Garros and his friends soon found themselves immersed in Viennese café society, a plunge led by *bon vivant* Charles Voisin. Later, Roland remembered fondly not any stimulating intellectual discussions in smoky coffee shops but rather the many restaurants and their hearty cuisine. Russian caviar, Hungarian Goulash, and Tyrolean roast goose topped the Viennese menus, all washed down with local white, not red, wine.

Daily newspapers of Vienna did not prominently feature the local air meet. The technical aspects of flying; horsepower, wing-warping, airspeeds, and altitude records, paled beside exploration of the human mind and the fierce debates about societal organization then underway in the city. Aviation activities at the exhibition consisted mainly of attempts to set altitude records, not only flying solo, but while carrying passengers. Much to Roland Garros's chagrin, Lieutenant Blashske of the Austrian army broke Garros's world record, despite lifting a passenger's weight. Clearly, this would not do.

Garros's Gallic pride would not permit another second placing. Before even leaving Vienna, Garros ordered yet another Blériot from the factory. The new craft would employ a Le Rhône engine churning out at least 80 horsepower, carried aloft by wings longer than any craft he had yet flown.

The city they left behind as the Frenchmen returned to Paris by train seemed quiet, perhaps too much so. The Emperor of Austria and King of Hungary, Franz Joseph, occupied the throne for 66 years, nearly all of them peaceful. Fitfully, the Empire kept a lid on regional tensions. But, in 1912, the strains were beginning to show. Around the Empire, trouble simmered, not yet on the boil. Russians stirred up trouble on the eastern border with their fellow Slavs. Ottoman Turks presented problems as they had for centuries. Multiple ethnic minorities chaffed under Austrian/Hungarian rule. The coffee houses of Vienna were hotbeds of political dissent.

Franz Joseph himself enjoyed popularity among his German-speaking subjects and commanded respect from his Hungarian citizens. Delivering over a half-century of peace and ever-increasing prosperity will do that for a king. The old ruler, 82 years old, still worked 12+ hour days, but in the government's upper reaches complacency slumbered at many desks. Austria-Hungary's army officers sported magnificent uniforms, showed wide mustaches, rode splendid horses, and danced at elaborate fancy balls. They did not fight wars. Alliance with Germany remained solid, but occasionally ordinary Austrians wondered if their militaristic Prussian cousins to their north would lead them into a conflict. Few in the Austria/Hungary orbit were prepared for that. Ironically, the Austrians, not the Germans, would toss a lighted match into the regional kindling.

Turmoil roiled under the placid surface in Balkan statelets. Daily turbulence between Orthodox Christians, Catholics, and Muslims generated rivulets of religious trouble. Serbs, Croats, and Albanians all hated each other. The mini-states in the area and their diverse peoples were too intermingled to be independent and too independent to get along with each other.

Years earlier, Otto von Bismarck, Chancellor of the newly-unified Germany, predicted when the inevitable European-wide conflict erupted, it would result from, "Some damn foolishness in the Balkans." His prophecy would prove to be accurate. In Vienna, magnificent orchestras played on. Colonels danced with their elegant ladies. Intellectuals, both actual and would-be, debated endlessly in coffee houses. The elderly Emperor worked tirelessly to keep the peace. He would fail, and soon.

Back in France, Garros regained his status as the world altitude holder with the new Blériot, but by only 60 meters, 200 feet. The bigger, more powerful engine and longer wings performed as expected, but both added weight to the aircraft. It was apparent to Garros that the Blériot XI reached the upper limits of both its development and altitude capability. Another plane would be needed if he were to continue to be competitive in the field of aviation record setting. However, Louis Blériot was profoundly uninterested in the expensive and risky process of developing a newer, higher performance aircraft. The business-oriented Frenchman focused on his bottom line, his flight school, and turning out evermore copies of the tried-and-true Mark XI.

Boredom eventually overtook Roland Garros, and he entered a routine air meet in the Alliers region, outside the town of Vichy. On 17 September 1912, Garros learned another French aviator, Georges Legagneux, beat his altitude record by all of 90 meters, 300 feet. Legagneux flew a Moraine-Saulnier. This constant swapping of the title of world altitude record-holder alarmed the grandees of the Aero Club of France. Pilots were regularly approaching 17,000 feet, 5500 meters, and striving for ever-more height. Doctors warned that the effects of these dizzying ascents, sustained flights at high altitude, and slow descents, on the human body were unknown, and potentially fatal. Aviators struggled to survive, to breathe, and to think clearly at heights above the highest peaks in the Alps. Who knew what would happen to men up that high? The Aero club announced there was no reason to fly any higher. Why go up there when the long-term physical changes could be catastrophic? The Aero Club's plea was ignored. In fewer than five years, combat pilots would be flying and fighting at over 21,000 feet, 6400 meters, without supplemental oxygen, *sans* heated cockpits, and with no better understanding of oxygen starvation, or hypoxia. The Great War provided a valid reason for flying over 17,000 feet; to kill other men who were also up there, waiting.

Lack of official support for height-achieved records did not faze Roland Garros, nor did it dampen his resolve to regain the title he considered his. It seemed to Garros the Morane-Saulnier aircraft possessed more potential performance than his Blériot XI. He set about teaming up with the new company.

Vichy is in the geographical center of France, south of Paris. During the Second World War, after the fast approaching first one, Vichy became notorious as the seat of the German-dominated Quisling French government. But in 1912, hot springs and a resort qualified as its claims to fame.

On the train back to Paris, Garros and Jules Hue discussed the transition to Morane-Saulnier; what was required, and how to approach the up-and-coming firm's owners. Later that night, Garros found in his apartment a telegram which to his shock announced the death of Charles Voisin. Driving his powerful Hispano-Suizza "Torpedo" automobile near Lyon in the Beaujolais region with "Baroness" La Roche by his side, Voisin passed a line of horse-drawn wagons and hit an oncoming Darracq automobile head on. Voisin died instantly. His lover, only recently fully recovered from injuries suffered in her crash at the Rheims air display two years prior, was seriously hurt. She would not fly again until after the Great War.

Garros immediately left for Neuville-sur-Saône to pay his last respects to his friend and sponsor. He later wrote that an aviator is used to death. But this time was different, Garros was unable to view Voisin's body. His grief overcame his wish to do the right thing for the family, to pay his respects. Charles Voisin was interred in the family cemetery in Neuville fewer than 10 km, 6 miles, from the scene of the wreck.

First John Moisant, then Charles Voisin. In 21 months, Roland Garros lost two close friends to violent deaths. You wonder if these two men, older and wiser in the ways of the world, served as substitute fathers for the young man from the colonies. Did they replace the biological father he never grew close to? His father's clumsy attempts to re-insert himself in Roland's life came to naught. The emotional gulf yawned too great. Moisant and Voisin introduced the younger Garros to a world of mature pleasures; fine dining, vintage wines, and beautiful ladies. Some of his female companions were sophisticated, some were of questionable virtue, and some displayed both traits. Garros senior's string-pulling from Saigon could not compete with an invitation to dine at the Ritz or a night on Bourbon Street in New Orleans.

Garros contacted the Moraine brothers, Léon, and Robert, along with their partner, Raymond Saulnier, and expressed an interest in flying one of their aircraft, perhaps to a new world altitude record. Their headquarters at the Villacoublay airfield southwest of Paris was more modern and better equipped than the older converted parade ground at Issy which the French army let deteriorate. To this day, the French Air Force flies out of Villacoublay. After a test flight, Garros offered to buy the machine on the spot and to join the Moraine-Saulnier team, leaving Louis Blériot. Garros signed a contract with the company as a test pilot and salesperson. When not trying to regain his altitude crown, he would be selling aircraft, reaping 500 francs for each bird sold.

Tired of the dreary Parisienne fall weather and again bored, Garros took his new aircraft south to warmer Marseille at the beginning of November. He would try to regain the altitude title, this time in a Moraine-Saulnier. The monoplane, while state-of-the-art, did not appear to be conceptually different from his old Blériot. It too employed a Le Rhône rotary engine, used wing warping for roll control, and mounted a tripod in front of the cockpit from which stretched wires holding the wing in place. Evidently, the similar design details came together well and the Moraine-Saulnier held the record.

However, Garros could only coax the new craft up to 4200 meters, 13,000 feet, before the severe cold became too much to bear, even over the south of France.

Garros wrote a friend that he could not see setting a record over *La Côté de Azur*, at least not in the winter. He left Marseille by sea on 20 November 1912 for Tunisia, across the Mediterranean, where he hoped to fulfill a secret plan for further aviation glory. More news was promised but for the time being Garros, now well-known in France, would travel to North Africa *incognito.*

CHAPTER TWENTY-THREE

TRIUMPH IN TUNISIA

Back on Top of the World

Roland Garros devised a plan to regain the world altitude record using a secret weapon – oxygen. Flying out of Marseille on a test hop, he secretly carried aloft a small metal canister of highly-compressed pure oxygen. Cracking open the bottle's valve at altitude, he sipped on a metal tube, inhaling the life-giving gas. In the highly competitive world of sport aviation, such a technical edge could not stay secret for long. Sport aviation was the only kind of aviation practiced at the time as no one had yet worked out a commercial use for airplanes, if he wanted to outwit the competition, he needed to keep his idea under deep cover.

Accompanied by Jules Hue and an assistant mechanic, he booked passage across the Mediterranean for Tunis, the capital of Tunisia, with his Morane-Saulnier monoplane disassembled and stored in the costal steamer's cargo hold. The ship's passenger manifest read, "M. Mandelson" not "Roland Garros" to avoid attracting public and competitor attention. Tunis would be much warmer being adjacent to the Sahara Desert's northern reaches. The French colony was not an aviation hotbed and was considered a backwater in the grand scheme of all things French. There, he could conduct his test flights and record attempts in relative secrecy, far from the prying eyes of other competing pilots.

Tunis is the northernmost major city in Africa and the African city closest to Europe. France colonized Tunisia in 1881, when the independent Arab country of Tunisia went bankrupt and could not feed or support its people. Paris encouraged French settlers to move across the Med and by 1910 over 35,000 French citizens called Tunisia their home.

Tunis is a city rich in history. Fifteen kilometers, nine miles, outside the capital lies the ruins of one of the ancient world's great cities, fabled Carthage. In the first millennium BCE, Carthage ruled most of North Africa and Southern Spain. It presented the only existential threat to the budding Roman Empire and to Rome itself. Rome and Carthage fought a series of long, drawn-out conflicts, the Punic Wars, over many decades. Hannibal of Carthage, one of history's legendary generals, crossed the Mediterranean to Carthage-controlled Spain with an army of foot soldiers, horse cavalry, and a troop of 38 war elephants. Hannibal, his army, and his elephants, crossed the Pyrénées Mountains into what is now southern France and trekked across snowy Alpine passes into northern Italy. He burnt wooden bridges behind him making a statement to both the Romans and to his own men about retreat. For fifteen years, Hannibal marched back and forth over large swatches of northern Italy. He never lost a battle, but could not win the war, not having enough men, or elephants, to overrun the city of Rome. The Romans fought a delaying war using scorched earth tactics and hit-and-run raids to slowly bleed Hannibal white. At last, he gave up, commandeered a fleet of boats, and took what was left of his army back across the wine-dark sea to Carthage. Rome eventually conquered Carthage in 165 BCE, razed the city, enslaved all the people, and legend has it (probably incorrectly), sowed the land with salt. For most of the next 1800 years following the sacking of Carthage, the Tunisian coast remained an afterthought in European affairs despite serving as the Roman Empire's breadbasket for nearly a millennium. Many commoners in Italy ate wheat grown across the Mediterranean by Roman colonists.

After arrival in Tunis, Garros introduced himself, using his real name, to the French Governor-General of Tunisia and revealed his plan to set a new aviation record. The fellow Frenchman saw in Garros a way to generate favorable publicity for the colony and for himself. He authorized free use of the local horseracing track and generously volunteered to pick up all expenses incurred during the attempt.

Before leaving Marseille, Garros inquired by telegraph as to the availability of an oxygen supply in Tunis, not wanting to be seen loading bottles of O2 on board the steamship along with his airplane. Watching eyes would have suspected the thrust of his plan. But when Jules Hue tried to buy oxygen, all he found was liquid oxygen, not the compressed gas needed for high-altitude flight. It is not known what liquid oxygen was used for in Tunis in 1912. Discouraged, the team had only one small bottle, maybe enough for one record attempt, maybe not.

On his initial test flight from the Tunis Hippodrome, Roland Garros climbed to 5000 meters, 15,500 feet, without using his precious supplemental oxygen. At this altitude, one-half of the Earth's atmosphere is beneath an aircraft. Gasping in the thin air, he became light-headed and almost passed out. A quick descent cleared his brain. The experience convinced him of the need for help in breathing. With only one oxygen bottle, he would have to make it count.

On 11 December 1912, he went for the record. Intermittently inhaling the bottle's last wisps of gas, he climbed to 5600 meters, a little over 17,000 feet before he descending to lower, denser atmosphere. He told the small crowd gathered to witness the record attempt he could have reached 6000 meters, 18,600 feet, had he more oxygen. Still, the record would be his again once the sealed barograph was removed from the aircraft and returned to France for the Aero Club of France's validation.

The French people of Tunis felt Garros put them on the modern map with his now well-publicized aerial feat. The Governor-General was pleased as well, basking in the reflected glow of success. However, this outpouring of Gallic pride awakened a long-simmering rivalry in European/Tunisian society. Three times as many Europeans of Italian extraction lived in Tunisia as folks speaking French. The government in Rome and the

Italians of Tunis long felt Tunisia should have been an Italian colony, not a French possession. They harked back to 165 BCE when the Roman army overran nearby Carthage. For over 800 years, what later became known as Tunisia was a Roman and hence an Italian city. The Italian community of Tunis wanted to re-live past days of Roman glory and the Frenchman, Roland Garros, would give them the opportunity.

Garros proposed a flight, the first flight from North Africa to Europe. The headland north of Tunis is but 150 kilometers, 90 miles from the Italian island of Sicily. With careful fuel management a Morane-Saulnier might fly from Tunis to Rome in three stages. Such a flight would symbolically re-establish the long-lost link between Tunis/Carthage and Imperial Rome. To his credit, the French Governor-General agreed to support the ex-pat Italian plan, and set about making arrangements through official channels. The Italian Consul in Tunis turned-to and obtained the Italian Navy's logistic support. The hastily-devised plan came together quickly on the political/military front. Now, all that was needed was an aircraft able to fly the distance.

Ninety miles, 150 kilometers, represented the Morane-Saulnier's extreme range when driven by the big motor, leaving no room for errors of navigation or headwinds. So, Jules Hue replaced the 80-horsepower mill with a spare 50 horse unit. Changing a rotary engine did not take long; unbolt a few mounting brackets, disconnect the cockpit controls, remove the air intake, reverse the process, and the job is done. Swapping out the Merlin V-12 in a WWII Spitfire took days, but in 1912 the task required a few simple wrenches, an hour or so, and a strong back. The spare engine saved some weight and offered greater fuel economy. Speed and maximum altitude were not part of the equation; Garros would be flying slowly at sea level. The more fuel-efficient engine afforded some extra margin of flight time if things went wrong during the crossing.

In case things went terribly wrong, Hue installed some additional emergency equipment. Behind the pilot's seat, he stored a pneumatic life raft and a signaling light. In the open space inside the rear fuselage, he mounted a float buoy with a long bamboo pole attached. At the pole's end was a red flag. If Garros went down at sea, he could remain afloat and signal for help. It is doubtful the little pilot wore any personal floatation devices. Pioneering American aviators ventured over open water with two partially inflated bicycle inner tubes crisscrossed over their chests like bandoleers. These improvised life preservers would keep even an unconscious aviator's head above water but looked silly in photographs. Fashion plate Roland Garros would have never permitted pictures of him wearing crossed bike tubes.

Finally, someone invented the cockpit seat belt and Hue bolted buckled leather straps to the pilot's wooden seat. Conventional wisdom at the time held that during a crash on land, it was best to be thrown clear of the plane's wreckage, hopefully before fire broke out. Water landings reversed this logic, fire being unlikely. Pilots hoped ditching at sea would allow the aircraft to crumple around them and float a few seconds before sinking; time enough to un-belt and swim away with the survival gear.

Showing no signs of jealousy of the Italian-sponsored event and wishing to support French aviation, the French Navy volunteered the services of a squadron of motor torpedo boats. A boat would be stationed every 16 kilometers, 10 miles, along the route of flight from Tunis to Sicily. In case of a ditching at sea, not unlikely given the reliability, or lack thereof, of the era's engines, rescue would be nearby. Also, the boats would provide navigational checkpoints, useful if the weather turned misty, as was often the case in winter over the sea.

With the best wishes of the Governor-General, the Italian Consul, and the local Muslim leader, the Bey of Tunis, Roland Garros launched at 0800, 18 December 1912, destination Sicily and Europe. He overflew Carthage to emphasize the political linkage between the ancient city and Rome. Then, the tiny monoplane was lost to sight, headed due northeast out to sea. The flight went smoothly, proceeding from one torpedo boat to the next. Entering Italian territorial waters, the Italian Navy took up escort duty and guided him until he neared the coast.

Low on fuel, he could not reach the planned stop at Trapani. Garros landed in a farmer's field as soon as he crossed the coastline. While a farm hand went to fetch gasoline, the farmer and his wife invited Garros in for lunch. Rural hospitality demanded no less. Following a long lunch with local wine, a small crowd watched and waved as Garros took off. Before engine start, the farmer, thrilled to be part of history, vowed to name his wine cellar after the famous French aviator and lunch guest, Roland Garros. Such were the trials and tribulations of flight at the dawn of aviation.

Garros flew west to Trapani, a fishing village on Sicily's far western tip, on the promontory pointing toward distant Spain. Surrounding a crescent-shaped harbor, Trapani would be the first stop for one night on the route to the Eternal City. From the air, the narrow beach looked like gray sand. It was not. Beaches on the Mediterranean's north shore tend to consist entirely of round stones, not sand, and are rocky. Volcanic Sicily's are the worst. Perhaps used to the wide expanses of flat, level sand on France's Atlantic coast or the equally ideal beaches of North Africa, perhaps due to too much wine at lunch, Garros set the Morane-Saulnier down heavily on a shelf of rocks in front of the local promenade. Wheels bent, their mounts shattered, and a few fuselage structural longerons cracked. Deposited in Trapani later by a French torpedo boat, Jules Hue examined the damage and informed Garros repairs would take at least 48 hours. Morane-Saulnier parts were hard to come by in the fishing village. Replacements would be fabricated from scratch.

Roland Garros was furious, mad at himself for cracking up his new aircraft, angry for spoiling what was turning out to be a perfect flight on a wonderful day. He was frustrated at the delay. Things seemed to be going his way again before the hard landing. He was back on top of the world, literally, with a new altitude record he believed was his to lose. In addition, he felt an urgent need to return to his beloved Paris in time to celebrate Christmas with his friends. But local dignitaries and the press wanted to meet him, to interview the pilot who just flew over from Tunisia. He was having none of it, locking himself in his hotel room until the unwanted attention subsided. Garros later that night boarded a train alone to Salerno and checked into a sea-side hotel under his assumed name to wait out the repairs to his crippled bird.

On 22 December, he took his newly-fixed aircraft airborne from the tree-lined road running in front of the Trapani hotel and headed due east toward the Italian mainland. Sicily is triangle-shaped and he flew along the long north side. Off to his right loomed the largest volcano in Europe, Mt Etna at 3330 meters, 10,925 feet, always active, always erupting, always beautiful, ever the symbol of Sicily. He crossed the narrow Straights of Messina, 3 km, 2 miles, wide before lunch and turned left, north, up the Italian coast. Garros stopped at Santa-Eufemia in Calabria, the Italian boot's toe, for fuel and a snack, then departed for Rome. He passed Mount Vesuvius, Europe's second largest volcano, near Pompei. The French pilot was the first human to view both from the air on the same day.

About 1445, 2;45, he touched down in Rome at *La Place d'Armes.* A jury-rigged wheel collapsed, pitching the plane forward on a wing tip and burying the propeller in the parade ground's dirt. The scene, viewed by thousands of Romans, presented an embarrassing end to an epic flight; 1148 kilometers, 700 miles, in 13 ½ total hours. While Hue and his assistant disassembled the crunched airplane, Garros enjoyed the hospitality of Rome's Mayor. A city tour preceded a lavish banquet, where he was given a gold medal awarded by the Aero Club of Italy. He returned the honor by giving the Club his damaged propeller as a trophy once it was cleaned and polished by Jules Hue. Garros noted years later he suffered from bad morale during the evening festivities in Rome. He wanted the flight to be uneventful, routine, conducted by a pro, instead of displaying two minor crashes for all the world to see. Italians for their part urged the Frenchman to forget the prangs. He had made it, and he should not worry about the details or the esthetics of hard landings, they told him. After a night of revelry and speeches, Garros and his ground crew hopped on the fastest train available; destination: Paris; objective: Christmas and New Year's Eve parties.

CHAPTER TWENTY-FOUR

A NEW PLAN

A New Love

Winter in 1913 gave Roland Garros time to think, to plan his next aviation quest, to enjoy the fame he earned by out-living some of his rivals, and to fall in love. His altitude record set in Tunis, was broken in March by an instructor pilot at the Blériot flying school outside Pau, France. "Pépé" Perreyon climbed to 5880 meters, over 18,000 feet, in a Model XI. Record books are silent if Pépé used bottled oxygen but you can assume he did. Nothing stayed secret very long in civil aviation. Evidently there was more performance to be wrung out of the old Model XI than Garros realized. That, or Louis Blériot reserved his best birds for his full-time employees and record attempts. Each aircraft, constructed by hand, differed slightly from the one produced before it and after. Tweaks for more performance were easily incorporated in production. No matter, Garros enjoyed his relationship with the Morane-Saulnier company and its supportive founders. His new aircraft felt familiar. Its handling characteristics were very similar to his old Blériot; marginally unstable in pitch, sluggish in roll, and hard to coordinate in yaw with the rudder. He did not know it at the time, could not have anticipated what was to unfold, but a similar Morane-Saulnier monoplane would carry Roland Garros into history books in less than two years.

Garros planned to enter those books earlier, in 1913, and stay there. He saw the scramble for altitude records to be a never-ending contest. Pilots claimed and quickly lost the title by scant hundreds of meters, trading the record back and forth. He hunted bigger game, a "first" which could never be surpassed. Garros devised a plan in his mind but needed to iron out the details and to develop enough trust with the

Morane-Saulnier company for the directors to approve and fund his efforts.

Spring, the middle of April, found Garros once again in the sunny South of France and once again air racing, but in a new type of contest and a new type of airplane. An air race was to be run from Saint-Raphaël, France on the Mediterranean east along the rugged coast to the Principality of Monaco. Only float planes would enter, takeoffs and landings would be on the sea.

In the early years of aviation, float planes gathered more attention than they do now. Adding canoe-shaped enclosed floats to a land plane gave it sea legs, literally. For a float plane, every substantial body of water became an airfield, no need to commandeer the local horse-racing track, to use a farmer's field, or to re-purpose an army parade ground as an aerodrome. Takeoffs could be virtually unlimited in length, a desirable feature for the under-powered craft of the day. If the lake or bay were large enough, landings and takeoffs could be directly into the wind with no tricky cross-winds to complicate things. For over-water flights the advantage of floats was obvious; emergency landings lost much of their danger. Float planes combined the attributes of watercraft and aircraft with obvious advantages. But, instead of results being greater than the sum of disparate parts, the finished devices ended up being worse airplanes and terrible boats.

Floats added weight and lots of it particularly when they leaked and took on water. Aerodynamic drag generated by floats cost airspeed and wasted fuel. On the water, the wind blew the aircraft around; even a light breeze could pivot and push a machine designed to use the wind, one bred to follow the airflow. Modern float planes have small rudders mounted on the floats' trailing edge for easier water handling. But in 1912, all the pilot could employ was the aircraft's own rudder, which was ineffective with the engine off and no prop blast to act on. Rough water prevented air operations, float planes needed calm seas. High waves tended to bang the delicate stick and wire airframes against solid, unforgiving docks. Float planes were a handful of trouble. However, like land planes, where there were float planes, there were float plane races. WWII's legendary Spitfire fighter began life as a float plane racer in the mid-1930s while float plane races were still popular.

Garros did well in his first float plane race, setting down in third place on Monaco's sheltered harbor. Overall, not a bad result for an aircraft not initially designed for water operations, flown by a pilot unskilled in aquatic takeoffs and landings.

After the race, Roland dined in Monaco with the second-place winner, Gabriel Espanet, friend from the aviation community. The two pilots met for dinner in an independent mini-state with its own ruling prince. Surrounded by the hills of France on three sides and the sea on the fourth, Monaco is a fairy tale kingdom. Then, as now, it served as a refuge and playground for the very wealthy. Money flowed through Monaco in route to other destinations, but substantial sums stayed. Local banks were stuffed with it, facilitated by use of the French franc as Monaco's currency.

Conversation over dinner between the two aviators, probably at l'Hôtel de Paris Monte-Carlo, turned from aviation to another common interest – automobiles. Garros voiced frustration with his once-trusty Grégoire sports car. It frequently broke down and not even the mechanical wizardry of Jules Hue could keep it on the road for long. Espanet replied, telling Roland he needed a newer, more modern motorcar and he, Gabriel, could arrange one. In the moneyed enclave of Monaco, the *nouveau riche* drove Bugattis. Espanet maintained solid contacts at the Bugatti factory, even knew Ettore Bugatti himself, and he volunteered to make the required introduction.

Italian-born Ettore Bugatti was a skilled engineer with an artist's eye for esthetics, two attributes not commonly found together. His automobiles resembled rolling works of art, not baroque ornamental art, but clean art deco designs long before art deco became a thing. He once pronounced, "If you have an opportunity to make something and to make it beautiful and you don't, what does that say about you?" Bugatti's design shop and factory hand-crafted his cars in Molsheim, a city in the Alsace region of France, now under Germany's rule. He spared no expense in designing and manufacturing his vehicles. Engines, chassis, bodywork, interiors, all were the very best which could be conceived and built. All the intricate pieces fit together like a watch from neighboring Switzerland, except for the brakes. Bugatti brakes were notoriously weak and not up to the task of efficiently halting his fast cars. Ettore Bugatti did not care, or perhaps he did, thinking of his cars' wimpy brakes as a branding technique. Another quote, "I build my cars to go, not stop."

Owning a Bugatti required a formal process. Prospective buyers did not casually waltz into a Bugatti showroom – there were none – plunk down a wad of filthy lucre and demand a car. That just was not done. A hopeful Bugatti owner must be properly introduced, vetted, and interviewed, often by Ettore himself. If *Le Patron* liked you, he would give his consent to commission a car. You would be notified when your vehicle was completed. Today, surviving Bugattis change hands, which they seldom do, for millions of dollars as collectors' items, works of mechanical artistry from *La Belle Époque*.

Summer passed quickly, not with intense aerial competitions but with lazy, peacetime exhibitions. In Paris, Garros flew in a mass gaggle of 68 aircraft staged by the President of France for King Alphonse XIII of Spain. Roland remarked that the roar of 68 un-muffled aircraft engines was something to hear. The clatter, unmatched in intensity at the time, was a precursor, the rolling thunder often heard before the storm. It would not be long until such aerial armadas were common, their aircrews airborne not to amuse, but to kill.

The day after the mass flyby, Roland put on a solo demonstration of what passed for aerobatics in 1913 for the Spanish King, after being warned by the French security service not to fly too low over His Majesty. Alphonse XIII recognized the name "Roland Garros" from participation in the ill-fated Paris-Madrid air race and complemented the young Frenchman in person on his prowess. On the Saturday ending the King's visit, the Aero Club of France, quite unexpectedly, awarded Garros a prize of 10,000 francs for excellence in aviation. It is not out of the question that a royal hand was in play. 10,000 francs would just about pay for a Bugatti if one did not specify custom coach work.

Garros flew in exhibitions in Vienna and Commercy, France, then traveled to Milan, Italy and agreed with the Aero Club there to help organize and participate in another float plane race. Racers would touch down on northern Italy's picturesque alpine lakes. It seems that once a colonial kid from Réunion and Saigon became accepted into the elite circles of France and Italy, doors opened for Roland Garros, doors he scarcely knew existed. The relatively relaxed summer also included an unexpected thunderbolt, or rather, a dart from Cupid.

Her name was Marcelle Gorge and she was stunning, with a flowing mane of honey-blond hair, a coquettish manner, and a mega-watt smile. Upon meeting her in Paris in May, Garros was smitten on sight. Not much is known about Marcelle other than her good looks. A woman of proper breeding would not have left a paper trail in the popular French publications of the times. Few well-bred women sported a visible public profile, nor did they desire one. It was a man's world. The few *femmes* who achieved fame tended to be entertainers who sacrificed their precious reputations for notoriety and money. That Mademoiselle Gorge was both beautiful and discreet speaks of her elevated social class. A love affair with a famous and daring pilot which did not make the newspapers speaks volumes about where she fit into society. Not for the last time would a comely lass be attracted to a gallant knight of the air. Garros's friends soon accepted Marcelle and she joined their social circle.

At last, Garros received an invitation to visit Molsheim, to be interviewed by *Monsieur* Bugatti. The usual process involved a train trip east to Alsace, but Garros preferred to make a statement on several levels, political and personal. He flew there in his private airplane. Nominally part of Germany for the time being, entrance into Alsace/Lorraine required showing a passport to the guards at the border. Flying into the region, as into Germany proper, involved obtaining prior permission from the authorities in Berlin. Garros did none of that, brazenly flying from Paris, crossing high above the frontier, and landing beside the Bugatti works. No Germans were consulted. From this, it is easy to discern Roland Garros's opinion of the political situation. Also, how better to display his credentials for owning a Bugatti and representing the brand than by a dramatic arrival from the sky?

Two days in Molsheim convinced the transplanted Italian automobile baron that Garros fit the Bugatti image, an important consideration for a luxury brand. While there, Garros took several factory supervisors up for short hops to see their workshops from the air, undoubtedly the first airplane ride for the craftsmen. His car was forecast to be ready by mid-September and the factory workers, impressed by their flights, vowed to make it a good one.

All summer, Garros traveled out to the Deauville aerodrome with Marcelle, consulting with the mechanics, making calculations, studying what was possible, and organizing the construction of two new, identical aircraft. Each was modified to mount tanks capable of holding 200 liters, 53 gallons, of gasoline, and 60 liters, 16 gallons, of lubricating castor oil. No aircraft to date carried so much fuel. Provisions for only one seat, the pilot's, were included. His covert plan obviously involved long-range flight, solo. Increasing the range of an underpowered, slow aircraft is not a matter of loading on as much fuel as can be lifted airborne. There is a point of diminishing returns. Lugging aloft too much fuel slows the aircraft down, reducing range. The over-burdened craft is spending fuel to transport fuel. The right amount to take on board should be just enough to achieve maximum range and no more. But what was Garros's objective? He seems to have shared it with Marcelle, which caused her to worry, but not so much as to discourage him from his dream.

And what a dream it was. Garros confided to a local journalist that he lay awake at night thinking on his plan, starring at the ceiling, and seeing his distant destination. This probably accounts for his confiding in Marcelle; she would have wondered why he was still awake yet oblivious to her charms. Thrilled to be in on the secret, the reporter agreed to keep the secret in exchange for exclusive access later. He also reminded Roland Garros the last man who attempted to fly across the Mediterranean disappeared, never to be seen again.

CHAPTER TWENTY-FIVE

SOUTH TO AFRICA

CONTINENT TO CONTINENT, BY AIR

Ronald Garros needed to be discrete, even secretive about his plan to stage the first successful flight spanning the Mediterranean Sea. Before television or even radio broadcasts, most French people consumed news via numerous daily newspapers, bought on the street one issue at a time. Papers competed in a battle for financial survival. Exclusive, exciting stories sold papers and public interest in aviation ran high. Higher still ran the curiosity in the exciting young men of the flying machines, who they were seen with, where they ate, what they said, and most importantly, what feat of aerial derring-do they planned next. When he flew as an unknown, under the press radar (although radar lay 30 years in the future), Garros operated without attracting unwanted attention. Now, he enjoyed fame as a well-known "knight of the sky." News hounds followed his every move hoping to scoop competitors.

Construction of new, long-range aircraft could be concealed, few journalists could identify a gasoline tank, much less an outsized one. Test flights at the Bac airfield went well, with Marcelle Gorge watching. There is no record of Garros ever taking off with the enlarged fuel and oil tanks full. Why practice a hazardous maneuver you must get right the first time? He knew of no criteria for choosing one aircraft of the two he had constructed over the other, both performed as expected; both engines hummed. Jules Hue, tasked with the final selection, knew both birds like the backs of his callused, greasy hands.

Official and military support presented more difficult liaison challenges. Garros avoided alerting the close-knit aviation community to his plan. Once the secret escaped through formal channels, others might beat him to his goal, or worse, die trying. He needed a secure departure point, on route navigation assistance, and possible rescue from the French Navy. Monitoring by the Aero Club was required to certify his hoped-for success. Not the least of his worries concerned weather, particularly prevailing winds. Flying an aircraft at 100 kph, 60 mph, and encountering a 31 kph, 20 mph, head or tail wind could reduce or extend maximum range by a third. Traversing the Med non-stop would be a close-run thing, fuel-wise. An unexpected wind on his nose could prove disastrous, probably fatal.

To keep his intent secure and to not alert the authorities prematurely, he elected to not consult government meteorologists, but rather looked up a bird migration expert. Birds, like light aircraft, are strongly affected by winds. Ornithologists counseled that Alsace's pale storks migrated across the Med from France to North Africa beginning in late September into October, riding a wind from the north, the famous Mistral. Garros's squadron in the coming Great War gained their nickname "The Storks" when ground observers likened the loose, flowing formations of white aircraft to a migration of Alsatian storks. But that was two years in the future. For now, Roland Garros would follow those same storks across the ocean.

Eventual contacts with the Navy went well; the admirals were happy to support highly-publicized French exploits. After all, they provided sea-borne escorts for his flight from Tunis to Sicily. The Aero Club, when finally contacted, proved equally cooperative, promising to send officials to the departure aerodrome. Garros elected not to inform the authorities in Tunisia having little confidence in the citizens there to keep a secret. When and if he touched down, he could notify them in person.

In late September, Jules Hue and his assistant disassembled the chosen airplane, traveled by rail to the naval base at Saint-Raphaël-Fréjus on the southern coast, re-assembled the bird, tested, and tuned the Le Rhône engine, and waited. Marcelle and Roland stayed in Paris to avoid alerting the prying reporters, who sensed something was afoot. Besides, his new Bugatti auto arrived from the factory and he had to try it out before leaving for the South. The motorcar was superb, all he hoped for. Ettore Bugatti and his team delivered a jewel of a car.

Roland was cautious about enquiring as to aviation weather over the Mediterranean; that would have been a clear tip-off. The meteorological folks could not be trusted to keep such questions to themselves when reporters were known to exchange money for inside information. Instead, Garros fell back on a time-tested weather forecaster. Each morning before first light, his lover watched him stand at his apartment window in the dark, staring at the barely visible leaves on the tree outside. On Monday, 20 September, the leaves rustled, disturbed by a north wind. The Mistral seemed to have arrived. The couple left later that day on a sleeper-car train for Fréjus, arriving shortly after noon. Two naval officers met them at the station.

Too late to depart, which would mean an arrival in Tunis after dark, Garros informed Jules Hue to prepare for a dawn takeoff and to dispatch his assistant to Sicily in case of an emergency landing there. The Navy issued orders to a torpedo boat squadron to put to sea. Roland and Marcelle booked a room in the Grand Palace hotel on the waterfront and enjoyed the most elegant, read expensive, dinner available, thinking, but not saying, it might be their last together.

Up before the sun, Garros and Marcelle arrived at the Fréjus naval base to find a crowd of Marines, local dignitaries, and Aero Club officials waiting beside the plane along with Jules Hue. The mechanic spent a sleepless night checking and rechecking the aircraft. Fair weather was forecast, but absent was the hoped-for north wind. Instead of immediately mounting up and cranking the engine, the aviator shook hands with each member of the *bon voyage* party. He kissed Marcelle a quick good-bye – she forced a smile of encouragement as if this was just another test flight back in Paris. Later, Garros wrote, despite his outward show of bravado, his stomach churned with concern, an understandable reaction from a young pilot who cheated death numerous times in the past and would again in the future, assuming he had one.

He saved his last and firmest handshake for Jules Hue, their eyes locking for long seconds with no words exchanged. Handing Hue a packet of telegrams, one to every prominent Parisian newspaper, he requested they be sent immediately after takeoff. The message, identical to each publication, announced his cross-Mediterranean flight and added his rationale for the attempt.

Garros's telegrams spoke of the future in elegant terminology using precise French. If aviation was to advance beyond its sporting phase, to progress from putting on displays of daring and death in front of (sometimes) paying customers, aerial art/science would have to prove useful in economic and human terms, he wrote. Communication and travel between far-flung communities would be key to aviation's destiny. He intended to prove travel between continents was feasible and to move the goal posts some ways toward that end. If he failed, attempts and progress must go on until successful. The messages sounded a stirring and unexpected clarion call from a young man best known to date for his Parisian playboy lifestyle, air races, and altitude records. The former car salesperson had grown up quickly. Later in the day, after publication of Garros's messages, it is not out of the question that the idealistic visionary Santos-Dumont read the newspapers and smiled.

Garros adjusted his flight gear, including spare goggles and a bulky fur coat, mounted to the cockpit, although the pilot's station was not called a "cockpit" at the time. That terminology would be applied later during the Great War. He nodded to Hue – crank the Le Rhône. Already warmed up, the engine caught on the propeller's first swing, roaring to life, blowing oil smoke over the crowd. The little Frenchman took a deep breath of cold, pre-dawn air and scanned the crowd for his lover. He spotted her easily, the sole woman in attendance, her lioness hair flowing in a "Gibson Girl" style. He looked forward, pointed straight ahead with his left arm, nodded, the Marines straining to hold back 80 horses released the shaking airplane.

The Morane-Saulnier monoplane laboriously gathered speed, held down by the equivalent weight of three passengers in extra fuel and oil. At last, a final bounce launched the laboring craft into the wet sea air. He was airborne, destination Africa. Garros turned over the ocean in a gentle bank, cleared the white surf line, and struggled for altitude. He kept the city lights of Fréjus on his tail. Higher up, enough pre-dawn light shown to allow him to read his hand-held compass. It read 180 degrees, due south. He turned 30 degrees left, to the southeast and the island of Corsica, birthplace of Napoleon. His destination was indeed due south, but there was nothing between him and a landfall but open ocean. Electing to divert eastward allowed Garros to hug the island coastlines in case of trouble.

After an hour and a half of cold, damp flying, he spotted the rising sun's rays over Corsica's central mountains. By this time, the adrenaline attendant to the public departure and heavy-weight takeoff had worn off. He was freezing and sleepy. Deep in the previous night at the Grand Palace, Marcelle bid him fare-thee-well with more than a forced, thin-lipped smile. Despite the resultant drowsiness, he felt no regrets, only sexy memories, perhaps his last of her.

A violent impact shook the light plane interrupting his revelry. A small piece of the whirling engine separated, exiting out the circular cowling, leaving a small, jagged hole in the thin metal. Soon freezing icicles of oil trickled out, driven by the propwash back to the cockpit. The Le Rhône vibrated, with a subtle shaking which neither improved nor worsened with time. He recognized the loss of one cylinder, a malfunction not unknown. The young pilot did not take this as a helpful omen.

To make matters worse, he was now only abeam Sardinia, a much larger island than Corsica, due south of Napoleon's home, and thoroughly Italian, not French. Comparing his actual position with his map, he realized his ground speed was slower by 25 kph, 15 mph, than planned, un-aided by north wind erroneously forecast by his favorite tree in Paris. Any margin of range he enjoyed for reaching Tunis just evaporated. Garros continued, past Sardinia, with Sicily far to the east.

A major decision loomed, a go-no-go point. He could land again in Cagliari, where his mechanic waited, for repairs and more fuel or he might press on across the wide Mediterranean with no place for an emergency landing. However, Sicily in the east was almost as far away as Tunis and equally risky to reach over open water. A diversion there to stay over land, would require a stop for fuel. With a sick motor and no fuel reserve, it would be difficult to reach Africa, maybe too difficult. He had already flown from Tunis north to the Sicilian island's western city. Doing the trip in the opposite direction would prove nothing, only a continental mainland-to-mainland flight counted as a true first. His telegrams to the papers blew the flight's secrecy. Now, every competent, and some not-so-competent, aviator in France could try to steal his thunder were he to abandon his current attempt. Roland Garros rolled the dice and pressed on, slowly climbing to 2500 meters, 5000 feet, to save fuel in the thinner air, ignoring the resulting increase in life-sapping cold.

Sicily shrank on the horizon behind him until only its volcanos' snow-covered peaks remained visible, then they too disappeared, sinking into the sea. Roland Garros flew on alone. For 360 degrees around, nothing was visible but an endless ocean, a hazy blue sky, and some scattered puffy clouds.

Consulting his hand-held compass, he seemed to be on course, but who knew where the needle was leading, or misleading, him. Given to him before the flight by his friend Edmund Audemars, it was a newer version than the compass left to him by John Moisant. Older models operated in air, the magnetic needle pivoted inside an empty, round case. Recently invented state-of-the-art compasses were filled with a clear liquid, usually wood alcohol. Slightly viscous, the fluid dampened the tiny needle's more extreme perturbations brought on by vibration, turbulence, turns, and dives. But nothing prevented distortion in the earth's magnetic field, a warp generated by the whirling mass of iron just in front of the cockpit and by its leaky spark ignition system. This was a physics problem that would not be quickly solved. In the early 1930's, famed writer/pilot Count Antione de Saint-Exupéry became lost over the Sahara Desert when his compass fluctuated by plus and minus 20 degrees. Saint-Ex wrote a best-selling book detailing the flight. But commoner Roland Garros, should he become lost, would vanish without a trace, literary or otherwise, to mark the corsairs' descendant's demise.

Enroute, he saw three torpedo boats spaced far apart making good time across the Med. Their Captains were instructed by the French Navy to head straight to Tunis at maximum speed. By aligning his fight path with the boats' foamy wakes, Garros judged his true course and calibrated his compass.

The hours droned on and the once-dispersed white puff-balls united beneath him, obscuring his view of the ocean and of any guide boats. Not for the first time, Garros sensed he escaped the chaotic world of humans and entered the peaceful realm of empty air, of birds, the sun, and clouds. Other times, he took solace in the isolation, away from the deaths and dangers below, knowing mother earth and a possible safe landing lay under the sheltering undercast. Not this time—only the trackless sea coldly waited. There was nothing to do but to hold his course as best determined, fight his worries, endure the cold, and fly on. He even stopped monitoring the decreasing fuel and oil levels. Reserves would get him there, or not, and nothing could be done about it.

It is a fall morning far out on the rolling sea. Pulling in their nets hand over hand, several fishermen strain against the wet weight, the frantically flopping fish, and their creaky old age. The wooden boat bobs in the offshore swell with land nowhere in sight. Early morning mist burned off with the dawn, scattered clouds briefly replaced the fog but then mostly dissipated, leaving a dim blue sky over an azure sea. In the light of the new day, a French Navy torpedo boat had passed off their starboard side, making good speed with a bone in its teeth, heading toward French colonies far in the unseen, distant south.

Naval exercises always generate gossip in home port waterfront bars, talk which linked the maneuvers with the faint rumblings of European war drums. The fishermen debate as they work whether conflict will come to the Mediterranean, and if it does, what would it mean? Can they fish during a sea war? It is hard enough to make a living on the water now with all those torpedo boats scaring the fish away. But, maybe a war would increase demand and improve the market for their catch, who knows?

Circling over the battered fishing boat, a squadron of white gulls waits for breakfast, squawking and complaining, hungry. The airborne scavengers expect discarded trash fish, the by-catch, to be thrown back overboard. Not that there will be many extra fish; the marketable species will go into wicker baskets down in the ship's shallow hold, most of the remaining sea creatures are destined for stew in a fish-wife's cauldron back on shore. Bony red rougets, greasy sardines, the occasional octopus or squid, all will wind up in a hearty bouillabaisse soup with garlic and potatoes accompanied by crusty baguettes. However, the birds wheeling overhead prefer their fish sushi-style and they keep orbiting.

Water lapping against the boat's planks, timbers creaking, the men's conversation in French, the gulls' incessant croaks, all are slowly overlaid by a drone, a steady mechanical hum. The fishermen scan the horizon, nothing there but emptiness in all directions. The noise seems to radiate down from the empty high sky. One old man spots it, points it out to the others, and they all squint into the heavens, shading their eyes with gnarled, weather-beaten hands. The source of the drumming appears to be not gull-shaped, although white like a gull, with wingtips spread for soaring. The strange thing is high and hard to see, but is indeed there and must be the noise's source. It follows the morning torpedo boat south-bound. The fisher-folk agree, it must be one of those aero planes everyone is talking about, but why is it so far out at sea, and why is it headed out even farther out, toward the continent of Africa? Africa, that exotic land rumored to be over the horizon, but never seen by the crew of elderly Frenchmen. What is an aero plane doing out here? No matter, there are fish to catch.

The gulls look up, spotting the interloper. Is it a sea-eagle? Another sort of gull predator? No, the strange creature is too high and seems to ignore the breakfast squadron and the long-awaited by-catch. Whatever kind of bird it is does not concern the gulls: it is not a threat nor a competitor. Soon, the noise dies, the thing disappears southward, the fishermen and the birds are again alone together on the trackless ocean.

The clouds beneath him thinned out, became widely scattered, then disappeared. Far ahead on the razor-slashed horizon he discerned through his oil-smeared goggles a smudge, a whiff of dirty gray smoke. Where there is smoke, there is land, or at least a large ship. Either one would mean safety. Soon, a thin, black line etched its way across his forward view through the propeller's dancing disc. Land! With the chimney smokes of village cooking fires rising from it. A quick look at his folded map, matching the terrain to the printed shoreline, identified the town as Bizerte, Tunisia. Bizerte sits on a flat, rounded promontory edging northward into the sea, the nearest town to Europe. Tunis, his original destination, lay 20 minutes father south, but Bizerte was Africa.

Half-frozen, almost out of gas, and with a lame engine, Garros declared victory and scanned the town for a hospitable landing zone. The French army's local parade ground offered obvious refuge. He touched down there unannounced, scattering a troop of drilling soldiers. The long-suffering Le Rhône clattered to a stop emitting a final metallic death rattle as the propeller swung to a halt. Roland Garros had survived flying for eight hours and 30 minutes, the longest airplane flight in history. Forever, he would be known as the first human to link two continents non-stop by air.

Wide-eyed soldiers gathered around the smoking airplane, its engine tinkling as it cooled. Their platoon leader strode up, eager to reasses command of the now disordered rabble and of the situation. On unsteady, cramped legs, the half-frozen pilot climbed down from the cockpit to answer the officer's shouted question.

"Vous venez d'où?" Where did you come from?

"En la France." Garros replied, trying but failing to hide a triumphant smirk.

Quickly arriving by car, the commander of troops in Bizerte listened to Garros's story and invited the pilot to a late lunch at his official residence. Shedding his flying gear, Roland offered to the general newspapers stuffed inside his fur jacket for added insulation. The crumpled journals carried the day's date, 23 September 1913, and were published in France, proving Garros had indeed flown across the ocean that day. Such a unique feat called for champagne to accompany lunch. Corks popped, many corks.

Military mechanics labored most of the afternoon repairing the engine, and Garros took off, unaffected by the champagne, and headed for Tunis where a large crowd, alerted by phone from Bizerte, waited. Roland landed at dusk and was escorted by the Governor General to the Bey of Tunis for an official welcome and obligatory banquet. Around 10 pm, a telegram arrived from Paris, announcing France and its newspapers had received news of his landing and confirming his aerial feat. Also presented was a note from the President of the Council of France who occupied the post of Minister for Public Education, congratulating Garros for his courage and skill. It seemed the troubles he suffered in the rigid French education system; the ignored "mandatory" dead language requirements, the refusal to learn fencing, and the failed attempt at the Bar Association were forgotten, wiped away by the oil stream from a Le Rhône rotary engine.

Garros left by steamship the next day for Marseille. He was greeted at the dock the morning of 25 September, 1913 by a throng of dignitaries. Aero Club Officials, Navy brass, the President of the French Cycling Union (who presented him with a proclamation outlining how a champion cyclist progressed to be a champion aviator), and hordes of reporters. Later, tired from numerous meetings and receptions, Garros still reserved time to sit down alone with the Parisian reporter whom he promised an exclusive interview. The following day, he departed by train to Paris, arriving at *Le Gare de Lyon* late in the evening.

The reception at the train station was, if anything more frantic than in Marseille. Reporters, each elbowing in for a quote, a scrum of photographers firing flashbulbs, Aero Club grandees, national politicians, Léon Morane – his aircraft's designer, members of the aviation elite, flying buddies, his café society friends, they were all there. Standing at the top of the railway car's steps he looked for her. Alone at the crowd's fringe, one of the few women present, stood Marcelle Gorge, waiting. Her radiant smile beamed, in no way forced.

CHAPTER TWENTY-SIX

LIVING THE GOOD LIFE

THE TOAST OF THE TOWN

Roland Garros's aerial conquest of the Mediterranean made him literally the toast of the town, the referenced town being Paris and the toasts being champagne. Wined and dined at the pinnacle of Parisian society, Garros "arrived" as a celebrity. Thanks to the newspapers, he became well-known by the public, not as just another flyer in the aviation community, but as a world-class aviator. Then, as now, French social pecking order reaches its zenith in Paris and radiates outward and downward across the country. Everybody who was anybody wanted to meet him, to shake his hand, to exchange pleasantries, to be his instant new friend.

His assigned table at Maxim's migrated upstream. Instead of being placed in front of a window so pedestrians could ogle Marcelle Gorge from the sidewalk, the couple found themselves seated in the center of the main *Salon* under the backlit, stained-glass ceiling. This horizontal movement of a few meters, or a few feet, in table positioning indicated a vast vertical leap in social status. For the *Mâtre d'Hôtel* to forgo window dressing in the elegant form of Mademoiselle Gorge and to elevate Garros and his lover to center stage, while not unheard-of, was highly unusual. Fine dining's epicenter tended to be reserved for captains of industry, minor royalty, high government officials, show biz personalities, and worthies for whom money was no problem. Mere airplane pilots, often considered along with racing drivers to be glorified mechanics, usually were not admitted into Maxim's at all until their exploits added to the glory of France.

Fame is not for everyone and Garros knew it. He resolved not to exploit his new-found status for unearned financial gain nor to attract unwanted attention. Yes, he circulated among the music halls, restaurants, and social events as before, but he strived to keep himself grounded, figuratively if not physically. His new friends, while entertaining, he found to be shallow and superficial. Garros much preferred the company of the local aviation community, his flying buddies. They spoke the same arcane language, shared the same experiences, faced the same dangers, lost the same compatriots in violent crashes. Men who frequently witnessed death up close and personal bonded like no others, their friendship made even more precious by the knowledge a loss could apart tear their circle the very next day.

Roland also spent more quality time with Marcelle Gorge, even considering making their relationship formal and permanent. This matrimonial idea went against the prevailing social convention. In 1914, upper-class men married within their own network, ideally to a virgin, and to a woman approved by their family. No one married their lover, it simply was not done in the circles Garros inhabited. With no family close, his father had dropped out of sight again and traveled back to Saigon, Roland was free to follow his heart.

Despite the spotlight of attention, the camaraderie of his fellow pilots, and the love of his lover, the young pilot still achieved a higher degree of happiness, of contentment, while airborne. This detached state of being was impossible to experience on the ground. Above the clouds, alone with the drone of his engine and the slipstream's rush for company, he was able for a short respite to depart the mundane world of men and women and to re-enter the airman's unique domain.

The serene rush lasted for a scant few minutes, maybe an hour or two, in a clean and cold place where life was simple. Solo pilots know this world well, but few can describe it accurately. The emotions run too deep and the words will not flow easily. It takes the soul of a poet to explain this domain of the air. Later in the 1930's, Count Antoine de Saint-Exupéry expressed in his books the pilot's state of mind better than anyone before. Few have surpassed his accounts. Saint-Ex's love of temporary existence in the air eventually killed him. That love and a German fighter pilot.

During the Winter and Spring of 1913/1914, Garros could have banked a great deal of money by cashing in on his fame. Every aviation-themed event wanted his presence and promoters were willing to pay for it. Roland declined to enter the offered exhibitions and races as a competitor, preferring instead to serve as a spokesperson for aviation in general and to collect a reasonable appearance fee. His altruistic motivation carried on the dream of Santos-Dumont; to use aviation as a tool to bring people together. Certainly, many of the day's aviators thought alike and flew to make it happen. From the air, for the first time in history, artificial political divisions did not seem to matter, as national borders were invisible from the air. The French countryside looked a lot like its German counterpart, which blended into Austria, which faded into Italy. It was hard to tell the difference from high altitude.

This was an era of grand tours by pilots. Not really races, these events demonstrated how airplanes linked people, cities, and countries. Louis Védrines, flying Garros's old Blériot XI, flew from Paris on 19 November 1913, touching down in Nancy (France), Prague, Vienna, Belgrade, Sofia, Constantinople, Konya (Romania), Tripoli, Beirut, and Jaffa, returning to Paris in only ten days. Another aerial rally took in London, Madrid, Vienna, Milan, Gotha (Germany), Brussels, and Marseille.

Garros did fly exhibitions over many of France's major cities. Adding to his repertoire, he learned to perform an aerial loop. This vertical circle in the sky appeared to be extremely dangerous with the aircraft inverted at the top, the pilot facing straight down. It was first performed by a Russian captain, Piotr Nesterov, in 1913. A French pilot, Adolph Pégoud, introduced western Europe to the new maneuver. Crowds loved it and once a pilot with a sufficiently powerful aircraft made up his mind to try, the loop proved to be easy to replicate.

Springtime 1914, and Garros again participated in the annual float plane race from Marseille to Monaco. Honoring a prior promise to a promoter, he entered and won the race-tour of Italian alpine lakes, an event which featured spectacular scenery rather than cutthroat competition. Awarded the race trophy by a questionable application of the rules, Garros pressed for a German lieutenant who logged the lowest elapsed time to be named the winner.

At each appearance, with every interview by the press, in all his public statements, Garros emphasized the message he transmitted to the newspapers before taking off across the Mediterranean. His statements were clear and simple; aviation must progress from being an expensive sport to a means for mutual understanding and commerce between people separated and isolated by the tyranny of distance.

Privately, to Marcelle and to his close aviation clan he expressed other, darker ideas. Drawing on his experiences in Texas and Mexico, he envisioned how aviation could revise some common techniques of war. He feared aircraft would be used in such a way soon. Did he hear the approaching European conflict and try to forestall with his speeches the war everyone feared and expected? If a man could take breakfast in Germany, lunch in France, and dine in England, wouldn't his view of Europe from above be peaceful by default? Why couldn't everyone share this vision? Garros's thoughts were coldly received and the winter dragged on, both politically and weather-wise.

Parisian weather took its toll on Marcelle Gorge. She was rarely well in the cold and gloom. At the time, coal fires provided heating in many cities, including Paris. The resulting smoke often rendered breathing difficult. Marcelle seemed to have more trouble coping than most and blamed the coal smoke. Sadly, the problem was worse than mere air pollution, but no one, not her, not Roland, knew at the time. Early in 1914, Roland Garros and Marcelle decamped from the cold capital and rented a cottage in Fréjus, from which his historic flight had begun. The sunnier clime and fresher air soon put her on the mend. She seemed much happier in the South.

During a short visit to nearby Marseille, Garros received a telephone call from Raymond Poincaré, the President of France, informing him of appointment as a Knight of the Legion of Honor. *La Légion d'Honneur* is the highest award given by the French government. Established by Napoleon, the honor is bestowed for excellence in professional fields and for valor. Poincaré informed Garros his award stemmed not only from his aviation exploits but was also due to his tireless campaigning for aviation as a force for peace and understanding. For the rest of his life, Roland Garros would be entitled to wear a tiny red rosette in his lapel signifying his membership in the Legion of Honor.

With warmer weather, the summer flying season took wing. In May, Garros accepted invitations to fly in two exhibitions, one at Buc airfield just outside Paris and the second a few days later at Juvisy, a suburb little farther from the city, easily reached by rail. The airshows consisted of three head-to-head, simultaneous competitions. Two pilots would race cross-country, then try to out-climb the other, and in the finale, perform aerobatics above judges. Garros's first opponent was his good Swiss Friend, Edmund Audemars. On the second weekend, he flew against the young British aviator, Gustave Hamel.

The airshows were boffo show business, large crowds loved the displays and gate receipts filled the coffers. Participation in airshows, which he had spent the last year avoiding, fitted into a plan. Garros was pleased by the turnout at the two events. Less thrilled was the Aero Club of France, who had not authorized the shows and received no cut of the profits. Objections by the Aero Club spurred Roland Garros to take on that august group as part of his campaign to legitimize aviation. To date, a committee of scientific-minded worthies had supervised French aviation, none of whom were pilots or aircraft builders, and few of whom had ever been aloft. This arrangement was identical to the organization running French cycling as with the *Tour de France*. The sport was managed by men who were not athletes or even ex-athletes and it was not run for the benefit of competitors—the real stars who brought in the money.

Garros felt strongly that aviation needed to escape the domain of idle sport and move to a mature commercial structure in which pilots and manufacturers played a major role. He made his position clear in an op/ed piece penned for a major Parisian newspaper, thus opening a front against the Aero Club. Following up on his plan, Garros formed a society, *Le Groupe d'Aviateurs,* not a union but a free association of pilots. Again, the established vested interest, the Aero Club, objected, but to no avail.

In mid-June, the pilots' association staged their own airshow at Juvisy. Fourteen of France's leading aviators participated and performed well, flying for themselves and not for pompous bureaucrats. Media reporters, ever eager to stir up controversy to sell more papers, called it the greatest exhibition of aviation in the history of France. That description was a bit over the top, but huge crowds of spectators attended. After the exhibition at Juvisy, Roland and the group's treasurer, Jacques Morane the aircraft builder, deposited 10,000 francs into a Parisian bank, establishing a fund for the benefit of pilots. Flying in 1914 remained extremely dangerous. Pilots were on their own; no medical plan, no benefits, no un-employment insurance, and no retirement plan. Few would ever need a retirement fund.

Garros's argument that aviation had matured was undercut when Gustav Hamel, the British national hero, disappeared without a trace over the English Channel on his flight back to the United Kingdom. Hamel was 25 years old. Local fishermen discovered his body in early July. While Hamel's death signaled the world of aviation was still hazardous and perhaps not as ready for prime time as Garros expounded, the Englishman's loss highlighted the need for some sort of benefit program, if only for burial expenses. The seamen returned Hamel to the ocean after identifying him. But the normal dangers associated with flying were not the only hazards of the day.

Drumbeats of war thundered louder and closer; the newspapers spoke of little else. Despite this hysteria, or perhaps because of it, Garros and a few of his band of pilots accepted an invitation to fly in an airshow outside Vienna, in Aspern, in eastern Austria. The team arrived by train on the worst possible day. The day before, an Austrian pilot managed to collide with a Zeppelin over the city. This was hard to do; airships are the size of airborne barns and slow. Nine people lost their lives in the resulting explosion of hydrogen gas. The airshow was cancelled. Visiting French pilots, including Garros, sewed wide black ribbons over the white wings of their planes and flew at low level over the open graves awaiting the bodies from the mid-air collision. Lt. Helmuth Hirth, the German army pilot Garros befriended during the Italian float plane rally, reported the Austrian pilots were touched by the French display of sympathy. Garros later judged that the Austrians, despite their gratitude, seemed a militaristic bunch of men, spoiling for a fight of some sort. They would soon get it.

On the morning of 28 June 1914, two shots from a pocket-sized automatic pistol rang out in Sarajevo, Serbia, killing a portly middle-aged man and his wife. Hot lead ignited a national political fuse which smoldered and smoked. It burned slowly for two or three days and few people noticed. French newspapers banished the story to page two. Unnoticed by the public, the covert fire raced faster and faster until reaching a powder keg filled with ill will and political rivalry. There, the flame of assassination touched off a conflagration which would eventually involve half the globe. At first, the event appeared tragic for the victims involved but not important on a European scale. In Vienna, the murdered couple's home, the bands played on and the warm summer continued.

Lt. Hirsch, ever gracious, invited Garros to visit Germany, of all places. Roland accepted, flying to Mannheim in the southwest for a short visit. Returning the favor, he invited Hirsch to visit France to participate in an air meet in Lyon.

Hirsch accepted, placed first in Lyon, and then toured the Morane-Saulnier factory outside Paris. The German pilot returned to *Deutschland* after extending a reciprocal invitation to Garros and Jacques Morane for a longer, more informative stay. You gather the impression Garros and Hirsch were personally working against the flow of history, trying to establish some sort of relationship before the coming explosion.

On a whirlwind tour, Garros and Morane visited every major aircraft factory in Germany; Albatross, Benz, Bosch, Gotha, Mercedes, Oberusel, LVG, they toured them all. Outside Berlin, at the Fokker factory, Hirsch persuaded Roland to pilot the heaviest aircraft he had yet flown, a 100 hp Albatross. It is remarkable that a Frenchman would have been allowed to fly such a beast, the Fokker factory specialized in military aircraft. It is not known if Garros met Tony Fokker there. If so, neither man could have known then their paths would cross again in fewer than 12 months and their second encounter would drastically alter the course of aviation forever. Once again, an albatross would signify a milestone in the life of Roland Garros.

CHAPTER TWENTY-SEVEN

ALL HELL BREAKS LOOSE

Then Things Get Worse

Archduke Franz Ferdinand, heir to the throne of the Austrian-Hungarian Empire, and his wife Sophie died in Sarajevo, Serbia on 28 July 1914, killed by a Serbian ultra-nationalist. Their open-top touring car stopped in front of a café where Gavrilo Princip sat drinking coffee, waiting for a chance to strike. Princip, a Bosnian Serb, belonged to the Black Hand Society, a radical underground group dedicated to the overthrow of Austrian rule in the Balkans and to the establishment of an independent Yugoslavia. His team of five assassins stationed themselves along the royal couple's advertised route hoping one would-be killer could act. The team's leader had already thrown a hand grenade at the couple's vehicle without considering the inherent time lag until detonation. The grenade exploded under the following car eliminating most of the police escort. The bomb thrower, seeing his mission failing, swallowed what he thought was a cyanide pill and jumped into the nearby river. However, the pill was a fake and the stream held only a foot, 25 cm, of water. The Serb was quickly captured.

Eventually, the motorcade stopped near the café while diverting to a safer route. Princip dashed to the car and fired one bullet into the Archduke's neck and aimed his second shot at the Mayor of Sarajevo riding in the front seat. He missed the mayor, killing Sophie instead, then tried to turn the pistol on himself but was unable to pull the trigger before being disarmed by bystanders. Princip swallowed his own fake cyanide pill, which again had no effect. As revolutionary movements go, the Black Hand Society terrorists did not appear particularly adept. For touching off a world-wide conflagration which killed 19 million people, Princip was sentenced to 20 years in prison, dying behind bars in 1918. In the 1920's, his remains, along with those of his co-conspirators, were interred in a Sarajevo chapel dedicated to Serbian heroes.

The bungling Black Hand band is blamed, or celebrated, depending on one's ethnicity, for igniting the Great War on that fatal day in the Balkans. German Chancellor Otto von Bismarck's earlier prediction came true: the war began over some foolishness in the Balkans. However, if not for the murder, some other reason would have soon presented itself. The Central Europe powder keg only needed a match.

Eager to squelch any Balkan revolt, the Austrian-Hungarian Empire demanded public submission from the Kingdom of Serbia and when imperial demands were rejected, declared war. The Serbs appealed to their fellow Slavs, the Russians, who began mobilizing their army and rattling their sabers. Germany, bound by treaty to support the Austrians, ordered the Russians to stand down and when Moscow did not acquiesce, declared war on Russia. France, locked in a mutual defense treaty with Russia, saw an opportunity to regain Alsace-Lorraine and declared war on Germany. The Prussians, finally involved in the war they prepared for, even hoped for, vowed to humble France for the last time and declared total war. Seen in retrospect, you are tempted to label these actions as an example of the domino theory, but dominos are better organized. By the end of the first week of August 1914, most of Europe blazed with the fires of war sparked by bungling incompetents in the Balkans.

The Germans, meaning the Prussians who controlled the levers of power in Berlin, long believed the French and Russians were conspiring to constrain Germany. In Prussian/German minds, the allies wanted to deny the German state its destiny as a, if not the, major power in Europe. There was some truth in this idea. France, since the Middle Ages, considered itself the premier country on the continent, the largest in land area, the richest, and the most powerful. Only a temporary moment of political weakness in 1870 allowed Germany to invade, to topple the Second Empire of Napoleon II, and to annex Alsace-Lorraine, according to the French. To the warlike Prussians, every political problem called for a military solution. Prussian self-image demanded the honor of conducting war, particularly since the memories of war's horrors had faded during 40 years of peace. Planners in Berlin knew war with France meant war with Russia and vice-versa. They also saw a prolonged two-front war was probably unwinnable. While they defeated one enemy, France, they would also have to fight in the East. This task would prevent them from exploiting their victory over the French; to pacify, read loot, the country. To achieve the European supremacy they craved, the Prussians needed to knock out one adversary quickly, occupy the defeated homeland, then take on the second adversary. Well-organized Germans judged the backward, agrarian Russians would take at least a year to raise and train a modern army. To avoid simultaneous heavy combat on both east and west borders, Germany must first defeat France and do it in much less than a year. Their Austro-Hungarian allies would take care of business in the South. Learning the wrong lessons from the 1870 war, the Prussians believed they could fight their way to Paris in a few months. Once there, they could impose terms of surrender before French reserves could be mobilized and deployed. They were wrong.

In Paris, the French perceived that this conflict as offering their best chance to recover Alsace-Lorraine. They immediately agreed to aid the Russians and declared war on Germany. Paris believed a quick thrust across the 1870 border would surprise the Germans and force a retreat by the German army back into Germany proper. They were wrong as well.

Taking to heart painful lessons taught by the1870 invasion, the French spent the last decades of the 19th century and the first of the 20th fortifying their border with Germany. This interlocking series of fortresses, artillery positions, and bases were designed to halt or delay the expected invasion long enough to mobilize the French army. Conscription, the draft, had been the law of the land in France since the 1880s and most Frenchmen gained some military experience. Many had mobilization posts pre-assigned. Perhaps blinded by opportunity, in early August French forces ventured forth from their redoubts and crossed the border, entering Alsace-Lorraine intent on recovering lands they believed to be theirs.

The Germans, during their decades of occupation, fortified parts of the region and knew it well. They mounted a spirited defense west of the Rhine River. The French seemed unable to coordinate their artillery fire with the rapid charges of their infantry, leaving advancing troops unsupported. Perhaps they were loath to pound into rubble the cities and towns they intended to welcome back into France. With losses mounting and the Germans outflanking them, French forces withdrew from Alsace-Lorraine vowing to return, someday.

Berlin considered the fighting in Alsace-Lorraine a diversion. The General Staff's aim was not only to keep the disputed provinces, but to march down the *Champs-Elysées* as conquerors. However, an impregnable line of French forts stood between them and Paris.

The German solution to the French cordon of concrete and steel lining the border was the Schlieffen Plan, devised during 1892-1905 by the Prussian Count for whom it was named. The plan called for a lightning thrust through Belgium and Luxemburg, then wheeling south into France behind the line of forts, and on to Paris from the northwest. That Belgium and Luxemburg were neutral countries did not concern the Germans. The Schlieffen plan was continually updated and fine-tuned for over a decade. The plan's detailed transportation schedule depended on hundreds of trains specified to the exact number of cars and timed to the minute. Each unit's movements were prescribed, every commander would know his assignment when the order to march rang out. On 2 August 1914, word came from Berlin to execute the plan. Soon the German army poured across the border into Belgium and

Luxemburg. On the other side of the English Channel this development did not sit at all well in London.

The British found themselves in a historically unusual situation. For over 1000 years, ten centuries, the English considered the French to be their natural rivals and enemies. But new alignments of countries were changing traditional alliances. The British fought an intermittent series of wars against the French beginning with the Norman invasion in 1066 (they lost) until the final Napoleonic war in 1815 (they won). British ties with Germany/Prussia were closer than with France throughout most of the 1800s featuring intermarriage between royalty and cultural exchanges. Indeed, the German Emperor, Kaiser Wilhelm II, was Queen Victoria's nephew and the British royal family sported a German last name, Saxe-Coburg/Gotha. The British initially welcomed the rise and unification of Germany in 1870 thinking the Germans would serve as a counter-weight on the continent to the rival French.

By the turn of the century, London started to worry that Germany was growing too strong. Particularly disturbing to the Admiralty was the rapid construction of the German Imperial Navy's High Seas Fleet. This force of battleships and cruisers clearly intended to challenge the long-held nautical dominance of the Royal Navy. A century of Pax Britannia, when Britain ruled the waves and much of the globe, established London as the center of a rules-based international order; rules which were enforced by the British. Seeing Germany invade neutral Belgium and Luxembourg was just too much for the government in Whitehall to accept. Responsible countries did not invade innocent neighbors just to obtain a tactical advantage. British diplomats worked through July trying to broker peace between The Central Powers, led by Germany, and the Allied Powers, led by France. They failed. The United Kingdom declared war on Germany and reluctantly aligned itself with its old enemy France on 3 August 1914.

Commander of the German army in the late 1800s, Field Marshal Helmuth von Moltke (the Elder), stated, "A battle plan never survives contact with the enemy." Ironically, his perception was proven valid in 1914 by his nephew Helmuth von Moltke (the Younger) after he assumed command of the army. The Schlieffen Plan worked flawlessly in Germany, not so well in Belgium. The out-gunned, out-manned, out-supplied, and unprepared Belgium army fought surprisingly hard on its home turf, delaying the German advance, and upsetting the plan's critical timing.

Crossing into France from Belgium, the situation worsened for the invaders. The plan depended on the rapid movement of men and material by rail and road for units to achieve their assignments on schedule. This elaborate scheme made sense in Germany where the planners knew every mile of track and road and the trains ran on time. In Belgium, and days later in France, the infrastructure was not as highly developed as in Germany with fewer railroad lines and muddier roads. German train drivers followed German orders. In France, the railroad workers were much less keen to cooperate, even sabotaging the network to stall the German advance. Even with the locals subdued, the plan was doomed to fail. The schedule was basically unworkable.

It was impossible to move that many men, that many guns, all those trucks and horses, and thousands of artillery pieces across France at the speed required by the plan. Schlieffen and later von Moltke underestimated the speed at which the French could mobilize and their ability to quickly mount a defense. As the Germans advanced, their supply lines became longer and their armies farther from home, increasing the area of hostile territory to occupy and control. The German units racing to the west then wheeling to the south had the farthest to go and the worst infrastructure to support them. The French, falling back, closed ranks into a smaller battle space, shortened their supply lines and solidified their positions northwest of Paris along the Marne and Somme Rivers.

At one point, reinforcements arrived from the capital in 600 Parisian taxis commandeered to transport troops to the front and to bring causalities and refugees back. Following regulations, the cabbies kept their meters running. 70,000+

francs settled the tab. Some German units made it to within 30 kilometers, 19 miles, of the French capital. There the invasion stalled, due in part to the use of air power, a situation Roland Garros predicted to his friends during those long nights in Parisian bars.

During the German army's advance across northwestern France, the nascent French Air Force tested the utility of scouting for the enemy by air. Pilots set out in slow, fragile monoplanes over battlefields, venturing behind the lines of contact, and looking down. Hundreds of thousands of men and their matériel are hard to hide and are easy to spot from the air. Many units moved their big guns and supply wagons with horses. Horse Cavalry was still in vogue, and large formations of horses were also visible from above. Their riders were not aware their replacements, i.e. pilots, looked down on them, literally and figuratively. With units of the German army approaching the outskirts of Paris, one French scout pilot spotted something unusual in one area of the German line of march – no Germans. A gap opened in the front, leaving a swath of countryside lightly occupied. Marshall von Moltke (the Younger) was unable to move all his men, artillery, and supplies at the speed required by the Schlieffen plan. The infrastructure assumed to be present, was not. French resistance forecast to be not there, was.

One army corps bogged down, unable to keep up with peers on its left and right flanks. Ignoring the military chain of command, the French scout pilot flew directly to Army Headquarters and sketched out on a map what he had seen, or rather not seen. Roland Garros's aerial scouting in San Antonio, Texas on maneuvers with the US Army was duplicated in Europe, this time for keeps.

Incredulous French generals did not know whether to believe this windblown flyboy or not. But what did they have to lose? The Germans drew closer to Paris by the day. Decisive action of some sort was needed or the war would be over by Christmas as many on both sides predicted. Desperate, the French army changed from a defensive posture and attacked into the gap in the lines. This surprising advance threatened to split the German army, isolating the western units from main force support. The isolated Germans, their backs to the Channel, would then be vulnerable to attack from an army crossing over from Great Britain. Alarmed at the prospect of bifurcation and with the Schlieffen plan now in tatters, the Germans retreated. They called off the planned attack on the defenses hurriedly thrown up around the French capital.

Once the Germans closed ranks, the two armies clashed in a titanic battle around the Marne River, neither side able to achieve victory. The resulting stalemate degenerated into trench warfare by the middle of September 1914. Front lines inched forward and back for the four long, appalling years. The agony of defeat weighed heavily on von Moltke. He suffered a nervous breakdown and his staff assumed command. With quick victory over the French now out of reach and a two-front conflict inevitable, von Moltke reported to the Kaiser in Berlin, "We have lost the war." This time, he was right.

In the 1920s and 1930s, Nazi propaganda blamed von Moltke claiming he was too timid, that he failed to advance, and in not doing so, compromised the Schlieffen plan. According to Hitler's flacks, the plan was not at fault because German plans are infallible, but rather von Moltke's indecision squandered the best chance to win the Great War. Not the only myth created by the Nazis.

Paris was saved, due in large part to observations made by a lone pilot peering over the side of his stick-and-cloth contraption and aided by Parisian taxis. In the relieved city, the French Air Force was about to gain another recruit, one from Réunion Island.

CHAPTER TWENTY-EIGHT

FLYING FOR KEEPS

WHAT IS A FIGHTER SQUADRON?

During the first week of August, 1914, the French government ordered a general mobilization; all able-bodied young men were to register for possible service in the armed forces. As a citizen of Réunion Island and not of mainland France, Roland Garros was exempt from these orders, but he felt intense pressure to volunteer from his peers and from himself. War with Germany brought forth conflicting emotions from Garros, feelings which surprised him. During his schooling in France, he was taught about the disastrous Franco/German war of 1870 and how Germany annexed the French departments of Alsace and Lorraine.

These regions bounced back and forth between France and various Germanic states for decades despite lying west of the Rhine river, the natural German border. Most residents touted German names and spoke a German dialect as well as being fluent in French, with an Alsatian accent. Place names there were, and still are, a curious mix of German and French. Perhaps more significantly, local wines were crafted from German, not French, grape varieties and bottles listed those varieties on the front label, a practice then illegal in France. No matter, French official policy held Alsace and Lorraine were French – period. Growing up, Garros believed this and internally demonized Germans. On his first steamship passage across the Atlantic, therefore he refused to share a stateroom with three other men who happened to be German.

However, contacts with Austrians and Germans on the European airshow circuit broadened his personal horizons. He enjoyed stays in Vienna and Lt. Hirsch, a German, came to be a close friend. The tour of German aircraft factories by Garros and Jacques Morane in July of 1914 further opened his eyes, showing him the human side of Germany as well as its industrial capability. Now, to Garros, Germans were not hyper-militaristic automations, but real people many of whom believed Alsace-Lorraine, although on the Rhine's west bank, belonged under German rule.

Eventually, Roland Garros became infected by the war fever rampant in Paris. Newspapers spoke of little else and the political maneuvers leading to armed conflict were constant topics of discussion. Garros signed up for service and was inducted into the army. He received a military haircut, donned an ill-fitting uniform, and joined a rapidly-formed squadron of aviators. Most of the pilots lived in the region around Paris, the *Ile-de-France,* and knew one another. Before flying off to fight a war he expected to be over by Christmas, he had one important task. Jules Hue finished his mandatory military service in 1905. Under the 1914 mobilization, he received orders to report to his old army unit at once. Garros, using his contacts in the French bureaucracy, rescued Hue and had him assigned to the new aero squadron instead of the infantry. One of the world's most experienced aircraft mechanics had no business carrying a rifle. Given the horrific loses to come, Garros probably saved Hue's life and at the same time insured his aircraft would be properly cared for.

It is difficult to overstate the enthusiasm, the thirst, for war in Central Europe at the time. Each country expounded its own reason. Germany wanted to flex its muscles and assume what it believed to be its rightful place, first among nations, *Deutschland Uber Alles.* France wanted both Alsace-Lorraine and its tarnished honor back. The restive Balkan states wanted independence. The rulers of Austro-Hungary wanted to keep their empire. Russia wanted to protect Slavs and extend its influence westward. The British wanted to maintain a balance of power on the continent and to continue to rule the seas. Everyone assumed the coming war would be short and relatively bloodless. It was neither.

For over 40 years, a peaceful time except for the occasional skirmish, war was perceived as a grand adventure, with magnificent uniforms, beautiful horses, parades, shiny warships, and glory for the taking. No one anticipated the changes wrought by modern technology. Rapid-fire artillery, bolt-action rifles, barbed wire, poison gas, torpedoes, submarines, and yes, aircraft would render modern war unimaginably horrific. No one saw the carnage coming.

Another unknown was how to structure a unit deploying aircraft, or even how-to best use airplanes. Considering pilots to be scouts, like cavalrymen, aero units formed themselves into airborne versions of the Cavalry, even using the moniker, "Squadron" or "*Escadrille*" for the basic unit. In Germany, most pilots came from the horse Cavalry. In France, the idea seemed to be to collect all the aircraft of one type and their pilots into one organization and call it a squadron. Thus, Roland Garros's unit was MS 26 for Morane-Saulnier as all its planes came from that company.

Elsewhere, air arms fell under army command. Uniquely in France, a separate *Aéronautique Militaire* avoided the smothering bureaucracy of a more senior service. The concept of a band of friends and aviators getting together and forming a squadron was not strange. Cavalry units were often formed the same way. In early 1916, American members of an Ivy League college flying club enlisted together in the French Air Force and formed the famous Layfette Escadrille. The 38 pilots, some of whom survived the war, are celebrated with a memorial and crypt outside Paris. Flying, fighting, and perhaps dying with one's friends provided instant *Esprit de Corps*, a necessary attribute of any effective combat unit.

Being Parisians, the pilots of MS 26 also exhibited a certain *élan.* They felt compelled to present an image worthy of the capital, the world's fabled fashion center. Roland Garros's baggy army-issued garb just would not do. His fellow pilots took Roland to a well-known haberdashery and kitted him out with proper stylish uniforms. Also, once it became known who this volunteer pilot was, i.e., a world-famous aviator, he was promoted to officer as a Second Lieutenant despite having no military training or experience whatsoever.

After a short work-up, the squadron flew to Mazéville, an impromptu airfield outside Nancy. Nancy, once the capital of the Duchy of Lorraine, lies in a point of the French geographic hexagon thrusting into Germany. Stalled front lines were not far away reaching across northeast France and into Belgium. Jules Hue led a convoy of trucks from Paris with gear and needed supplies. For Hue, setting up operations at a makeshift airfield was no different from organizing hangers and shops at a major airshow. This time, he enjoyed French government support and the stakes were much higher. For a time, squadron personnel were quartered in a local manor house, *Le Chateau de Mazéville*, proving war does not always have to be about hardship and suffering.

As the fall of 1914 approached, the MS 26 squadron learned how to fly combat missions. Aping the soon-to-be-obsolete horse Cavalry, pilots scouted out enemy movements and fortifications, ranging along the trench lines, and at times venturing behind those lines. Once communication was established, this real-time intelligence flowed up the chain of command to French army headquarters.

Slowly, lessons of the failed Schlieffen Plan penetrated military minds. Aerial scouting had identified a gap in the German lines which the French exploited with British help. The German advance stalled and the invaders fell back. From this, it became readily apparent information gathered from the air revolutionized maneuver warfare. No longer could an army group in-mass and attack, surprising an unaware enemy. The result was the stalemate of trench warfare with neither side able to prevail through movement. Even the trenches were easily visible from above and any change quickly identified.

For decades, tethered hydrogen-filled balloons provided a means of adjusting artillery fire. Balloon crews would signal to gunners where their rounds fell in relation to the target. Aircraft, lacking air-to-ground communications, were less useful in this role, but could supply long-range target locations.

Roland Garros and his squadron mates flew a variety of missions; scouting, intelligence gathering, artillery spotting, and even lobbed a few hand-held bombs over the sides of their monoplanes. These bombs' tactical utility approached zero.

Early in the war, opposing pilots held no great animosity toward their counterparts on the other side. The fraternity of aviators, established during peacetime, remained in effect. There were reports of German pilots waving to French aviators as they passed each other. French and British flyers returned the courtesy. These *bon temps*, good times, did not last long. Once the importance of air operations became evident, each side grasped the necessity to eliminate the other's scouts, to blind the enemy's spying eyes.

But how could fighting be conducted in the air? Pilots, quickly forgetting friendly hand waving, took aloft all manner of weapons. Rifles (single-shot, bolt-action long guns), carbines, revolvers, even hand grenades were pressed into service to try and eliminate the other side's airmen. Nothing worked. In the three-dimensional world of the air where aircraft turned, climbed, and dived at speed over 100 kph, 62 mph, single bullets could not be aimed with any degree of success.

The obvious answer was employment of the recently-perfected machine gun. A spray of lead might be able to seek out and destroy an airborne target when fired from another aircraft. But early machine guns were heavy, their belts or drums of ammunition had to be inserted by hand, and they jammed often requiring an operator to clear the blockage. This situation called for carrying onboard a dedicated gunner in addition to the pilot, who had his leather-gloved hands full flying the aircraft. Machine guns were too heavy to hand-hold. A circular mount allowing the gun to be panned and aimed needed to be installed in the aircraft. This meant a larger aircraft with a structure stout enough to mount a machine gun and to adsorb its considerable recoil. Quickly, such "gun tub" biplanes were converted from two-seat craft previously designed for aerial photography. Results were not good on either side. Machine-gun-equipped planes with two men aboard, a gun in a ring mount, and ammo were heavier and thus slower than the planes intended to be shot down. Not a recipe for success; to shoot down an enemy, you must first overtake him. Another limitation involved the field of fire with the gun mounted in the rear of the cockpit. The gunner could only engage targets off to either side and above the aircraft. Two wings and a propeller blocked the forward view, the tail occupied the six o'clock position, and the guns could not be depressed much over the cockpit's sides. To shoot down an enemy, the pilot needed to fly alongside his target at short range allowing the gunner standing up behind him to fire. This tactic assumed the intended victim would allow such close formation flying to take place, which they never did.

Pusher biplanes were also tried. These mounted their engines and propellers behind the cockpit between the wings and the tail, affording a clear field of fire from the forward cockpit. However, the aerodynamic drag of this configuration made pushers even slower than the "tractor" planes. Few pusher fighters ever got within firing range of their faster would-be targets. The British even tried a "pulpit" fighter, mounting a separate gunner's cockpit on cantilevered struts inches in front of the whirling propeller. Only one was built and it is not known if anyone ever flew in the front cockpit. In 1914, aviators were brave but not, as a rule, stupid.

A two-man fighter plane required close coordination between the seated pilot and the standing gunner behind him. The pilot's role was to maneuver the craft to give the gunner a clear shot, not an easy task with a roaring, unmuffled engine nearby, a howling slipstream, and fur-lined flying helmets. Aircrew depended on hand signals to communicate with each other. All these limitations added up to significant failure to shoot down other aircraft. Nothing seemed to work. Air arms struggled to invent what would later be known as a "fighter Plane" although no one knew it at the time.

An obvious solution was to mount a machine gun rigidly to the aircraft's fuselage forward of the cockpit. This configuration offered low aerodynamic drag, no second crewmember required, minimal weight added (a Hotchkiss gun weighed 53 pounds, 24 kilos, plus ammunition), and the pilot could clear jams with the gun right in front of him. The gun would be aimed by pointing the whole airplane. The only drawback, and a serious one, was the propeller whirling in the line of fire. Somehow, the machine gun would have to be synchronized with the prop so the steel bullets would not impact delicate wooden blades.

August Euler, a German pilot, and engineer, proposed such an installation in 1910 but his idea fell on stony ground. Technical hurdles seemed insurmountable. Propellers turned at 1000 rpm or more and their rotational speed varied greatly. Early machine guns fired erratically, their rates of fire varying by hundreds of rounds a minute. Any mechanical linkage between the two systems would have to function at a high rate of speed and never malfunction. One steel-jacketed bullet into the base of a wooden propeller would splinter the blade, separating it from the hub. The resulting imbalance would wreck the engine, probably separating it from the airframe, which would spin out of control after losing the engine's balanced weight.

When war broke out in 1914, Auler's concept experienced a revival. Driven by the failure of existing designs with flexible, crew-served guns, several manufacturers played around with synchronized guns, an activity unblemished by success. Metal-bashing boffins attempted to interrupt the gun's firing whenever a propeller blade passed in front of the muzzle. With the speed of the spinning prop and the gun's relatively slow rate of fire, few bullets made their way past the engine cowling. Guns spent most of their time interrupted.

You get the idea now that this synchronization invention activity was pursued rather indifferently, perhaps as a sideline. It was not at all clear to the aviators or to their superiors that a fixed, forward firing machine gun represented a good idea. One senior RAF commander complained the concept required the pilot to point his craft directly at another airplane at close range, which was not advised. Also, many flyers doubted their chances at aiming a whole airplane with the precision required for accurate shooting. Flight controls were rudimentary and unbalanced. The effects control surfaces exerted on a flight path were sketchy and hard to predict on a small scale.

Aircraft of the period suffered from a condition known as adverse yaw. When the airplane was commanded to bank right with wing-warping, the nose tended to yaw in the opposite direction, left. Introduction of ailerons for roll control helped somewhat, but the condition remained. Pilots had trouble conceiving of being able to control their craft with a marksman's accuracy. So, men in stick and cloth crates continued to bang away at each other with flexible-mount guns while swirling in three dimensions and trying to maneuver abeam of their targets, whose aircrew were not about to give them the chance.

The Morane-Saulnier monoplanes of Garros's MS 26 squadron were too light, too flimsy to mount a machine gun ring. Carrying a second crewmember, gun, and ammunition was probably an aerial bridge too far. But, Roland Garros, Jules Hue, and Jacques Morane had what they thought was a better idea. It is not known who exactly dreamed up their solution to the forward-firing-gun problem. It was one of those ideas so crazy it might just work.

CHAPTER TWENTY-NINE

BACK IN THE CITY OF LIGHTS

FAILURE IN PARIS

In November of 1914, Raymond Saulnier and Charles Morane welcomed Roland Garros and Jules Hue at their workshops in Villacoublay just outside Paris. Their mission – approved by French Air Force Headquarters – find a way to fire a machine gun though a rotating propeller. Many other engineers in France, England, and Germany were trying and failing, a fact not unknown to French leadership. The concept of a fixed, forward firing gun was in danger of entering the crackpot realm; few thought it possible. One senior officer took the position that aircraft were forever destined to be little more than unarmed scouts. Indeed, the general went on, arming scouts might cause scout pilots to neglect their primary mission in favor of firing at the enemy. The utility of denying the other side its scouts by shooting them down does not seem to have been considered.

Partly for military security reasons, no one was eager for the Germans to find out that the gun/propeller synchronization effort continued and partly to avoid criticism as being a waste of time and money, the work was to be kept secret. Even Garros's old friend Edmund Audemars remained in the dark. A Swiss citizen, Audemars was compelled to be as neutral in the conflict as his country. In fact, due to traditional Swiss antipathy toward German overreaching ambition, he supported the Allied Powers but could only participate in the Great War by ferrying new aircraft to front line airfields.

Each day at dawn, Garros drove his Bugatti Type 18 to pick up Hue, then on to Villacoublay for more testing, more inventions, more trial-and-error, mostly errors. Even the educated efforts of the best Morane-Saulnier engineers and the practical knowledge of Jules Hue failed to produce a workable synchronization mechanism. Either the gun refused to fire reliably or bullets shattered spinning prop blades.

The team, working in a closed-off secret workshop and hanger, blasted to bits dozens of wooden propellers when they were able to get the gun to fire at all. Trashed props represented a major research and development cost. A decade earlier, the Wright brothers determined a propeller is really a rotating wing. As such, props need an airfoil-shaped cross-section. Because the tips pass through the air more rapidly than the sections near the hub, the airfoil varies along the blade's length. In 1914, propellers were carved from long, expensive pieces of closed-grained wood, usually walnut, by highly trained craftsmen following detailed templates. Props were not cheap and the frustrated team's errant designs splintered many.

When not testing the latest (non-functional) model of the synchronization gear, Garros flew "show the flag" missions over Paris during good weather, providing a visible presence overhead to a fearful public. Looking up from their boulevards, Parisians felt a little more secure knowing a veteran pilot was aloft watching for approaching Germans.

When he arrived back in Paris, Garros found Marcelle Gorge waiting for him, having abandoned her recuperative stay in the south of France to be with Roland. The couple resumed their previous, pre-war life, dining frequently at Maxim's and Le Couple restaurants. This luxuriant life style was not a conscious choice for them. Parisians of their age, status, and class did no cooking at home. It is doubtful their apartment even boasted of a kitchen or that either knew the first thing about food preparation. An apartment was for sleeping, dressing, and sex; every other activity took place in public venues. Paris was their living room, dining room, and study. But something was amiss in the City of Lights.

The government of France had decamped to Bordeaux in the country's far southwest corner to avoid possible capture by a victorious Germany and to conduct war from there if necessary. Otherwise, Paris carried on as before, maybe even more intensely, either to show the Germans they would not be cowed or to enjoy life before the darkness descended as in 1870.

Paris had not changed, but Roland Garros had. In his four months at the front, he experienced the horrors of modern war. From above, he saw the bright lights of gun flashes and saw the shells' impacts erupting in mushroom clouds of dirt, mud, and blood. The damage being done to the revered French countryside, *La France Profonde*, was appalling and clear. He witnessed endless trails of dead and wounded men streaming back from the trenches, some to hospitals and some to graveyards. The bright and beautiful people in Parisian salons, bars, and theatres not did see these sights firsthand, only through the sensationalistic newspapers' partisan lens. Common people fought in the war, not the diners at Maxim's. If they cared, it was not obvious to Roland Garros. Now, he saw Parisian nightlife and its people in a new light. He met and got to know some talented, aware people, such as Isadore Duncan the dancer and Jean Couteau the writer. There were also poseurs, fakes, and dilettantes; shallow people to whom the Great War represented an unwelcome distraction from the good life of *La Belle Époque.* He wondered how people could debate the latest music hall review, perhaps *Le Can-Can*, when less than an hour's taxi ride away men were living and dying in muddy, fetid trenches. It became too much to bear.

Garros, Marcelle Gorge, and Audemars left Paris for the home of old family friend Jean Ajalbert, *Chateau Malmaison,* where Garros spent several happy, carefree summers. Ajalbert lost his son, age 19, at the end of November in a battle in the Argonne forest. He welcomed Garros, his lover, and his Swiss friend to partially assuage his own grief. But the news relayed from Garros's squadron was not good. Losses mounted, he lost friends and squadron mates. Yet, every day, he returned to the workshop to try once again to solve the problem of arming a single-pilot airplane.

Roland knew he must eventually leave Marcelle and his friends and return to the front. He realized the war would not be gloriously won by Christmas and his chances of survival in it, when he returned to fight, grew slimmer by the day. When confronted by their own mortality, some men ignore the situation hoping to literally dodge a bullet by mental avoidance. Others try to settle their affairs. It is common for men, and in much later years, women, when entering combat to write farewell letters to loved ones. Roland Garros penned such a letter in late December to his father in Saigon. No answer had come back by year's end.

New Year's Eve of 1914 was a somber occasion at *Chateau Malmaison*. Instead of enjoying the usual gourmet feast prepared by the numerous servants, Roland Garros, Marcelle Gorge, Edmund Audemars, and Jean Ajalbert ventured into the chateau's extensive wine cellar. There, four despondent people found, opened, and tasted the oldest bottles in stock. 1915 promised not to be a good year.

At the end of January, Garros received orders to report back to his squadron. Money men behind the factory did not believe the experiments on gun synchronization were leading anywhere and they terminated program funding. Development of the synchro gear held up delivery of 12 would-be fighter aircraft. The financiers wanted to book the sale.

Garros, Hue, and Saulnier could not argue with the green-eyeshade men. They believed deployment of a single-seat fighter plane would change the war but could not demonstrate a working synchro device. The team fell back on plan B, a method of firing through the propeller which, while not an elegant engineering solution, did work after a fashion. Garros hoped to prove the combat utility of a fixed gun with the jury-rigged mechanism. Success would open eyes and wallets for more development. Together with his trusted mechanic, Garros reported back to MS 26 and obtained permission to try his idea in combat, the only pilot authorized to do so. In his absence, the squadron moved to the town of Saint-Pol-sur-Mer, two kilometers south of Dunkerque, near the English Channel.

When not flying, Garros worked with Jules Hue in a hanger used to store spare parts, determined to solve the propeller/gun problem. They fabricated two triangular steel plates fixed to the rear surface of a propeller. Each plate would shield the fragile wood underneath from bullet impact. The plates' surfaces featured metal grooves designed to catch a bullet and sling it outward instead of allowing a ricochet back at the pilot. The miniature shields were attached to the propeller hub by steel straps. The whole assembly needed to be carefully balanced to prevent violent rotational forces. Raymond Saulnier calculated only 5-10% of the gun's hot lead output would strike the propeller. The plates did not need to deflect constant impacts. Deflector plates were a brute-force method of firing through a prop arc by diverting a small number of bullets, but would they work in combat? Remarkably, Garros and Hue's original device survived the war intact and is on display in Germany, of all places. How it got there is a story in itself.

February and March saw poor flying weather and when aircraft could take to the air pilots were committed to scouting and the occasional bombing mission. Garros's and Hue's first gun-equipped aircraft was rolled up into a crumpled ball by a thunderstorm while the craft was parked outside. They salvaged the modified propeller and mounted it on another airframe, the first true fighter plane.

The first of April 1915 dawned clear and cool. It was time to try the deflector plates, which had only been ground-tested. Garros and Hue knew their bit of ironmongery did not represent the final solution. Its purpose was to demonstrate the tactical utility of the true fighter plane to the generals and the money-men. They would be wildly successful, just not for the side they fought for.

CHAPTER THIRTY

THE TASTE OF BLOOD

DEATH OF AN ALBATROSS

Clawing for altitude, Roland Garros climbed into the dawn as the morning sun's rays sliced through low costal clouds. He flew north, toward the French border, toward the front lines, toward the Germans, toward occupied Oostende, Belgium, and toward history. He crossed over the spider web of trenches near the Oostende railway station, bombed the previous night without effect, as usual. Hunting, he searched the lightening sky for prey.

Something moving in the west caught his eye, an aircraft at 1500 meters, 5000 feet, altitude over the beach called *La Panne* by the Belgians. Against a background of featureless sky, an object's movement is easier to discern than its discreet shape. Peering intently to the west, he could barely make out a white aircraft about 500 meters, 1650 feet, above him. The plane was following the surf line below south toward the front lines. Prominent black Maltese crosses marked the stranger as a German Albatross observation plane, exactly the quarry he sought. Garros turned left and continued climbing, pointed his aircraft's nose at the enemy's predicted future position. As he neared the intruder's altitude, he spied a two-seat French aircraft, a Voisin biplane, also trailing the German. The French gunship, lugging two crewmembers plus a ring-mounted machine gun and its ammo cans, had no chance to catch the Albatross and to pull alongside to give the gunner in the rear cockpit a clear shot. Indeed, as Garros watched from his ascent, the distance between the two aircraft grew greater. You could not script a more definitive scenario to demonstrate the aerial superiority of his lighter, faster, single-seat monoplane.

The German crew didn't catch sight of Garros climbing from beneath until he closed the distance between them to several hundred yards/meters at their altitude and approached firing range. Distracted, they were busy keeping a watchful eye on the Voisin falling further behind. The German aircrew was probably not worried and saw no need to take evasive action when they finally spotted Garros. They just out-ran one French plane and Garros's Parasol Type L craft presented no threat as long as its nose stayed behind their tail, or so they thought. The leather-coated observer turned, readying his bolt-action rifle, intending to compel this cheeky Frenchman to keep his distance.

Now in close trail with the Albatross, Garros struggled to bring his rigidly-mounted machine gun precisely to bear. He needed to aim the whole airplane in the process. The scout plane was ultra-sensitive in pitch, the nose bobbing up and down, over-controlled by the all-flying tail plane. Roll control was another story. The aircraft did not like to roll and when it did, the rate of roll varied unpredictably. Wing warping for roll control caused the wings to flex, the degree of flex depending on the airspeed. Adverse yaw sliced the nose left and right opposite to each roll input further complicating matters. A German test pilot later stated a lightning bolt traced a straight line in the sky compared to a captured aircraft with "Morane" controls. Garros fought to place his makeshift gunsight, just two wires in a ring sight, over the Albatross' profile ahead. His breath came in gasps, partly due to exertion, mostly due to excitement; this was the moment he anticipated for months. Concerned by the Frenchman's close approach, the German observer fired a shot from his rifle, the slipstream whipping away the muzzle smoke. Garros felt the bullet's impact on his plane's right-wing spar, a sharp crack. He ignored it, this was no time to back off and check for battle damage, not with a potential kill in hand.

Roland Garros opened fire at 30 meters, 100 feet, spraying a 24 round cannister of ammunition toward the Albatross in two seconds. The barking gun's recoil shook the lightly-built craft from nose to tail. When he and Jules Hue fired the gun on the ground, the plane's structure, braced by the ground, vibrated, but not like this shaking. If any bullets struck the deflector plates, he did not notice. The cracked wing spar held fast.

Amazed and frightened at the sight of a stock-appearing aircraft shooting forward and seeing the machine gun's muzzle flashes attenuated by the spinning propeller, the Germans turned right and down hoping to dodge the lethal bullet stream reaching for them. The observer jerked off rifle round after round at the little Frenchman, his aim spoiled by the steep turn. Garros followed the Albatross in its right spiral as he wrestled another heavy can of ammo into the gun's breech in front of him. Both aircraft mounted rotary engines. The German mill was a direct copy of Garros's Le Rhône. The spinning steel cylinders' rotating mass acted as giant gyroscopes with attendant precession. Each bird wanted to turn right much better than left and the two, hunter and hunted, entered a descending right-hand spiral. Aircraft of 1915 did not have enough power to turn tightly and maintain altitude, so the fight descended. Once he re-armed his gun, Garros found his lighter, more agile aircraft was able to turn inside the Albatross. He steadily cut across the circle and again reached a close-in firing position. Able to pull lead on his turning target, he pointed his craft ahead of the fleeing, panicked Germans as a hunter aims in front of a flying duck, or an albatross.

Stick and cloth aircraft of the era had few vulnerable points where machine gun bullets could do serious damage. Most of the structure's outline was vacant, covered only by doped muslin cloth stretched over a wooden frame. The only kill zones; the fuel tank, the engine, and of course, the crew, were all concentrated in one small section of the plane, a difficult target.

Garros's second 24-round burst found the Albatross' engine. He saw a quick flash of red flame followed by black castor oil smoke as the engine came apart. Once again out of ammunition, he leveled his wings, and watched with horror the German plane's death throes. The doomed Albatross tightened its turn, its nose pointed steeply downward. It appeared the pilot hoped to regaining control of the plunging aircraft. The right wing and nose would rise for a few seconds, the plane would stall, and fall again. All the while the west wind carried the two adversaries back over French territory, one dying bird trailing smoke, the other circling it as ground troops watched from their trenches.

Thousands of troops, some speaking German, some French, some English, turned their faces skyward. Most had seen the occasional aircraft fly over the battlefield crossing no-man's land but no trooper ever witnessed a battle in the sky like this. Two droning planes locked in mortal combat, one a winner, the other losing everything. The outcome clear, the triumph of one over the other transfixed the troops in their muddy slits in the earth. Now, here was a war scene they could understand.

Finally, the German plane seemed to give up and pitched nose-down vertically. It impacted the earth in a field behind the front lines, the unused fuel igniting in a miniature mushroom cloud of flame and smoke streamed away by the wind. Roland Garros flew low over the crash site, circling once, twice, turning right, peering at the wreckage, now just a blackened pile of burning sticks. A thin smoke plume rose from the pyre, blowing eastward, carrying with it the spirits of two human beings home to Germany. For the first time in history, a true fighter plane had shot down an opponent in armed combat. Never had a lone pilot hunted down other aviators. It would not be the last time.

It is not an easy thing to do, to kill other men with a machine gun at close range. Infantry gunners fired at enemy soldiers scarcely seen through the dust and smoke at long ranges—ghostly figures moving in the distance. Airborne death was up close. In a dynamic, swirling dogfight, with only a primitive gun sight, point-blank range was the only viable technique. Later, German flying ace Oswald Boelcke remarked he knew when he was within range when he could make out the leather strap of the enemy pilot's goggles on the back of his opponent's head.

The next day, Roland Garros drove one of the squadron's vehicles out to the crash site. The dead Albatross lay well back from the front-line trenches, a crumpled, charred mess, like a white bird hit by a truck. Looters visited the scene first. The wreckage had been picked clean. Insignia, side arms, emblems, anything perceived to be of value was gone. Two bodies were in a horrible state. The observer had been consumed in the fire, mutilated beyond recognition. The pilot, thrown clear by ground impact, suffered a bullet through his head. Death came instantly to him. The futile attempts at regaining control Garros witnessed in the air were probably the observer, not the pilot, trying to pull out of the dive with the pilot's body slumped over the controls. Finally, probably wounded himself, the observer accepted his fate as the ground rushed up to meet him.

Garros wrote Ajalbert that he took no pride in his work after viewing the crash site. The grisly sight sickened him. His only source of satisfaction was proving the utility of a forward-firing gun in a single-seat fighter plane. Perhaps using a mental rationalization, Garros believed his death-dealing demonstration would shorten the war. It did not. Industrialist Alfred Nobel entertained the same delusion. The Swede believe the explosive power of his invention, dynamite, would make war obsolete. It did not either, but did make Nobel even richer.

Garros wrote his mother in Saigon he expected no royalty compensation for the deflector plates he and Hue installed. Raymond Saulnier conceived the original idea as a safety back-up in case the synchro gear failed and applied for a patent.

Garros's revulsion at killing two human beings did not prevent him from killing four more. Such is the blood lust of war. On 15 April 1915, Garros's Hotchkiss machine gun found another Albatross. He notched a third kill three days later. At this time, the entire French Air Force had managed to down five German planes. Roland Garros accounted for three of these.

In Coleridge's classic poem, "Rime of the Ancient Mariner," a sailor shoots and kills an albatross, a flyer usually associated with good fortune. To punish the shooter, the ship's other crew members hang the dead bird around the offending sailor's neck as penance for his deed. After killing three Albatrosses and their human crews, Roland Garros's life took up a new, darker path. Subsequent events make you wonder if the first fighter pilot, who unleashed true air-to-air combat on the world by downing Albatrosses, carried their metaphorical bodies with him in spirit around his neck, unseen, but there all the same.

Flying a second sortie on 18 April 1915, behind enemy lines, at low altitude, looking for victory number four, Garros's engine quit. Some accounts attribute this to a plugged fuel line, other, mostly German, reporters say he was shot down by ground troops, that a bullet severed a soft copper tube. In either case, he was forced to glide to a landing behind the lines in occupied Belgium. Aviators of the Great War carried matches for just this situation. They were to torch their aircraft preventing the bird from falling into enemy hands. Destruction was supposedly easy to do with dry wooden structures covered with highly flammable doped cloth. Garros set his Type L alight, but the fire did not burn quickly enough. German foot soldiers soon came running, captured Garros at gun point, and extinguished the flames. Cold, wet spring weather probably dampened the craft's fabric, preventing a quick bonfire. Crucially, the armored propeller and gun survived. Both were forwarded up the chain of command, the ground troops were clueless as to what these strange devices meant to the war effort, but they sensed the bits of ironmongery were important. They were indeed.

Roland Garros's exploits, the downing of three observation planes in less than three weeks, attracted the attention of French command authorities. He received a commendation from General Foch, the Deputy Commander of the French army. However, for some reason, his exploits were treated as an outlier, the actions of a random hero, not the start of a new phase in warfare.

The Germans, on the other side, paid close attention to the tactical implications of Garros's successes. It was their men and aircraft that were shot down. Garros's propeller with its deflector plates was, after removal from his aircraft, closely examined by an intense young man with a reputation as a brilliant engineer, a good pilot, a smooth social operator, but a man with questionable business ethics. His name – Anthony Fokker. After learning of Garros's skein of kills and viewing the armored propeller, Tony Fokker sprang into action. His success resulted in a disaster for Allies and a triumph for the Central Powers. Fokker, a renegade Dutchman, soon unleashed the infamous Fokker Scourge.

CHAPTER THIRTY-ONE

ANTHONY FOKKER

FATHER OF THE SCOURGE

Anthony "Tony" Fokker was a piece of work. Despite sharing some common history with Roland Garros, Fokker turned out entirely different as an aviator and as a human being. Like Garros, Fokker was born in a far-away colony, the Dutch East Indies, modern-day Indonesia. His Dutch parents moved back to the Netherlands to provide young Tony with a proper Dutch education, which evidently did not take. Fokker never graduated from high school. Also, like Garros, Fokker was a pioneer aviator. He taught himself to fly in 1910 in an aircraft he designed and built himself. By all accounts, Tony was a superb flyer. Later, he personally demonstrated new aircraft designed by his workshop for military brass and dazzled watching dignitaries and pilots alike with his skill in the cockpit. Fokker, like Garros, was a hail-fellow-well-met, liked and accepted by the upper crust of society, able to charm and impress people when he needed their help.

There the similarities with Roland Garros ended. Fokker treated the engineers who worked with and for him miserably, taking personal credit for their successes, and blaming others for failures. He claimed their inventions as his own and constructed elaborate tales starring himself about how new designs came about. In 1912, despite the growing tension between Germany/Austria/Hungary and the rest of Europe, Fokker persuaded the German government to fund an aircraft design shop and factory for him outside Berlin. Fokker spoke German; Dutch is a Germanic language, a close relation to High German. All during the Great War, Fokker turned out military planes for Germany.

The original Schlieffen Plan called for an invasion of the Netherlands enroute to capturing Paris. By the time war broke out, the German staff decided to forgo that portion of the plan hoping to keep the Dutch neutral. This worked, the Netherlands stayed out of the war, allowing Fokker to keep working for Berlin as long as he did not engage in combat. Dutch neutrality later worked to Roland Garros's advantage as well.

You get the impression Anthony Fokker would have happily performed the same role for the French or British government for the right price. Fokker aircraft, while sometimes innovative in design, suffered from poor quality control in the factory, resulting in inflight failures that could and should have been avoided. Tony Fokker refused to reinvest the considerable profit he collected from the German war ministry in his factory and his production numbers never reached promised rates. German Air Force pilots loved Fokker's planes, but throughout the war they experienced a shortage of flyable airplanes due to Fokker's trousering of his factory's money.

The situation grew so corrupt the authorities in Berlin prepared embezzlement charges against Fokker. Only Germany's timely defeat and a forced change of government saved Tony Fokker from jail. Immediately after the war, Fokker violated the terms of the armistice signed by the combatants. He shipped three trainloads of aircraft engines, tools, manufacturing equipment, and factory gear, all owned by the German government, to the Netherlands to re-establish Fokker aircraft in his home country. That bit of industrial theft came later; in May of 1915, Tony Fokker became the father of the "Fokker Scourge."

Alarm spread among German airfields all along the western front as a mysterious Saulnier-Morane monoplane shot down German aircraft seemingly at will. If the French authorities did not grasp the tactical importance of denying the skies to enemy scouts, the

Germans certainly got the point. When the mysterious, predatory aircraft crash-landed behind German lines in Belgium, interest grew. Had the French discovered a way to fire a machine gun through a propeller? Identification of the marauding pilot as the famous pre-war aviator Roland Garros heightened the intrigue. It seemed to the Germans this new weapons system had been entrusted to one of their best pilots for combat testing. Garros and Jules Hue labored alone, ignored by French officialdom.

In a biography written in 1928, Tony Fokker tells a tall tale of how he rushed to Garros's burning aircraft, salvaged the propeller and gun from the Type L Parasol with his bare hands, and instantly grasped the device's importance. He goes on to say he took the propeller back to his workshop on a train and singlehandedly invented a functioning synchronization mechanism, working 48 straight hours on the project. Not much of this story holds up to the light of history. The truth is more pedestrian. Garros barely-scorched plane was quickly repaired and its insignia painted over with Maltese crosses. It flew to Berlin where Tony Fokker and his team examined the modifications.

In contrast to the French and British, the Germans understood how combat aviation had just profoundly changed. Garros proved a single pilot could aim a machine gun by aiming an entire aircraft and a fighter pilot could attack other aircraft at short range without colliding with his targets. Furthermore, lumbering two-seat observation aircraft were clearly vulnerable to faster, lighter, agile single-seat fighters. An effective fighter plane, firing through its propeller, could put out the eyes of an airborne enemy. However, crude metal deflector plates were not the ultimate solution, a proper synchro gear was needed.

Tony Fokker later claimed to have perfected the synchronization mechanism, but the device was probably invented by one of his engineers, Heinrich Lubbe. Lubbe had worked on the problem for at least six months, albeit half-heartedly and with little success. Now, the High Command and

Tony Fokker wanted a device that worked and they wanted it now.

Lubbe and/or Fokker, under pressure by the brass and now knowing the tactical concept was viable, encountered a blinding flash of the obvious. Previous trials in three countries and numerous patents attempted to interrupt gun firing when a propeller blade passed in front of the muzzle. At Fokker's Berlin workshop, the engineers reversed the mechanism's logic. They converted a machine gun from a fully automatic device which fired bullets if the trigger was held down into a single shot device, one trigger pull, one bullet launched. Then, the Fokker technicians arranged a series of rods and bell cranks such that propeller blades themselves pulled the trigger when the way forward was clear. Once the gun fired and reloaded a round, another blade fired the next round. This scheme held the added advantage that the faster the propeller turned, the faster the gun operated.

In one of history's ironies, back in Vilacoubly, Raymond Saulnier came to the same conclusion at about the same time. Only, he could not make this idea work either. The clunky Hotchkiss guns used by the French employed a heavy firing mechanism which could not respond quickly enough when commanded to shoot by a passing propeller blade. Fokker worked with the lighter, faster-firing Spandau and Parabellum guns which could answer to quick firing impulses.

Tony Fokker, ever the hustler, fine-tuned the synchro gear and used its success to help sell more airplanes. He would not have profited much by installing a system of rods onto existing airframes. Fokker's new bird was the *Eindecker* or "monoplane." He essentially copied the captured French Saulnier-Morane monoplane, but optimized the design for air-to-air gunnery. Mounting the wing mid-fuselage improved visibility for the pilot and made room for the gun. Strangely, Fokker kept the "Morane" control system which gave Garros so much trouble in sighting the gun.

Tony Fokker demonstrated the new plane and its armament for the German Air Force in Berlin mid-June 1915.

The brass insisted on Fokker flying the new bird himself. If the synchro gear failed, the designer, not a service pilot, would be in jeopardy. Instead of flying the aircraft into the demonstration airfield, Fokker towed it behind his touring car to the aerodrome for a dramatic entrance. Piloting the new aircraft, he easily perforated targets on the ground while firing through the propeller. Regardless of what you think of Anthony Fokker's character, he and his team designed a weapon which would rule the skies for six months of the Great War, the first aircraft designed from the outset to be a fighter plane.

Ministers in Berlin were impressed and ordered Eindeckers into production. However, Fokker's factory could only turn out one or two a week. Around mid-July, the new fighters began showing up at the front lines, two assigned to each squadron. No local commanders knew how to best employ this unique weapons system. Fighter planes appeared on daily flying schedules seemingly at random. A pilot might fly on a scout mission with an observer, or an artillery-spotting sortie, or he might go it alone in an Eindecker. The German Air Force which invented the purpose-built fighter plane, did not know how to invent the dedicated fighter pilot. That role fell to two junior officers.

Lieutenants Oswald Boelke and Max Immelmann were the most experienced pilots in their squadron stationed at Daouri in occupied France. In June 1915, each was issued his own personal Eindecker, the only two possessed by their unit, and were ordered to develop tactics exploiting the device. Boelke took the lead and worked out a way for the two to coordinate their attacks on French and British planes. Instead of flying random gun passes in a swirling melee, the two young Germans learned to work as a team. Their aerial maneuvers were planned and understood before takeoff. Intra-plane communications were limited to hand signals, hard to see while fighting, as this was long before plane-to-plane radios.

While one pilot engaged a target, his wingman maneuvered to follow up and to protect his leader. If the attack failed, the wingman rolled in on the target aircraft while the leader positioned himself for another pass. The Allied aircraft could not easily escape being under attack almost continuously. Boelcke was the thinker, the tactician, while Immelmann was the consummate stick-and-rudder man. Immelmann perfected a maneuver, a half loop followed by a half roll which positioned an aircraft quickly for a re-attack. The Immelmann turn, as it became known, is still practiced by student pilots today.

Eindecker deliveries picked up in July; more squadrons received their allotment of two aircraft and pressed them into combat following the example set by Boelcke and Immelmann. Appearance in the skies over France and Belgium of the new fighters using the new tactics unleased what the sensationalist French and British newspapers labeled "The Fokker Scourge." The Allies could not cope; their aircraft and tactics suddenly became obsolete. Army planners went blind with observation craft falling like burning leaves. Germany established air superiority over the war zone. The only respite came from the Germans themselves. To prevent the secret synchronization gear from being compromised by an aircraft forced down and captured, German pilots were forbidden to venture past the forward line of German trenches. True fighter pilots at last, a few Germans gleefully ignored this dictate in pursuit of ever-more victories. Blinded by bad weather in December, a German aviator landed his Eindecker at a French airfield by mistake and the secret of how to shoot through a turning propeller was quickly revealed. French test pilots quickly flew the Eindecker, finding it to be no better or worse than their own Morane-Saulnier craft. It did not represent a leap ahead in aircraft performance. The Fokker Scourge lived by the gun.

Using their well-practiced tactics, Boelcke and Immelmann continued to rack up kill after kill during the second half of 1915. By year's end, the Fokker Scourge accounted for 28 British and French planes shot down. Boelcke and Immelmann together accounted for 17 of these. Both earned the *"Pour le Merite"* medal, the highest honor the Prussian military could bestow despite its French title. The equivalent of America's Congressional Medal of Honor or the British Victoria Cross, the

Pour le Merite featured an enameled blue Maltese Cross on a neck ribbon. It instantly became known as "The Blue Max" after Max Immelmann, the first pilot to receive it.

Boelcke published a set of rules for air combat, the *Dicta Boelcke,* in a pamphlet distributed throughout the German Air Force. Read today, some of the rules seem self-evident, i.e., "Don't lose sight of the enemy," but the eight statements were the first formal treatise on fighter weapons and tactics.

On 18 June 1916, the two fighter pilots attacked a British observation plane. Immelmann's synchronization gear malfunctioned. His gun shattered a single propeller blade and the unbalanced rotating engine shook the aircraft apart. The tail broke off, the airplane pitched up, both wings separated, and Max Immelmann plunged to his death, conscious to the end. He was 25 years old. He who lives by the sword or gun....

Max Immelmann fell to earth because he was not issued a parachute. Had he one, he could have simply unbuckled his leather seat belt, stood up, let the airflow suck him out of the cockpit, pulled the ripcord, and floated to earth to fly and fight another day. Instead, he and many of his contemporaries on both sides were doomed to ride wrecked planes down, knowing for long, agonizing minutes full well what lay in store – sudden death by impact. The worst cases involved fire. Wooden airplanes covered with cloth painted with highly flammable dope burned furiously in a 75 mph, 120 kph, slipstream. When an enemy's bullet found the fuel tank or if leaking fuel dripped on the hot engine, a raging fire erupted instantly. A terrible choice confronted the poor devil in the cockpit; burn to death over several minutes or leave the aircraft and fall for half a minute, waiting on the crush of death. At this point in the war, no fixed-wing pilot on either side could bail out of a stricken airplane. A major malfunction, battle damage, or an onboard fire usually resulted in aircrew fatalities. The loss rate among aviators reached horrendous levels. At one time, the average life span of a Royal Air Force fighter pilot at the front was three weeks.

Parachutes had been in existence for over a hundred years, perhaps even since the time of Leonardo de Vinci. The name is French, *para* from the word for "to protect," and *chute* from the French word for "fall" – protection from a fall. By 1910 many people had demonstrated successful parachute drops, usually from balloons, sometimes from aircraft. The first parachute descent from the Eiffel Tower came in 1908, involuntarily by a dog. Parachutes were not unknown, unproven technology. Militaries of the era possessed parachutes; crews of observation balloons counted on them for quick, safe escapes. Therein lay the problem.

Senior officers stationed well back from both sides of the trenches during the Great War cannot be accused of either original thinking or of caring overmuch for their men. Why else would they order human wave attacks against machine gun nests or deny their aircrews parachutes? In the case of aviators, the answer comes in two parts and balloons play a major role in one. None of the commanders, none of the staff officers, none of the planners, nor any of the men who wrote regulations had ever commanded a fixed-wing aviation unit. Flying squadrons did not exist when these men came up through the ranks nor when they attended service academies. Few ever flew in an aircraft. It is safe to assume none understood the mentality of the new breed of warrior, the fighter pilot.

What the brass did grasp was the actions of balloon crews when under attack. Suspended beneath thousands of cubic feet of flammable hydrogen gas in a wicker basket hundreds of feet in the air, balloon crew members were sitting ducks to air attack. When a fighter plane appeared on the horizon, crews quickly considered four options. One; hope the anti-aircraft guns on the ground around the balloon could shoot down the attacker or scare him off without putting any stray rounds into the explosive balloon. Two; hope the balloon's ground crew could winch the gas bag to earth in time for the crew to run out from underneath it. Three: hit the silk and float to earth. Four: hope the fighter pilot would not get enough hot lead into the balloon to touch off a fireball. Balloons were extremely vulnerable; an American ace, Lieutenant Frank Luke, the "Balloon Buster," torched 14 balloons in less than two months. It is no surprise balloon crew members tended to quickly choose option Three, escape by parachute.

Generals tended to put all airmen into the same category perceiving no differences between balloon observers and pilots of fixed-wing aircraft. The pseudo-logic ran, "Airmen will bail out at the first signs of approaching trouble if parachutes are available. Therefore, if we equip pilots with 'chutes, they will not stick around and fight."

Another bogus rationale, probably a cover story to disguise the point about parachute-induced cowardice, involved saving a stricken or malfunctioning airplane. Aircraft cost money and were in short supply. Better to have the aircrew try to save the airframe instead of bailing out when an engine quit, a commonplace occurrence. This thinking was also highly suspect. In the hundred and twenty-plus years of military aviation, pilots have tended to stay with a doomed aircraft too long, trying the save the bird.

For whatever reason, it was not until 1918 when the German High Command, facing a critical shortage of pilots, issued parachutes to aviators. Ernst Udet, later commander of all German fighter forces in World War II, and Herman Goring, ultimately Hitler's Deputy Fuhrer, owed their survival in the Great War to parachutes. French, American, and British pilots never received them until after the war when it was too late.

Max Immelmann's death received wide coverage in newspapers and not only in Germany. Parisian and London broadsheets featured what to them was good news. By this time in the war, fighter pilots on both sides acquired a mystical public status. Everyone who read the papers knew who the leading aces were, and now many kills each racked up. The press fed this public fascination focused on a handful of men, none over 30 years old. Fighter pilots seemed to represent what each country's citizens felt were their national core values or at least what the newspapers told them those values were.

At the time, newspapers were both the prime source of news and the main distributors of propaganda and it was not easy to tell the difference. The idea of a free, independent press, which reported only facts became lost in wartime fever. Little separated the editorial pages from hard news. Indeed, the same men sometimes wrote both. They were always men. Each paper, whether in Paris, London, Berlin, or Vienna, slanted war news to reflect the owner's political views and the respective governments' official positions. Reporters were tradesmen, not professionals. Most beat reporters worked their way up from messengers or delivery people. None were college graduates. The concept of a well-educated, independent reporter who related the news without fear or favor lay in the future. Thus, war news, whether censored for security reasons, slanted by politics, or dictated by an imperious owner, rarely gave an accurate picture of developments on the battlefield.

This was not surprising as the news from the front was never good. Armies were slaughtering men by the thousands, an average of over 3000 per day, for little gain. The "Great War" bogged down in the mud and blood of the trenches. No one wanted to report on that situation and no one wanted to buy papers and read about it. Instead, the papers gave top billing to stirring accounts of the latest victory, the most recent triumph, and the grandest exploit. During a global war of much complexity with stalemate on the battlefield, the public wanted heroes. Heroes who did things people could understand easily. Fighter pilots filled the void. What better symbol of a county's finest than dashing, photogenic young men who flew and fought alone, assuming the role of the single-combat warrior? Part knight errant, part old west gun fighter, aviators fought battles anyone could understand with definite, immediate winners and losers. The public lapped it up and the authorities, aided by the docile press, fed the interest.

Bowing to the public's demand for heroes, papers did not let facts get in the way of a good story. Parisian papers reported Roland Garros's first air combat victory came about when he rammed his monoplane into a dirigible. How he survived the inevitable fiery explosion (like observation balloons, dirigibles floated on hydrogen) was not related. This bogus account must have been good copy. It still exists in reference material.

The Fokker Scourge did not make the English or French papers while it occurred. The ever-present censors had no interest in publicizing the fact that German aircraft were wreaking havoc with Allied observation planes. Only after Allied synchronizer-equipped fighters began to turn the tide after the first of the year did the term "Fokker Scourge" appear in the broadsheets as a menace dealt with and dispatched.

For Tony Fokker, the scourge generated more sales than his factory could produce. It also kicked off a technology race which continued throughout the war. Every aircraft maker in the West set about to build and field airplanes with higher performance than the Eindecker and equip them with synchronized guns. They succeeded in the main and by year's end 1915, the Fokker Scourge began to abate. Tony Fokker fielded his own improved models, which were again countered by the Allies, and so it went for the rest of the war. A particular aircraft would gain the upper hand only to be overcome by the other side's improved models. The result was rapid progress for four years in the field of aircraft design and performance. Roland Garros would experience this technology leap for himself, but first he had to cope with prisoner of war camp.

CHAPTER THIRTY-TWO

PRISONER OF WAR

AND NOT A HAPPY ONE

Roland Garros found himself once again in Germany, this time as an unwilling visitor. Instead of touring aircraft factories as a guest, as he had done less than a year prior, he toured a succession of prisoner of war camps as an inmate. The shock of captivity must have been intense for the free-spirited Garros. He transitioned from enjoying the many carnal pleasures of Paris to forced detention somewhere in Germany. Accounts of his life in various prisoner of war camps come almost entirely from Garros himself in his published memoirs (written while a prisoner) and later press interviews. He took great pains describing how he refused to submit to his guards, denying them respect and disobeying them whenever possible. Coming from a relentless self-promoter, these stories must be taken with a grain of salt. However, there is some history backing up his claims of passive resistance – his frequent transfers. For his efforts, he was transferred from camp to camp; Kustrin, Treves, Bourg, Opiniatree, each one harsher than the last, until he was locked up in the ancient fortress of Zorndorf near the Polish-German border.

The Germans reserved this pile of rocks for what the French labeled *"Fortes Tetes"* or "Strong Heads." Life there was not easy, bordering on brutal. Garros said his life in prison was harsh, at times desperate, but he was never intentionally mistreated, tortured, or singled out for abuse.

Conditions in Zorndorf prison gained such a bad reputation the French began working with the International Red Cross organization, based in neutral Switzerland, to alert the Swiss to the situation. Government authorities in Paris complained to the authorities in Geneva, claiming internment in Zorndorf constituted a war crime. The Germans, conscious of bad publicity they were already getting about this medieval lock-up, closed it down, and transferred Garros to Gnadenfrei back in Alsace. Roland wrote his family he thought he died and gone to heaven, the conditions there were so much better, almost like a summer camp with armed guards. Following more pressure from the Red Cross, German jailers allowed prisoners of war to receive an unlimited number of packages and letters and to retain their personal effects such as books.

As days stretched into weeks, weeks into months, and months became years, Roland Garros continued to hold out hope of release or escape. He wrote his mother, telling her the letters and books sent to him by friends and family kept him going, kept his spirits up, allowed him the luxury of thinking he was not forgotten.

His father, working with his high-level contacts, tried to get him released to asylum in Switzerland using the help of Swiss friend Jacques Quellennec, but to no avail. The Swiss government, scrupulously neutral, only accepted POWs whose health was so poor they might not survive further captivity. An exchange of captive officers between Germany and France was discussed but also went nowhere. In both cases, Garros's basic health and fame worked against him. He was too well for the Swiss, and too well-known for the Germans to release or to trade in exchange.

Despite the improvement in his living conditions, after two years Garros's morale seems to have finally flagged. Perhaps he saw the war's non-progress for what it was, a futile stalemate. The two sides, mired down in never-ending, never-progressing trench warfare, were no closer to victory or defeat than when the Schlieffen plan failed in 1914. The only changes evident were improvements in the techniques of mass slaughter. Tanks, poison gas, flame-throwers, barbed wire, and tightly choreographed artillery barrages were unleashed with lethal effects. Zeppelins bombed London by night, killing thousands of civilians in the densely-packed city. Widespread panic ensued. London's population had not been hounded by the dogs of war for centuries, and sudden death had never fallen from the sky. Germany built massive, railway-borne siege guns capable of shelling Paris from behind the front lines. These too operated under the cover of darkness. When buildings began to explode and crumple without warning, Parisians wrongly attributed the carnage to unseen Zeppelins hovering above. Still, the Great War dragged on and on.

In early January 1917, the despondent prisoner penned a final heart-breaking letter to Marcelle Gorge. On the hand-written note the low state of his morale leaps from the page. He tells Marcelle the war will go on for much longer and he does not expect to return anytime soon to Paris. Do not waste the best years of your life, of your youth, which can never be recovered, he tells her. He releases her from any obligation to remain faithful and to follow her heart wherever it leads. He seems to understand the young lady's carnal desires, and why not, he shared those urges along with her bed. Garros closes with, "*Vis raisonnablement, mais vis. Suis tes gouts et tes instincts: sois libre pour nous deux.*" Screw reasonably, but screw. Follow your tastes and your instincts. Live free for both of us. Perhaps not the most elegant choice of words to give someone their freedom, but Garros's message is as clear as his love for Marcelle.

The Gnaderfrei prison was probably converted from a school. It boasted a tennis court, one of the few POW camps to have one, ever. Newly cooperative, or perhaps scheming, the little Frenchman befriended the camp commandant and obtained permission to receive two racquets and some balls. The racquets arrived via the Red Cross, as did all the packages and letters delivered to the camp. Both leather-wrapped, wooden handles were hollow and in them were stashed maps of Germany and a miniature compass. One problem inherent with escape from a POW camp is knowing where you are and the direction of safety.

This curious episode indicates forces and people at work under cover, behind the scenes. There is more to this story than meets the eye. How would Garros know to look inside the racquet handles? Like all packages, the sporting equipment was subject to inspection upon arrival by the guards yet the contraband slipped through. Garros later hinted at coded messages he sent and received via letters while in prison. Who set this system up? Who managed the process which went on to deliver more forbidden goods? Garros also received boxes of civilian clothes sent from France. A picture exists of him along with two compatriots taken while they were POWs. All three, two Frenchmen and a Russian officer, are well-dressed, as if out for a night on the town. Undoubtedly, his captors took the photo to prove to a skeptical world conditions in POW camps were not as dire as feared. But still, natty attire is not normal in prison.

By this time in the years-long conflict, conditions in Germany were deteriorating rapidly. Cut off from overseas supplies by a Royal Navy blockade and with dwindling stocks of food, rations in Germany were short. Compounding the problem was the fact that most, if not all, young men were away at the front or were dead. Few able-bodied men were available to farm or to process food. Women pressed into rural service could not keep up with the hunger of a million-man army, particularly in a time when refrigeration and cold storage were not widely available and wastage was common.

Garros's status as a famous pre-war aviator and national hero generated numerous food parcels mailed by private citizens and delivered by the Red Cross. He boasted his food deliveries were feeding half the prisoners in camp. Probably an exaggeration, but not by much. On the other side of the barbed wire, the guards were starving. Garros remarked that the rations provided to the staff would not be fed to dogs in France. Even allowing for traditional French cuisine snobbery and the fact that dogs were, and are, fed in restaurants, this comment is interesting for two reasons. The first speaks well of the Germans. Despite their miserable rations, the guards seem to have obeyed all the protocols for POW treatment and did not confiscate or interfere with food shipments. This ultra-humane and honest policy fell into disfavor in the 20th century's later wars when combatants regularly denied POWs needed nourishment. Secondly, excess food delivered from France via Switzerland prove how hungry guards might be bribed. Garros knew food was gold in a POW camp and could be exchanged for favors and access.

The tennis racquet caper and subsequent actions strongly speak of a covert, underground network established by the French and operating in Germany and Switzerland. France and various Germanic states including Swiss cantons shared a border and mutual suspicions for decades, even centuries. Yet, travel between the rival states was easy and frequent. French people toured Germany and Germans strolled the Champs-Elysees. Two world's fairs in Paris entertained thousands of Germans and their Austrian/Hungarian allies. Given the long history of rivalry, including the war of 1870, any responsible government would have established a network of agents across the contested border. It is reasonable to assume the French did just that.

A possible source of spies, for both sides, would have been the disputed provinces of Alsace and Lorraine. Most citizens there spoke both German and French fluently and they could pass for either nationality. History books are rife with examples, mostly of agents working inside France for Germany or innocent folk suspected of divided loyalty. "Mata Hari," an exotic dancer turned *femme fatale,* and a Dutch citizen like Tony Fokker, was convicted of spying for Germany and executed by firing squad in France. Earlier, Alfred Dreyfus, an Alsatian French army officer, found himself framed and sentenced to Devil's Island prison for passing secrets to Germany. Dreyfus was innocent, but his trial exposed the widespread belief that German agents were active in France.

We must assume similar networks operated in Germany sponsored by the French who have a well-deserved reputation for *sub-rosa* expertise. However, as winners write the history books and presumably wish to replicate such successes in the future, covert operations inside Germany were kept secret long after the war. Accounts and techniques were buried in the archives of the DGSE, the *Direction Général de la Sécurité Extérieur*, the French counterpart to the CIA and the British MI6 organizations. All we can follow now is washed-out tracks in the sands of time. Garros's eventual escape and evasion display all the hallmarks of a sophisticated covert operation orchestrated by a French government who very much wanted its national hero back. Today, 100 years later, the official French position is that Roland Garros operated alone. Perhaps the French are even now running agents in Germany.

When not pretending to play tennis, Garros managed to corrupt a guard, perhaps with food, perhaps with gold coins smuggled in, the record is not clear. For his efforts, he was transferred again, to Magdebourg, an ancient city situated almost in the geographic center of Germany on the Elbe river and as far from any border as possible. He was allowed to take along his personal effects and books. The Germans' objective, to keep Garros in captivity and if he did escape, to hunt him down in Germany, proved to be harder than anticipated. One reason was the quality and dedication of the guards, or lack thereof.

By early 1918, living conditions in Germany and Austria were worse than ever and were going downhill rapidly. A harsh winter and poor harvest almost exhausted food stocks in civilian areas. Germany was cut off from the breadbaskets of Poland and the Ukraine by the Russians. Not just hunger, but outright famine, stalked the land. People were starving to death. If malnourishment did not kill, it weakened civilians and disease did the rest. Morale in the armed forces was also undernourished. The High Seas Fleet, bottled up in the north German port of Kiel by the Royal Navy, refused to put to sea. Berlin began to transfer reluctant sailors to the infantry to help alleviate a crisis in manpower. In this environment POW camp guards were not a high personnel priority. The military's dregs; the infirm, the weak, the dim-witted, the old, found themselves guarding Allied prisoners. Opportunities for compromise abounded.

In his dreams of escape to date, Garros lacked one essential component, a German-speaking compatriot. Germany is, for the most part, densely populated. Unaided cross-country evasion and undetected travel in winter were almost impossible, even in 1918. Escapees could not have crossed farmland without contact with the natives, so public transportation would have to be used. Train schedules, streets signs, directions, all in German, needed to be understood by escapees. Interactions with locals could not attract suspicion and ID card checks were everywhere. Undoubtedly, Garros picked up some of the language during three years of captivity, but his accent would have stuck out on German streets like a French beret on his head. He needed someone who could pass for German, who could speak the language, and could execute a cover story. That man was Anselme Marchal.

Marchal, another French pilot, met Garros in Magdebourg. Early in the war, he flew a nighttime mission in a long-range aircraft from Nancy in France to Berlin dropping propaganda leaflets calling for the German people to reject their leaders' attack on Russia. His engine quit before he was able to continue to Poland as planned and Marchal entered the miserable world of the POW. A relentless escaper, Marchal once made it all the way to the Dutch border; freedom lay on the other side of a deep canal. His traveling companion, a non-swimming Royal Air Force pilot, managed to fall in the water. The banks were too steep to climb; Marchal could not swim either. He confronted an awful choice. Abandon his friend to drown and he could probably reach safety in the Netherlands over a nearby bridge or call for help. He chose the honorable path and German forest rangers came running, fished out the Brit, and returned both POWs to the authorities. Besides Anselme Marchal's unquenchable thirst for freedom, the native Alsatian possessed one other key attribute. He spoke perfect German.

Marchal and Garros obtained two German officer's uniforms, according to later accounts. How this feat of subterfuge was pulled off is not known with certainty, but speaks again of the existence of outside, covert help. At the time between the dog and the wolf, i.e. twilight, they walked purposefully toward the camp's main gate. When challenged by a guard, Marchal, in his best imperious German, told the sentry to mind his watch. The two Frenchmen walked out unmolested. Once out of the guards' sight, they ditched the uniforms and donned civilian clothes, soon blending in with the natives. It was St. Valentine's Day, 14 February 1918. Roland Garros had been a prisoner for nearly three years and at last he was free, as free as you can be deep inside your enemy's home country,

What followed was, by contemporary accounts, an epic journey. Garros, led by Marchal, passed through Magdebourg, Brunswick, Cologne, and occupied Aix-la Chapelle, until reaching the Dutch border. Newspaper accounts told of them sleeping in cemeteries, who wants to search there at night, and hiding in dark cinemas while waiting to catch the next train. All this travel, mostly by rail, required money and identity cards. Food, which was not cheap, needed to be purchased, and admission to cinemas, if such occurred, was not free.

This trip across Germany has all the characteristics of a well-planned and well-run operation by a network of French agents operating under deep cover. How could two POW's acquire realistic officers' uniforms, cash, ID cards, even watches needed to catch a train on time? Marchal's language capability undoubtedly played a part, but he and Garros needed help and lots of it. Cover stories published later by newspapers were designed by either intent or by planted information to sow confusion. According to the popular press, Garros attempted several prior escapes, including digging a tunnel which ended in failure in a cemetery just outside the wire. The public was led to believe that finally one of his escape capers paid off.

If a prisoner did have a history of trying to flee, what are the chances the authorities would allow such a hard case to possess civilian clothes and to play tennis? In fact, his one escape attempt proved successful, another indication of outside forces at work. Garros himself let the curtain of deception slip once during an interview with the New York Times. In the published piece, he states all accounts of his escape from Germany were inaccurate and how he achieved his freedom was secret. When they read this statement, intelligence operatives at the DGSE *Quai d'Orsay* headquarters in Paris probably choked on their espressos.

It is 15 February 1918. The scattered crowd of Germans waiting in the cold for the train include some old men, a few young boys, and women of all ages. Men of military age are conspicuously absent. On the platform, most remain silent, with the hang-dog expressions of beaten people. These are folk who are going about their business regardless of the news from the front, which they have learned to distrust, while ignoring the hunger they all feel inside. Hunger for proper nourishment certainly, Germans love to eat, but also a longing for better times, for a future without never-ending war, for their few surviving young men to return.

The old man is slightly built, of average height. He wears a rumpled brown suit, a worn overcoat, a narrow-brimmed felt hat, with black shoes run down at the heels. Wire-rimmed glasses frame an expressionless face with a bushy-grey mustache. His silver-tinged hair is cropped short. He is the sort of man few notice, one who melts into a crowd, a man who escapes attention, which is precisely the point. He could be anyone or no one.

A worn, leather satchel dangles from his right hand, perhaps containing a clean shirt and some bread and sausage. Maybe a revolver. His left hand holds an unlighted cigarette dangling between his middle and ring fingers, an unusual way to hold a smoke, one which escapes notice unless you are looking for it, which is also the point.

Two young men mount the stone stairs to the platform, the taller one in the lead, the shorter, darker one following. Both are sallow, unused to the light of day, with sunken cheeks and pinched lips. Their clothes, suits and ties covered by cheap cloth coats, fit poorly, hanging on frames which once were robust but now are gaunt. If anyone cares to notice, their eyes set them apart, the haunted eyes of the hunted, eyes searching for danger where none is apparent. In normal times, such stark visages would attract attention, but not now, and not in Germany. The two have the look of men who had seen too much, done things which sickened their spirits, who have experienced the horrors of modern warfare. The fact that they do not stand out speaks volumes about the quality of life in Germany in 1918.

Both men search the crowd, looking left and right without moving their faces, only their darting eyes. The leader quickly spots the nondescript old man leaning against a faded wooden sign displaying train schedules. The old man raises his left hand, the one holding the still-unlit cigarette up to his face, making it more visible. The two nearly pass the silent man who seems to ignore them. They look up and down the platform both ways, then stop and slowly approach him.

The tall one speaks with a hint of an Alsatian accent.

"*Hast du eine extra Zigarrette? Ich bin anscheinend draubben.*" Do you have an extra cigarette? I seem to be out. The shorter traveler remains silent, a half-step removed, his dark eyes never stop scanning the crowd.

"*Nimm die Packung, ich versuche aofzuhoren,*" Take the whole pack, I am trying to quit, the older man replies with the same regional inflection. He reaches into his inner coat pocket and withdraws a cardboard cigarette box, slightly crushed, and hands it to the supplicant.

"*Vielen Dank,*" Many thanks. The taller one speaks.

"*Gute Reise.*" Good journey, comes back the reply, with a slight edge of irony.

The two travelers walk to the end of the platform, turn their backs on the crowd, and open the cigarette pack while facing each other. When they glance back to the billboard, the old man has disappeared, faded into the cold. They divide between them train tickets, two ID cards, ration cards, and a flattened roll of tattered German Marks. In the distance a steam train rounds a curve, chugging into view, slowing for the station with screeching brakes. The train is west bound, toward the Dutch border and freedom.

However they did it, the two fugitive travelers somehow managed to cross the frontier between Germany and Holland avoiding the guard towers and coiled barbed wire. By the first of March, they were back in Paris, feted by officialdom, the press, and the public alike.

Almost three years of captivity had not been kind to Roland Garros. His eyes sunk in their sockets and his cheeks were sallow. Gone were the flamboyant mustache and the wild mop of curly hair. He was thinner than usual. Usually outgoing and friendly, he was reserved, cautious in his interactions with others. Prison will do that to a person. Starting to recede, his hair was slicked back, set off by a pencil-thin mustache. In photos taken in Paris, Roland Garros has an uncanny resemblance to another French aviator and author who would gain fame after the war – Antione de Saint-Exupery. Garros and Saint-Ex were to share more than similar appearances.

CHAPTER THIRTY-THREE

BACK TO THE FRONT

WHY?

Why did he volunteer, even demand to fly combat missions again after such a long, forced lay-off? Was it a thirst for revenge, a long-awaited payback for his prolonged misery as a POW? Did he now hate Germans and Austrians, the very people he socialized with in 1914? Was he bored? Did he miss the excitement of air combat, the thrill of contested flight? Did his adrenaline addiction reappear? Did he want to make up for the wasted years of whiling away time in prison reading books, writing letters, and pretending to play tennis?

Perhaps he missed the macho camaraderie of a combat squadron. Life in a fighter squadron is like no other professional relationship. Pilots get to know their squadron mates better than their siblings, sometimes better than their spouses, a fact not admitted easily, particularly to said spouses. Life-long friendships form with mates who could be dead tomorrow. Maybe he missed the emotional intensity of that unique environment. Patriotism undoubtedly played a part. He was not compelled to sign up for military service as a citizen of Réunion Island, but he did, twice.

You could speculate he wanted to prove something to himself if not to the public. Getting shot down in1915, if that is indeed what happened instead of engine problems, represented a personal failure of sorts. Also, notching two more kills would make him an ace, an honor few pilots attain and would represent a redemption of sorts for the humiliation of being captured.

Maybe his corsair heritage asserted itself. Did he need to prove himself worthy of his sea-faring ancestors featured in tales told by his father? Being a pilot captured by the Germans might have reminded Garros of a corsair captain apprehended by the Royal Navy, without the waiting gallows. It could be he wanted to sail the sky as a modern corsair once again before the war ended his opportunity. Germany was clearly defeated, with mutiny in the Navy, starvation in the cities, and chaos on the battlefield. This could be the last hurrah for a corsair/pilot. A few last sorties, a few final chances for glory and redemption. Or, it could have been a broken heart that drove him back to the front lines.

His physical recovery and re-immersion into Parisian society did not go as he hoped. Marcelle Gorge remained in the Pyrénées still in medical care and not improving. He never saw her again. In September of 1918, Garros enjoyed a brief dalliance with the famous exotic dancer Isadore Duncan. Dating the *Belle Époque* version of a stripper probably fulfilled fantasies with which he entertained himself during long nights in captivity. Duncan later wrote she danced for Garros one night in a fountain in the *Place de la Concorde,* at the foot of the *Champs Elysées.*

It is early September in Paris and the days are getting shorter. It is pitch-dark at midnight. Traffic in *La Place de la Concorde* is light and due to gas rationing, limited to official vechicles and taxis. The streetlights for which the city is famous are extinguished and the few cars' headlights are dimmed. Paris is blacked out to make bomb-aiming by German Zeppelins and Gotha bombers more difficult. Two bodies are silhouetted against the sheets of water spouting from one of the two fountains in the plaza. One person, a female, stands in the knee-deep pond, the other, a man, sits on the circular stone rim. The woman in the pool twirls, pirouettes, and poses, her silk dress clings like a second skin, revealing her voluptuous figure. The slender man watches silently but intently.

"Tu me fais peur, mon amour." You are frightening me, my love, she says after a particularly provocative move.

"Pourquoi?" Why, the man asks.

"I look into your eyes when we are alone and instead of my reflection, I see the fires of war."

"You know I must go back." The man replies.

"No. Why must you? Germany is beaten. The war is all but won. The President himself has offered you an important staff position. Why do you return?"

Her tears mingle with the spray from the fountain and fall unnoticed. The man's answer is to look skyward, into the black night, toward the unseen horizon in the northeast. Off in the far distance, over the rattle of the occasional passing car, an aircraft engine drones in the dark.

In grainy black-and-white photos of Garros taken in mid-1918, gone is the intense stare into the camera so evident in pre-war shots. He appears to be looking past the camera, into the middle distance. At what? During another war, World War II, or was it the same war continued, Saint-Ex experienced the same cognitive disconnect and employed the same solution, volunteering to fly in combat.

Garros made the long boat trip across the Atlantic, fighting seasickness all the way, dispatched by the French government to New York to publicly thank Americans for entering the global conflict, and for tipping the scales of battle in the Allies' favor. Usually adept, even enthusiastic, at interacting with the press, his interview with the NY Times shows him being irritable and curt. Gone is the self-promoting former car salesperson and pioneer aviator pushing for faster progress in flight. You get the impression he wanted to be somewhere else. Of course, he may have been merely repelled by the lack of professionalism shown by local reporters. One article listed him as born in South Africa. For a French colonial, being erroneously traced back to a British Crown Colony was the ultimate slight and one which could have been prevented with a simple question.

Strings were pulled, phone calls made, contacts exercised, chits brought in, and Roland Garros got assigned back to the front lines. French national authorities must have been reluctant to risk a hero, whose name everyone knew, in the crucible of combat. The debate went all the way up to the summit of French political life. Senior politician Georges Clemenceau and the President of France, Raymond Poincaré, became involved. Viewed from another more cynical, perspective, why should Roland Garros be sheltered from danger? Many other famous French aviators had risked their lives for France and the war was not quite over.

By this time in the war, the French Air Force had established tactical flying schools to teach the latest techniques to young pilots before plunging them in the maelstrom of combat. In August 1918, Garros spent some time in such a school in Pau near the Spanish border and the site of Louis Blériot's flying schools before the war. He flew the Nieuport XVII, a graceful but fragile machine, one fast becoming obsolete in squadron service. In mid-September, he returned to his old Squadron, SPA 26, "The Storks."

Garros found none of his old squadron mates still in SPA 26; most were dead. Also gone was the air war as he remembered it. Three years is a long time when rapid technical and tactical changes are afoot. The squadron was equipped with SPAD XIII's with triple the horsepower; 220 hp versus the Morane-Saulnier's 70 hp, he last flew. SPADs were sturdy biplanes instead of flimsy monoplanes, the technology had moved on rapidly. Wing warping for roll control was out. Proper ailerons flexed on each top wing's trailing edge. Old Le Rhône rotary type engines were obsolete, The SPAD XIII mounted a mighty Hispano-Suiza liquid-cooled V-8.

Aircraft performance in 1918 must have seemed breathtaking to Garros. Before the war, he abandoned his quest for the world altitude record due to oxygen starvation at 16,000 feet, 4800 meters, due to the resultant loss of cognitive ability. Now, SPADs regularly flew patrols over 21,000 feet, 6600 meters, where the air was even wispier and the temperature was far below zero, whether measured in Fahrenheit or Centigrade. It is doubtful if Garros ever experienced 100 mph, 160 kph in his old crates. A SPAD XIII could clock 135 mph, 218 kph, in level flight and approached 240 mph, 400 kph, in a dive. Pre-war monoplanes were barely aerobatic; loops and rolls were a challenge. In 1918, biplanes could do most aerobatic maneuvers easily and recover. Instead of one clunky, long Hotchkiss machine gun, the SPAD mounted twin .303 caliber Vickers "modern" guns each with 400 rounds and firing, hopefully, through the propeller. Roland Garros must have felt catapulted into the future. In a way, he was. The SPAD XIII is everyone's mental image of a World War I fighter plane. When asked to picture a flying machine from that era, most people will mentally draw a SPAD and why not. All the French aces alive at war's end and most of their American counterparts flew the SPAD XIII. Several still exist in various museums around the world.

One area untouched by technical progress was the cockpit. Aircraft were unpressurized and would remain so for the next two and a half decades. Cockpit heating was a distant dream. Parachutes still did not figure into the picture. Even given the rapid progress in aerodynamics, WWI biplanes and triplanes were a handful to fly; evil-handling beasts requiring the utmost in piloting skill and care. The SPAD XIII was better, or rather less bad, than most and certainly a more honest airplane than the famous British Sopwith Camel. Camels tended to be unstable in roll, neutral in yaw, and divergent in pitch. Reliability continued to be a problem with engine failure a constant worry, particularly in the SPAD.

Add up the miserable human factors features of the era's airplanes, the treacherous handling characteristics, the highly flammable structures, the unreliable engines, the flights in marginal weather without instruments, the sketchy maintenance, and you get a period when fighter aircraft killed nearly as many of their own pilots as they did of the enemy, whoever that was. Just under half of the pilot deaths during the Great War were due to accidents.

Roland Garros plunged headlong into this hazardous world of fighter aviation; one for which he was ill-prepared. Piloting is a skill which rusts with neglect and he had not flown in three years. His physical condition had deteriorated. He lost weight and with it muscle tone. Hand-eye coordination is not enhanced by captivity in a cell. Perhaps due to a POWs' poor diet, his eyesight was fading. Garros smuggled eyeglasses into his cockpit and donned them under his flying goggles when he thought no one was watching. Fighter pilots live on their eyesight, coordination, physical conditioning, confidence, and training. In the fall of 1918, Roland Garros fell short in four of the five attributes.

Why did he do it? The question bothers us today. A national hero, he could have remained in Paris attached as an advisor to the French General Staff, a position he was offered and turned down. No one would have faulted him for taking the post. He paid his dues as a POW and was the inventor of true air combat. He delayed his entry into the future world of aviation, a world he promoted and helped create. Garros was destined to participate in the advances of the 1920s, as did Saint-Ex, and then retire to a life of renown as a senior *Legion d'Honneur* member. But he did not wait safely on the ground until the war's end. He could not. The headstrong rebel who avoided traditional education in Saigon, who refused to learn swordsmanship in Nice, a lawyer who did not know Latin, a successful car salesman who ditched his lucrative business for aviation, the socialite playboy who contemplated marrying his lover, just could not back down. Garros told the NY Times he expected to re-acquire his flying skills in less than a month. That estimate proved to be wildly optimistic. He rejoined the Storks as the wing moved from Nancy to Noblette in the Champagne region. Garros returned to the locale where he first acquired a taste, a burning thirst, for flight years before in Reims.

When he arrived back at his squadron after a three-year hiatus, few things remained unchanged. Besides the leap in aircraft performance, fighter plane tactics had evolved rapidly. Instead of parceling out fighters in ones and twos among general purpose squadrons, wings of fighters took to the air flown by full-time, dedicated fighter pilots. Concentrating their expertise together facilitated exchange of information and tactics among the pilots both formally down the chain of command and informally around the officer's club mess tables and bar. Particularly the bar.

Hard tactical lessons taught years earlier by Boelke and Immelmann, had been hoisted aboard by both sides. Flights, squadrons, sometimes whole wings, flew and fought as organized teams. The lone-wolf fighter pilot's time was rapidly ending. Germans with their more hierarchical mentality took this concept further yet. They anointed their best, or most experienced, pilots as "*Chasseurs*" or "Hunters." These aces sought easy targets while the rest of the flight protected the hunter, allowing him to concentrate on logging a kill without the necessity of watching behind his aircraft for the enemy. Hunters soon ran up impressive kill totals and even aviators of marginal talent, such as Herman Goring, could become famous aces. The French tried to emulate the Germans with some success despite lacking the requisite love for discipline and for assigned airborne roles. However, the German Air Force committed a serious mistake, an error they would replicate with similar consequences during the 1940s and round two of the Great War.

German pilots were assigned to combat squadrons for the war's duration or until they were killed – the usual outcome. This scheme did not allow experienced pilots the opportunity to transfer back to training squadrons to pass along their hard-won knowledge and to share evolved tactics with their students. Why? No self-respecting Prussian warrior would not be at the front and fighting. Relegation to a pilot-training role invited dishonor among the German jocks. In the short term, this plan produced good results. The more experienced German pilots were more than a match for their French and British opponents. As the fighting dragged on, this idea fell apart as tactics and techniques became more sophisticated and thus harder to learn literally on the fly.

Junior pilots reported to their squadrons with little knowledge of how to fight, only how to die. Critical expertise did not filter back to the training bases. The Fokker Scourge became Fokker Fodder as Allied pilots took the measure of green-as-grass Germans. To their credit, the French and British set up a rotation system so experienced combat veterans, or those with frayed nerves, were sent back to the training command on a regular basis. This paid off equally well for the allies in the 1940s. The Germans, to their disadvantage, continued making the mistakes of the Great War. Some lessons must be learned the hard way.

The German High Command saw this trend developing and instead of correcting the dire situation, doubled down as 1917 became 1918. The shortage of qualified pilots was exacerbated by a lack of candidates for pilot training. Prussian cavalrymen, ideally from the upper reaches of German/Prussian society, Berlin's preferred solution, made things worse by getting killed and thus unavailable for pilot training. Instead of relieving their experienced pilots and sending a few back to train others, they concentrated all their best aviators into just a few wings. This misguided scheme produced several units of very proficient fighter pilots and more numerous wings of "nuggets," with little hope of either combat effectiveness or survival. Elite units ranged along the front lines wherever tactical needs were the greatest. Wings sometimes moved weekly, trying desperately to stave off, or delay, defeat.

This nomadic lifestyle reminded folks of prewar displays put on by "flying circuses" living and flying out of tents, constantly on the move. Baron Manfred von Richthofen's circus is the most famous of these elite units. They took on the title with gusto and painted their aircraft in wild colors like circus entertainers. Gaily-painted Fokkers also allowed closer teamwork in the air as identifying teammates was a snap. Protect the blood-red triplane! (the Red Baron).

For the Allies, Germany's concentration of talent into circuses produced a situation in which adversaries did not know what to anticipate in the air. Attacking a formation of

Fokkers might result in easy pickings from the low-skilled wings, or a fight to the death with aces, like the Richthofen outfit. Leave the red airplane alone and go after ones with standard paint jobs.

Not much is known about Garros's return to his old squadron, and particularly what training he received there, if any. The German army was falling back, finally losing the war, on the verge of collapse, and the Storks were in great demand for combat missions. No longer a war of trenches, it became a conflict of maneuver, highlighting the mobility of aircraft. French, British, and American generals finally ran the war they wanted and planned for. A self-taught pilot, Garros the old aviator was not used to being instructed on matters aeronautical. It is not clear how receptive he would have been to advice from pilots 10 years younger and with far fewer hours in the air.

On 2 October 1918, Garros, flying with his new squadron mates, shot down one German plane, which was confirmed as his fourth victory, adding to his three kills in 1914. He claimed another kill the same day, but this one, which would have made him an ace, could not be verified by neutral observers. Flying a SPAD XIII whose capabilities he was just learning to employ, these two engagements represented quite an accomplishment. Roland Garros, the oldest pilot in the squadron, out of shape, wearing glasses, his reflexes slowed by captivity, managed to down two enemy fighter planes in mortal combat. You would be forgiven for believing he happened upon two nuggets, German pilots of little experience and less training. In the fighter pilot community to this day, the motto, "A kill is a kill" remains extant; they all count regardless of the quality of the opposition.

Later that week, on 5 October 1918, Garros flew as number two, wingman to his Flight Commander, who was leading a flight of seven SPADs. Evidently, his victories on the 2nd convinced the Squadron Operations Officer that Garros was up to speed and capable as a Number Two in formation. Over the Ardennes forest, behind the fast retreating German lines, five

314 | ED COBLEIGH

of the formation's pilots separated, against orders, to attack a lumbering German observation plane. In what was probably a pre-planned trap, the two remaining SPAD XIIIs were jumped by at least seven Fokker VIIs. These Germans played on the first team. Both desperate French pilots flew for their lives as the Germans, operating in unison, split up into two flights, each taking one opponent. This well-honed tactic prevented the Frenchmen from providing mutual support to each other.

World War One dogfights played out at close quarters, usually inside of 50 yards, 50 meters. With unstable gun platforms and no lead-computing gunsights, only crude wire crosses, it was extremely difficult to hit a moving target outside of point-blank range. Air combat was up close and personal, with adversaries in full view of one another. There is nothing like having an enemy 100 feet, 30 meters, behind your aircraft shooting at you with twin machine guns to get your heart pumping. This proximity made for frantic action, yet due to the slow speeds involved, an engagement could take 5-10 minutes. Five minutes of twisting, turning, climbing, and diving, dodging bullets while trying to get a shot off when a aircraft passed in front of your guns. Physical courage was not enough, good physical conditioning was essential.

A fighter pilot needed to keep his wits about him when maneuvering against a foe. Turn too tight at too high an airspeed and you could pull the wings off your aircraft. Too fast a dive could shed the wings' fabric. A stall, from too tight a turn at too slow an airspeed would result in a spin. A spin is a predictable flight path, aiding a shooter. All this raced through a pilot's mind as bullets raced toward his body.

The French flight commander lost sight of Garros during the swirling, turning *mêlée,* and barely managed to escape his three attackers. The SPAD XIII was faster than a Fokker and its pilot was able to disengage and run for the safety of the front lines the Germans were forbidden to cross. Looking back over his shoulder, he tried in vain to spot Garros's plane among the now-scattered Germans buzzing about like angry wasps.

French civilians in the forest town of Saint-Morel, who watched the dogfight with great interest, saw a SPAD explode in mid-air, an incendiary bullet finding one of the SPAD's three fuel tanks. The resulting fire torched the aircraft almost instantly. According to German records, Garros was probably killed by Lt Herman Habich of *Jasta* (Squadron) 49.

The end came quickly for Eugène Adrien Roland Georges Garros. He was a day shy of his 30th birthday and just over a month short of the peace treaty ending the Great War. Perhaps he fought to fly again in combat as a moth flies circling a candle, close enough to feel the heat but striving to skirt the flame. The fires of war Isadore Duncan saw in his eyes that night in Paris were the fires which attracted him, fires he could not avoid, fires which ultimately consumed him literally and symbolically. The pilot who survived crashes without number, forced landings, engine failures, storms, and rickety airplanes could not survive when four younger men were determined to kill him.

Villagers recovered his body and interred it in Vouziers, a nearby larger town, where it remains today under a modest stone obelisk. The corsairs' descendant was laid to rest far from the seas where his ancestors sailed and over which he flew to fame and glory, but under the skies where he belonged.

At 1100 on the 11th day of the 11th month, a peace treaty was signed in a railway carriage beside the River Oise. The Great War was over. The conflict claimed an average of 3000 lives every day for more than four years. Roland Garros was but one of millions. Large swatches of northern France and Belgium lay in utter devastation. Starvation stalked German cities. The governments of Germany, the United Kingdom, Belgium, and France were virtually bankrupt. The "War to End War" settled nothing. The peace treaty sowed malignant seeds of retribution, repayment, and revenge which bore poisoned fruit in World War II. The fighter plane which Garros and Jules Hue invented and demonstrated would play an even greater role in the coming conflagration. But that is a story for another time.

THE END

EPILOGUE

In 1943, Count Antoine de Saint-Exupéry was racked with boredom and tortured by guilt. The French nobleman and pioneering pilot spent most of the 1920s flying for Aeropostale (the airline, not the clothing company) and developing air mail and passenger routes from France down Africa's west coast, over the South Atlantic to Brazil, and from there to the extreme tip of Argentina. He wrote literate books about his many and sometimes painful adventures, books which gained popular and critical acclaim. Around 1930, he abandoned commercial aviation for life as a man of letters, or so it said in his passport. He went on to write *The Little Prince*, a literary aviation novel which became the third bestselling book of all time.

With the fall of France in 1940, Saint-Ex and his wife fled to New York City. They set themselves up in exile, living in luxury, occupying twin penthouses on Central Park South. Like Roland Garros in 1918, Saint-Ex eventually found comfortable life in a big city to be stifling. Once again, a war raged over the future of Europe in general, and for Saint-Ex, for France in particular. His inner demons compelled him to return to the fight, to do his part. Petitions were written, telegrams sent, contacts exercised, debts called in. The issue went all the way to General Eisenhower, Supreme Allied Commander in Europe, who authorized Saint-Ex's return, probably to get the vexing issue off his desk. The parallel with Roland Garros's demands to return to combat is uncanny.

Antoine de Saint-Exupéry was assigned to a reconnaissance squadron flying an un-armed version of the P-38 Lightning. He was 43 years old, fat, with a body wrecked by numerous airplane crashes and by days and nights of riotous living. He could barely fly the P-38 and was no match for the German fighter pilot who shot him down. Saint-Ex disappeared into the Bay of Carqueiranne off the coast of Toulon, France, where Roland Garros began his flight across the Mediterranean over

30 years previously. The Luftwaffe pilot who unknowingly terminated Saint-Ex's final flight had read all his books.

Five years after Roland Garros's death, a small monument was dedicated to his honor on the Champs-Elysées in Paris, but this was not to be the most famous remembrance to his memory. During the first decade of the 20th century, Garros played on the French national rugby team with another athlete, Emile Lesieur. Lesieur also flew as a *Pilote de Chasse* or fighter pilot during the Great War. He survived and after the war took up a senior position in the French amateur athletic community. Lesieur remembered fondly his association with Garros on the rugby field and as a fighter pilot. He understood the key contribution Garros made to the world of tactical aviation.

The older Frenchman felt Garros lacked the recognition he deserved. French flying aces like Nungesser, Fonck, and Guynemer were national heroes celebrated throughout the land while Garros remained a footnote. Roland Garros entered the history books as one of a few early aviation pioneers and as the first pilot to span the Mediterranean by air. However, according to Lesieur, the world's first fighter pilot deserved more credit for showing the way for those who came after.

During the 1920s, France was a powerhouse in international tennis, winning the Davis Cup in 1927. To defend the cup, Lesieur was commissioned to build a new clay tennis court and stadium in an eastern suburb of Paris. He did so and demanded the facility be named after Roland Garros. The Roland Garros National Tennis Center is there today and is the site of what the world calls the "French Open," but is known in France as *"Le Tournoi de Roland Garros."* Over the decades the center has grown to occupy a city block in area with multiple courts, grandstands, a gift shop, a gourmet restaurant (after all, this is France), and supporting buildings. The memorial has outgrown its subject. The tennis world knows of "The Roland Garros" but few in that world know who he was. Even fewer care.

★★★

Delving into the life of Roland Garros, I was surprised to learn of Garros's flying exploits in New Orleans, Louisiana where I was born, and in Chattanooga, Tennessee where I grew up and the city I call my hometown. As a boy, I heard tales of Mountain Cove Farms, home of the drunken, rowdy cowboys who perforated the grandstand's tin roof at Warner Park in Chattanooga. They deployed their six-shooters when John Moisant's flying circus air show was cancelled due to bad weather. On one of my many trips to the City of Lights, I dreamed of visiting the center court stadium at the Roland Garros tennis complex. There I would yank out a Colt revolver and put six holes in the roof in remembrance of that long-ago dark and stormy night in East Tennessee. However, I had an uncharacteristic onslaught of good judgement. I thought better of it and wrote this book instead. My notional celebratory gunfire plan was, I later discovered, unworkable in any case as the center court at *Stade Roland Garros* lacks a roof.

There is something poetic, if not ironic, about a national center where tennis, a most civilized and genteel sport, is played named after a man who, along with Jules Hue, invented a graceful and terrible new weapon, the fighter plane. I believe that somewhere, Roland Garros and Saint-Ex are watching tennis matches, the French Open perhaps. The two pilots are probably laughing and drinking champagne.

Ed Cobleigh
Lieutenant Colonel, United States Air Force
Fighter Pilot

BIBLIOGRAPHY

Schiff, Stacy. *Saint-Exupéry: A Biography*. New York. Holt. 1994

Garros, Roland. *Mémoires*. Paris. Phébus. 2016. (in French)

Lemaire, Vincent. Feldzer, Gérard, Lovera, Jean. Et al. *Roland Garros : L'Homme Qui Flirtait avec les Nuages*. Paris. Federation Français de Tennis. 2018. (in French)

Fleury, Georges. *Roland Garros: Un Inconnu si Célèbre*. Paris. Bourin Editeur. 2009. (in French)

Raismus, Ed. Olds, Christina. Et al. *Fighter Pilot: The Memoirs of Legendary Ace Robin Olds*. New York. St. Martins Griffin. 2011

Lee, Arthur Gould. *No Parachute: A Fighter Pilot in WWI*. New York. Time-Life Education. 1991.

Lee, Arthur Gould. *Open Cockpit*. Grub Street Publishing. London. 2012

Boyne, Walter J., The Smithsonian Book of Flight, Smithsonian Books, Washington DC, 1987

Rickenbacker, Capt. Eddie V. *Fighting the Flying Circus: The Greatest True Air Adventure to Come Out of WWI*. New York. Doubleday. 2011.

Tallman, Frank. *Flying Old Planes*. New York. Doubleday. 1973.

Gibbs-Smith, Charles H. *The Invention of the Aeroplane (1799-1909)*. New York. Taplinger Publishing. 1966

Christienne, Charles and Lissarague, Pierre, translated by Kianka, Francis. *A History of French Military Aviation*. Washington, DC. Smithsonian Press. 1986

RG Magazine, Roland Garros Tennis Center, Paris, *Un Homme en Guerre, Roland Garros*. (in French)

General Dynamics, *Aces High*, General Dynamics Corp, Fort Worth, TX, 1977

Reichl, Ruth. Remembrance of Things Paris. Random House, New York, 2004

Various. New York Times.

Various. Chattanooga Daily Times

Memphis Commercial Appeal

Various. New Orleans Times-Picayune.

AUTHOR'S BIOGRAPHY

Ed Cobleigh flew 375 combat missions in the F-4 Phantom earning two Distinguished Flying Crosses and the Air Medal. He has flown fighter planes with the US Air Force, the US Navy, the Royal Air Force, the French Air Force, and the Imperial Iranian Air Force. His log book shows time in the F-104 Starfighter, F-4 Phantom, A-4 Skyhawk, GR1/T2 Anglo-French Jaguar, and F-16 Viper. As an instructor, he taught student pilots at the USAF Fighter Weapons School, the USN Fighter Weapons School (Top Gun), and the RAF Qualified Weapons Instructor Course (Jaguar). He co-authored the US Air Force air-to-air tactics manual.

Serving as an Air Intelligence Officer, he worked with the CIA, FBI, and MI6 on a variety of classified intelligence projects. He has visited 50 countries in various capacities and France 50 times.

His memoir, *War for the Hell of It: A Fighter Pilot's View of Vietnam*, is an Amazon #1 bestseller. *The Pilot: Fighter Planes and Paris*, his literary aviation novel, has gained excellent reviews. Cobleigh has been on the faculty of the Central Coast Writers Conference and his op/ed pieces on fighter weapons and tactics have been published in numerous professional journals and popular magazines.

Ed and his wife, Heidi, live in California's wine country with their horses and dogs.

ACKNOWLEDGMENTS

The following people were instrumental in this book seeing the light of day.

Doris Badger provided grammatical, punctuational, and inspirational assistance. Admiral Sir Frank (Skip) Bowman, USN Ret, and Lt. Gen, David A. Deptula, USAF Ret, prized open publishing doors. Special thanks to Michaël Guittard of the Roland Garros Tennis Center in Paris for key information. Also, thanks to the Tennessee Aviation Museum for providing reference material. John Koehler of Koehler Publishing made targeted suggestions to improve the book's commercial appeal.

Dr. Ben Lambeth provided motivation and an example of learned erudition. Walter, "Buck" Bender relayed knowledge of flying floatplanes. Dr. Tilar Mazzeo's course on narrative non-fiction writing and her bio of the widow Clicquot were very helpful in setting standards to strive for.

The book could not have been written without the support of my wife, Heidi. She tolerated my late hours and swearing at the computer, not to mention the process expenses.

Book Reviews

Readers are invited, requested even, to post a review on the book's home page at Amazon.com. Reviews need not be lengthy, but they should be honest accounts of how the reader perceived the book, the good and the bad, the highs and the lows. Reviews will allow prospective readers to make an informed buying decision.

Thanks in advance,

Lt/Col Ed Cobleigh, USAF (Ret)
Fighter Pilot, "Fast Eddie"

Lightning Source UK Ltd.
Milton Keynes UK
UKHW011853190721
387438UK00001B/51